Firing Lines

Firing Lines

Three Canadian Women Write the First World War

DEBBIE MARSHALL

Foreword by Anna Maria Tremonti

DUNDURN
TORONTO

Copyright © Debbie Marshall, 2017

All rights reserved. No part of this publication may be reproduced, stored in a retrieval system, or transmitted in any form or by any means, electronic, mechanical, photocopying, recording, or otherwise (except for brief passages for purpose of review) without the prior permission of Dundurn Press. Permission to photocopy should be requested from Access Copyright.

Cover image: istock.com/Branislav Zivkovic
Printer: Webcom

Library and Archives Canada Cataloguing in Publication

Marshall, Debbie, 1959-, author
    Firing lines : three Canadian women write the First World War / Debbie Marshall ; foreword by Anna Maria Tremonti.

Includes bibliographical references and index.
Issued in print and electronic formats.
ISBN 978-1-4597-3838-6 (paperback).--ISBN 978-1-4597-3839-3 (PDF).--ISBN 978-1-4597-3840-9 (EPUB)

    1. Moore, Mary MacLeod, 1871-1960. 2. Nasmyth, Beatrice, 1885-1977. 3. Montizambert, Elizabeth, 1875-1964. 4. Women war correspondents--Canada--Biography. 5. World War, 1914-1918--Journalists--Biography. 6. World War, 1914-1918--Press coverage--Canada. I. Tremonti, Anna Maria, 1957-, writer of foreword II. Title.

D632.5.C3M37 2016   070.4'499403   C2016-906317-8
                                       C2016-906318-6

1 2 3 4 5   21 20 19 18 17

  Conseil des Arts   Canada Council
     du Canada   for the Arts

We acknowledge the support of the **Canada Council for the Arts** and the **Ontario Arts Council** for our publishing program. We also acknowledge the financial support of the **Government of Ontario**, through the **Ontario Book Publishing Tax Credit** and the **Ontario Media Development Corporation**, and the **Government of Canada**.

Care has been taken to trace the ownership of copyright material used in this book. The author and the publisher welcome any information enabling them to rectify any references or credits in subsequent editions.
— J. Kirk Howard, President

The publisher is not responsible for websites or their content unless they are owned by the publisher.

Printed and bound in Canada.

VISIT US AT

Dundurn
3 Church Street, Suite 500
Toronto, Ontario, Canada
M5E 1M2

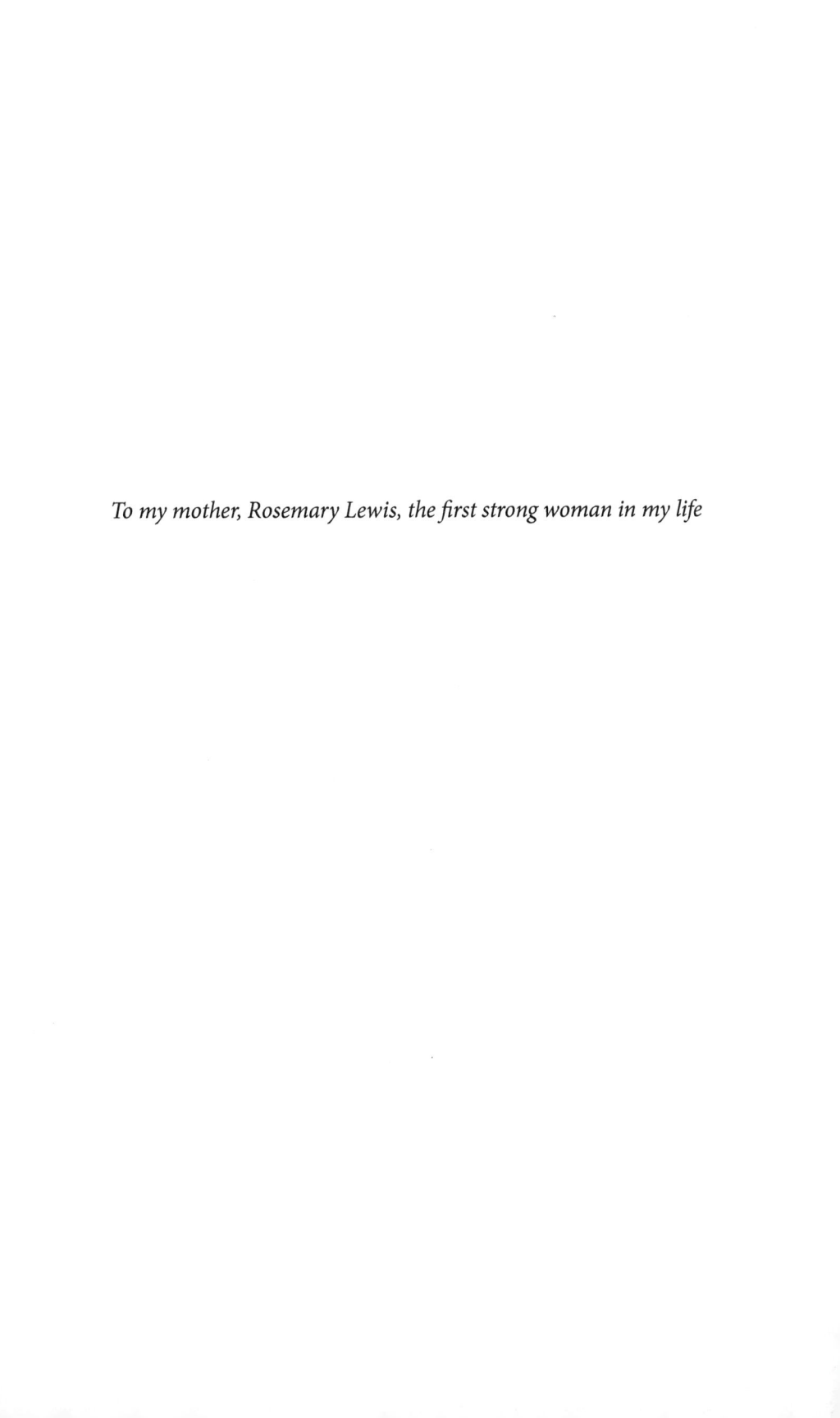

To my mother, Rosemary Lewis, the first strong woman in my life

A condensed story of the war from the personal viewpoint should contain not only a day in the life of a sailor, a soldier, and others serving in His Majesty's forces, but a day in the life of a poor mother whose husband was fighting, who could tell of waiting in queues for food which was rationed … a day in the life of voluntary workers among the families of the fighting men; of a nurse behind the lines and a nurse in a London hospital; of someone who was out-of-doors when an air raid was on; of women of wealth and leisure in ordinary times, working hour after hour in war supply depots; of a girl driving a motor ambulance in France. One could go on for a long time noting aspects of the life at home and abroad during the war, all of which were part of the great story of endurance and suffering.…

— Mary MacLeod Moore, "A Happy New Year! The Story of Our Times," *Sunday Times*, December 30, 1934

Contents

Foreword	By Anna Maria Tremonti	9
Prologue	Reclamation	15
Part I	Prelude to War	
Chapter 1	The Suffragette	23
Chapter 2	Military Daughter	38
Chapter 3	The Aristocrat	54
Part II	Behind the Lines	
Chapter 4	Called to the Colours	75
Chapter 5	Total War	97
Chapter 6	Who Dies If England Lives?	123
Chapter 7	Women's Work	151
Chapter 8	Lines of Communication	170
Chapter 9	When Your Boy Comes Back to You	183

Part III	Last Words	
Chapter 10	Beatrice Nasmyth	203
Chapter 11	Mary MacLeod Moore	220
Chapter 12	Elizabeth Montizambert	247
Afterword		271
Acknowledgements		275
Notes		277
Bibliography		299
Image Credits		303
Index		305

Foreword

I was not the first Canadian journalist to look to the small number of American and British women reporters during the Second World War as role models for their "firsts" in conflict coverage. The fact that three Canadian women chose this same path at the beginning of the last century — to cover what would later be known as the First World War — has been buried by time. And yet Mary MacLeod Moore, Beatrice Nasmyth, and Elizabeth Montizambert went to extraordinary lengths and put themselves at risk to document what was happening to civilians and soldiers throughout Britain and France from the very start of that war.

One hundred years after these three women forced themselves onto the front pages of Canadian newspapers as war correspondents, author Debbie Marshall has pieced together the stories of their lives and their work, resurrecting their legacy. Marshall has hunted down dispatches and combed through personal letters to offer a picture of who these women were and what motivated them.

Among them, these three women published thousands of stories that were dispatched to Canadian publications — from the *Vancouver Province* to the *Montreal Gazette* to the *Toronto Star* and *Saturday Night Magazine*. Those stories included interviews with high-ranking officers and often heavily-censored coverage of the Allied military. But it was the dedicated attention to regular people — alternately defiant and fearful, living in the midst of violent attacks, personal loss, deprivation, and uncertainty — that comprised much of their work at the time and continues to set them apart today.

As blackouts were imposed across London, as German bombs fell, as Parisians formed long queues for food and Zeppelins buzzed the skies above, these women kept moving around the cities and travelling into the countryside, reporting, offering a glimpse of civilian life amidst the disruption and danger. What was unfolding on the front lines was secretive and censored — one of the women appeared to get around that by speaking to the wounded soldiers at hospitals, learning more about actual battles and also about the vulnerability of Allied soldiers, six million of whom would perish during that conflict.

All of this is very significant. For many of us who came of age covering wars in the 1990s, the American journalist Martha Gellhorn was *the* war correspondent to emulate: she had disguised herself as a nurse to board a British naval ship headed for the beaches of northern France at the time of the D-Day invasion during the Second World War. Her work, which centred on women and children and on the wounded in hospitals, stood out from the coverage of so many male reporters at the time, which focused almost exclusively on front line battle information and, for the most part, ignored the plight of civilians. Gellhorn brought a humanity and empathy to the coverage of conflict, and she was revered by journalists, male and female, for decades, credited with changing the face of war reporting. Unbeknownst to us all, three Canadian women had begun that change one war earlier, to little fanfare.

Nasmyth, Moore, and Montizambert came from different backgrounds — from privileged to poor — and were anomalous among women of the day because they pursued full-time jobs. They each began their journalism career in the "women's pages" of newspapers, covering fashion, gossip, and household issues, writing columns and so-called "lighter fare" directed at female readers; for almost all women of the time, that was the only way in to the male-dominated field of journalism. That is not the typical path to assignments in conflict zones today, but this was the early 1900s: the working assumption was that only men were capable of hard-hitting coverage. The women Debbie Marshall profiles were part of a small cadre of females breaking new ground and changing the rules.

By the standards of journalism today, some of what they did raises eyebrows. For example, Mary MacLeod Moore made it clear she — and many in the British press — initially had no problem with the rampant censorship, which extended beyond security to propaganda efforts to try to control public morale. For her part, at the end of the war, Beatrice Nasmyth was acting as the "publicity secretary" for an official Canadian delegate to the Paris Peace Conference while continuing to write articles about the conference and the signing of the Peace Treaty at Versailles. Remarkably, Marshall suggests Nasmyth's articles appeared without a byline because of "the old prejudice of female journalists not being able to write 'serious news,'" rather than the problem of her blatant conflict of interest, which would surely not be tolerated today.

Even with these missteps, the women's contributions to conflict journalism were significant and have been ignored for far too long. To learn of their dedication to the story at times of great hardship is both an inspiration and, admittedly, a bit of a surprise for me. The fight for women to be taken seriously as journalists covering all topics of weight has been a long one.

In fact, it would take another eighty years for the numbers of women covering war to truly expand. Yes, women were reporting through the Second World War, and of course many covered the Vietnam War. But I belong to that first generation of women to be assigned to conflict zones in large numbers by major western news organizations. We were reporters, photographers, producers, editors, sound technicians, and translators. It felt, at the time, as if our (almost exclusively male) news bosses had no choice — there was simply no reason to think that women already covering politics, the military, finance, foreign affairs, and domestic unrest would be anything but capable in the field of conflict. To deny us was unacceptable.

In the early 1990s I was dispatched by *CBC Television News* to cover what became a growing array of troubles that involved military might and citizen rebellion: from the U.S. invasion of Panama (1989–90) to the Israeli-Palestinian conflict to the collapse of the Soviet Union and the resulting civil war in Georgia. The desire for independence that saw success in the former Soviet republics such as the Baltics and Ukraine was also confronting Eastern Europe and it was ripping through Yugoslavia one republic at a time. Croatia was still smouldering when I began chronicling the viciousness in the Bosnian countryside and the siege of Sarajevo.

My first trip into Sarajevo was harrowing: our van was loaded with a backup fuel supply of eight jerry cans of gasoline as we drove across the tarmac of the Sarajevo airport from the Serb-controlled outskirts toward the centre of the city, which was controlled by the Bosnia army. By darting behind the French armoured personnel carriers of the United Nations peacekeeping force, we were able to avoid the barrage of machine gun fire unloaded in our direction that most certainly would have sent us up in a ball of flame.

On that first trip, the team was one of gender parity: I was accompanied by editor and sound technician Kathy Durnin, of the CBC's Moscow bureau, as well as photographer Louis DeGuise and producer John Scully. During my first year covering the Bosnian war, I encountered a who's who of western female journalists: fellow CBC-er Gillian Findlay; Canadians Sheila MacVicar (ABC), Hilary Brown (ABC), and Jackie Shymanski (CNN); Christiane Amanpour (CNN), Janine di Giovanni (*Sunday Times*), Maggie O'Kane (*The Guardian*), Barbara Demick (*Philadelphia Enquirer*), Angela Rodrigo (TVE); as well as fearless photographers such as Alexandra Boulat (Sipa Press, VII Photography), Corinne Dufka (Reuters), Margaret Moth (CNN), and freelance translators such as Canadian Sonja Pastuovic and Aida Alibalic. And, of course, there were even more women than the ones I mention here.

Since that time, far too many wars have raged, and women have continued to distinguish themselves as journalists in every one.

During my time covering the Bosnian war and other conflicts, I would receive calls from journalism students from various cities across North America — all of them women — who were working on a Masters degree and writing theses on the work of women in battle zones. In many of these conversations, the students seemed in awe of the very idea that women were working alongside men in such dangerous places. These calls continued for years, and I was incredulous that anyone would still see women as separate when it came to journalistic pursuits and assignments. That is perhaps why it remains so important to highlight and celebrate those women who really were at the vanguard of such reporting; to understand what is possible gives new generations of women the inspiration to pursue their own journalistic paths.

My own career ambitions were sent in a new direction when I watched Ann Medina reporting for *CBC News* out of Lebanon in the early 1980s. The Lebanese civil war would drag through fifteen long years, with what seemed at the time a confusing array of factions inflicting endless damage on a vulnerable population. Ann brought great clarity to a complex conflict, finding the heartbeat of the story, using images that remain with me until this day. I thought she was fearless, and I hung on to every word, watched every story that she filed. It was her reporting that made me want to cover war. At that time, I had no idea what that would truly entail, nor did I have any idea how I would go from a local reporting job to something as seemingly unreachable as a foreign assignment. But I had seen what was possible, and my work from then on drove me toward that goal.

Since that time, I have kept a close watch on the women around me, and before me, who also believe in the importance of documenting the consequences of conflict. We have been smuggled across lines, talked our way through checkpoints, and found endless ways to get close to the fighters waging the wars and those civilians suffering the consequences of those battles. Today there are many women whose fearless and exemplary journalism informs us all of the horrors of war, while exposing the politics behind it and the toll it takes on those caught in the middle.

Individuals and news organizations in most western nations recognize and celebrate famous war correspondents as people whose storytelling in the first half of the twentieth century became a part of the history of those wars. With the exception of a few Canadian men whose names are on that list, we mostly hear of American and British journalists. Debbie Marshall's research highlighting the lives of Beatrice Nasmyth, Mary MacLeod Moore, and Elizabeth Montizambert during the First World War enriches our view of our own journalistic history.

Anna Maria Tremonti
JOURNALIST AND HOST OF *THE CURRENT* ON CBC RADIO ONE
NOVEMBER 2016

Prologue

Reclamation

A group of women wrapped in furs and warm winter cloaks stands on the quay at Boulogne. Around them surges a blue, red, and khaki sea of French, British, and Belgian soldiers. White-veiled nurses run alongside patients being carried on stretchers onto waiting ships. There are shouts, marching orders, and whistles as the women stand silently watching, absorbing the details of what they are seeing, overcome by the reality that they are on the doorstep of the Great War.

They are the first party of female Canadian journalists allowed into France to visit the lines of communication. Only a small group of accredited male journalists is now based in France, watched over carefully by the British army and stationed a comfortable distance from the front. Women journalists are frowned upon by military leaders, and only one other such party has been allowed into the country before — a group of British women led by the famous anti-suffragette, writer Mary Augusta Ward.

At last, with the support of military authorities and prominent politicians, female writers from Canada are to be allowed to view life behind the veil that separates the home front from the war front. The party includes Beatrice Nasmyth, Mary MacLeod Moore, and Elizabeth Montizambert. They are "special correspondents," posted overseas to provide a female perspective on the conflict. At a time when fewer than two hundred Canadian women are working as journalists, compared to about 1,500 men,[1] they are members of a small and elite group. The three are also friends and colleagues, whose paths have crossed many times in women's press clubs in Canada and Britain. And unlike Ward, they are thoroughly modern feminists, ardently championing the vote for women at home and abroad.

At thirty-two, Nasmyth is the baby of the party. The tall, slender, square-shouldered woman with the mischievous glint in her bright blue eyes is the assistant editor of the *Vancouver Province*'s women's page. Her colleague, Mary MacLeod Moore, is forty-six and the most experienced writer of the group, having made her living as a journalist for the previous twenty years. She pens a weekly column for the *London Sunday Times* and *Saturday Night Magazine*. Curly-haired, forty-two-year old Elizabeth Montizambert, dressed in exquisite furs and one of the new military-style hats, is fashion editor turned war correspondent for the *Montreal Gazette*. The descendant of a wealthy, aristocratic Quebec family, she writes — not surprisingly — under the nom de plume Antoinette. She is stationed in Paris, while the others make London their home base.

The only surviving photo of the women's tour. Elizabeth is holding the muff in the front row. Beatrice (left), Roberta MacAdams (right) in the back row. The woman dressed in furs may be Mary.

16   Firing Lines

A car with a bright red cross on its side pulls up to the quay, and a young officer steps out and hails the women. They bundle inside; as it draws away, its headlamps gleam off the helmets of soldiers marching into the darkness. They are singing, and the echo of "Take Me Back to Dear Old Blighty" drifts into the women's car and then fades away as they pass through cobbled streets lined with shuttered houses. A cloth-sided ambulance moves slowly past them in the opposite direction, a lantern casting shadows on the four men lying within.

Nasmyth, Moore, and Montizambert were part of a small contingent of female writers and journalists covering the Great War — both on the front lines and on the home front. Each had tens of thousands of readers, yet today few people know these women's names. The cause of their anonymity may lie in the pervasiveness of Great War histories that focus on the literary output of male luminaries such as Siegfried Sassoon, Robert Graves, and Wilfred Owen while overlooking female literary figures, such as Edith Wharton and Helena Swanwick. Women like Wharton and Swanwick were immersed in the war from its outset and recorded their experiences in popular magazines, newspapers, and books. Their writing was accessible, and their work often focused on women's experience of the conflict — topics that until lately have not been deemed serious enough for consideration by historians and literary scholars. Fortunately, in recent years, writers such as Margaret Higonnet and Joyce Marlow have begun to examine and publish women's wartime writings, and in the process are slowly beginning to expand our understanding of the impact of the Great War.

One area, however, that has received scant attention from scholars of every stripe is the wartime writing and journalism of Canadian women.[2] Between 1914 and 1919, Beatrice Nasmyth, Mary MacLeod Moore, and Elizabeth Montizambert wrote thousands of accounts describing the war and its impact on those who fought it *and* on those who never carried a gun.

Like their male colleagues, these three women wanted to get as close to the front as they could. They faced formidable obstacles. From the outset of the conflict, Britain's secretary of war, Lord Kitchener, had made it clear that journalists — male or female — were a security risk. Correspondents were banned from entering a military zone around the British Expeditionary Force, and any dispatches from France had to be submitted to the War Office before publication. The War Office established its own Press Bureau; this bureau censored news and reports sent from the British army and then chose what to release to the waiting press in London and around the world.[3]

The home front wasn't exempt from Kitchener's attentions, either. The government passed the Defence of the Realm Act (DORA), making it illegal to publish anything that directly or indirectly aided the enemy. As historian Martin Farrar points out, this included "information on any troop or naval movement, any description of war and any news that was likely to cause a rift between the public and military authorities."[4]

Canada quickly established its own complementary system of press censorship. Historian Jeffrey Keshen says that at the front, "military escorts guided the movement of journalists, photographers, and filmmakers, while specially assigned officers checked everything they produced. If a reporter was cunning enough to avoid submitting copy to military authorities, his ability to promptly transmit the account still depended upon one rigorously monitored undersea cable linking Canada and Britain.... Meanwhile, for the Canadian based correspondent submitting a disheartening story, not only did there exist the potential obstacle of a patriotic editor, but more important, the presence of Lieutenant-Colonel Ernest J. Chambers, the country's Chief Censor."[5] Chambers even went as far as banning material in Canada that had been passed by censors in Britain, "reasoning that the mother country's proximity to the war zone had partially accustomed its citizens to the grittiness of war — at least more so than geographically-sheltered Canadians who, he suggested, were tied to combat more by idealistic sentiment than any imminent concern about national survival."[6]

As the war progressed, however, access to the battlefront began to loosen. Governments began to face the fact that those at home wanted to know more about what was happening to their relatives, lovers, and friends serving overseas. Besides, war news was already leaking home in the form of poetry, essays, and letters from soldiers and nurses. In order to keep public opinion on their side, politicians and military leaders allowed a small group of male journalists into France, provided they agreed to wear military uniforms and submit to military authority in exchange for limited access to the battlefront. Many would spend much of the war behind the lines in the cozy French village of St. Omer.

The same cushy offer wasn't extended to female journalists. Popular opinion and government policy officially excluded them from the terrors of the conflict simply because they were considered too emotionally and physically fragile to withstand its effects. This masked the reality that women were already on the front lines. French and Belgian women, medical staff, the new women's military auxiliaries, women whose soldier relatives were seriously wounded in hospital, female writers from other countries who were living in France, influential upper-class women with military connections, and even female soldiers (such as Irish sergeant-major Flora Sandes) were facing the bullets and bombs of total war.

Despite the obstacles placed in their paths, many female journalists from Canada did manage to cover the war in Britain, and in France as well. Moore, Montizambert, and Nasmyth were among their number. The stories they sent home were a far cry from those of their male colleagues. Instead of heroic (sometimes fabricated) tales of battles won, their stories were intimate, compelling views of a devastating war and the human wreckage it left behind.

Women's wartime lives are recounted in detail, from homemakers to ambulance drivers, nurses to factory workers. Not only did Moore, Montizambert, and Nasmyth write about the war's impact on combatants and non-combatants alike, they also participated in the war effort as hospital visitors and canteen operators (sometimes near the front lines). One even played a small role in the making of history — Nasmyth engineered the election campaign of one of the first women elected to a Canadian legislature. In reviewing the phenomenal wartime output of these three women, it becomes clear that for them, war was women's work as well as men's. If we want to know more about how *both* sexes experienced the war, then we need only turn to the reports and surviving letters of these journalists to expand our understanding.

The "Great War," as it was known, would be the pivotal experience in all three women's lives. Although Moore, Montizambert, and Nasmyth were established writers by 1914, covering the conflict gave them a much bigger stage on which to perform and would lay the groundwork for the work they would do after the war. And it would — as war often does — help them clarify their priorities. Later in life, they would look back on their careers and see their early years in journalism as preparation for covering the conflict, and their later years as filled with work that was never as thrilling or fulfilling as their wartime experience. Their Great War writing reveals journalists who were deeply engaged with the subjects of the stories they were writing. They weren't just witnesses — they were participants in a cataclysmic drama.

In December 1917, Nasmyth, Moore, and Montizambert visited the ten-thousand-bed hospital base at Étaples and interviewed the women who were working there. As Moore would later tell her readers, "I wish you could see with me the Motor Ambulance Convoy, where girls, some of them Canadians, are driving the wounded men, day and night, to great hospitals. I wish you could walk with me among the ambulances and see upon them the names of Canadian towns and counties and societies.... Would you could be with us as we visit in the moonlight on a crisp, frosty evening — so many of my memories are of moonlight and ice and the sun on the snow — a famous Canadian base and see the crowds of Canadian boys sauntering about and laughing and calling to one another...."

Today, by exploring their early lives and excavating their wartime experience, we can accept Mary's invitation and walk with these three Canadian women as they wrote the First World War.

Part 1
Prelude to War

Hail, hail,
The gang's all here,
Never mind the weather,
Here we are together;
Hail, hail,
The gang's all here,
Sure we're glad
That you're here too!

Hail, hail,
The gang's all here,
We're a bunch of live ones,
Not a single dead one;
Hail, hail,
The gang's all here,
Sure I'm glad
That I'm here too!
— D.A. Estron

Chapter I

The Suffragette

> Women have a much better time than men in this world; there are far more things forbidden to them.
>
> — Oscar Wilde

VANCOUVER, British Columbia, August 3, 1914. Twenty-nine-year-old Beatrice Nasmyth waved to her parents from the porch of the crowded observation car of the CPR train as it pulled out of the station. When they had disappeared into the distance, the tall, auburn-haired journalist stepped inside to find a comfortable spot to sit. She was surprised to see old friends from the Alpine Mountain Climbing Club sprawled in some of the comfortable maroon leather seats. They were on their way to Alberta, and invited her to join them for a climb in the Rocky Mountains. She wasn't interested. "The *Province* is sending me to London, in case there's a war."

"There isn't going to be a war. If there was, I'd know about it," drawled a red-haired Englishman from across the aisle. Beatrice looked the stranger up and down, smiled, then turned back to her friends with an airy, "The Prince of Wales, incognito!"

The "Prince of Wales" turned out to be wrong. When their Montreal-bound train stopped in Calgary a day-and-a-half later, Beatrice stepped outside to stretch her legs. On the platform, newspaper boys were waving copies of the *Calgary Herald* and shouting, "War declared! Great Britain's at war!" as customers lined up to buy a paper. Bea stared at the tall black headline — "Britain Will Fight Unless Germany Evacuates Belgium." She felt a rush of adrenalin at the thought of what lay ahead of her when she arrived overseas. There would be no lack of stories for her to file for the *Vancouver Province*. Her only worry was that she might not reach England before the war was over.

Beatrice wasn't alone in her excitement. The news of the war had rushed through the train. The young Brit who had teased Beatrice was now planning to curtail his vacation in Canada and return home to enlist. But before he got home, Guy Mackenzie Furniss wanted to get to know the sparkling young woman from across the aisle a little bit better. As their train cut its way across the prairies, he and Beatrice met for meals as often as they could, laughing and chatting long after the white-jacketed waiters had removed the fine bone china and silverware from their tables. They discovered that they had much in common. Guy was also connected to the newspaper world, but as an artist, not a journalist. He was professional engraver and the son of one of Britain's most popular illustrators, *Punch* cartoonist Harry Furniss. To Guy, Beatrice was a revelation — a woman who could hold her own in any conversation, sophisticated, yet refreshingly idealistic and filled with a spirit

The Nasmyth home in Stratford, where Beatrice was born.

24   Firing Lines

of adventure. He could think of no one with whom he'd rather cross an ocean; when they arrived in Montreal, he purchased a ticket for the *Calgarian*,[1] the same ship on which Bea planned to travel.

STRATFORD, Ontario, August 12, 1885. In the second-floor master bedroom of a modest red brick house on a quiet street in Stratford, Deborah Nasmyth gave birth to a daughter whom she and her husband, James, would name Beatrice. Her father immediately felt a special bond to this little newcomer — he and Deborah already had two sons (and would have two more), but this would be their only daughter.

Baby Beatrice was part of an extraordinary family, whose ancestors included artists, inventors, and politicians. Their influence would filter down and shape her life like the wide lakes that formed the rocky landscape of her beloved northern Ontario. She would inherit a deep appreciation for art from her paternal great-grandfather, Scottish landscape painter and portraitist Alexander Nasmyth. It was his brush that created one of the most famous portraits of Robert Burns — a head-and-shoulders profile of a youthful poet that hangs today in Scotland's National Gallery. Beatrice's grandfather George and his brother James were more interested in science than art, and would establish their own machine tool firm in Manchester in 1834. In 1842, James patented the steam hammer — an instrument that paved the way for the steam locomotive and, some would argue, the Industrial Revolution itself.[2]

George Nasmyth eventually used his stake in the business to immigrate to Canada. He settled in Woodstock, Ontario, where he met and married fellow Scottish immigrant Jessie Hay. The couple had seven children — Alexander, William, James (Beatrice's father), Charles, Jessie, Mary, and Jack.[3]

Both James and Charles Nasmyth studied pharmacy in Toronto, and by 1871, James was living and working as a druggist in Stratford, Ontario. Within ten years, his sister Jessie and brother Charles joined him.[4] Each brother established his own separate drug store in the booming young city. Charles's shop was on Downie Street, right across from the brand new neo-Gothic city hall, while James's pharmacy was located in an elegant three-storey brick office building on Ontario Street in the city's busy retail district.[5]

There was more than enough business for both brothers. Stratford was a prosperous community founded in the early nineteenth century by the Canada Company — a group of British investors who made money by promoting settlement in Upper Canada. The first waves of settlers arrived in the 1830s and included English, German, Irish, and Scottish immigrants.[6] A town site was developed and named Stratford, after the birthplace of Shakespeare. However, at this early stage in its development, it was not literary pretension that drove the town's economy — it was the community's location at the heart of southwestern Ontario and at the hub of two great railway lines, the Grand Trunk Railway and the Buffalo and Lake Huron Railway Company. These connected the town to larger centres, such as Toronto and Goderich. Manufacturers could easily ship their products across the country, and Stratford became a major producer of household furniture — from sideboards to sofas. In the late nineteenth and early twentieth centuries, seven factories would be built there, producing roughly one-sixth of all furnishings manufactured in Canada.[7]

As workers and their families poured into the community, there were more people to buy the pills and potions produced by local pharmacists. From all accounts, James became a prosperous businessman[8] — so prosperous that by the mid-1870s he was able to purchase and furnish the two-storey red brick house in which his daughter Beatrice would one day be born. James had fallen in love, and wanted to provide his future bride with a comfortable home that reflected his status in the local community.

James's fiancée was Deborah Eliza Dignam. Deborah was a short, slim woman with a round face, dark hair parted in the middle, determined-looking eyes, thin eyebrows and a rosebud mouth. Like James, she had a distinguished lineage. Her grandparents, Hugh and Ann Dignam, had emigrated from Ireland to Canada in 1839. They were staunch Methodists, and their son William became a saddlebag preacher. On one of his many trips preaching the gospel in the remote clapboard churches of southern Ontario, he met and married Elizabeth Sifton, the daughter of John Sifton, another Irish immigrant.

John Sifton had arrived in Canada in 1818 and was one of the first to settle in the Talbot Settlement — a community developed by the eccentric Anglo-Irish aristocrat Thomas Talbot. A military man and former secretary to Governor Simcoe, Talbot became an official settlement promoter, establishing a dozen townships in the London area.[9] John Sifton received one hundred acres of land under Talbot's settlement scheme. In 1821, he married Irish-born Deborah Hardy. The couple had four children before Deborah died in 1830, perhaps in childbirth.

Elizabeth Sifton was only five years old at the time of her mother's death, but there is little doubt that as she grew older, she would have been expected to help care for her younger siblings. Such responsibilities trained her well for life with her future husband, William Dignam. The couple would have ten children in all. Deborah, their third-born daughter, would be named after her maternal grandmother.[10] It was she who would marry James Hay Nasmyth on July 11, 1877.

Deborah Nasmyth's Sifton cousins included Arthur and Clifford Sifton. Between 1896 and 1905, Clifford was Prime Minister Wilfrid Laurier's

Deborah Nasmyth, Beatrice Nasmyth (with doll), and three of Bea's brothers.

The Suffragette 27

controversial Minister of the Interior.[11] He was a man considered by many to be the primary architect of western Canadian settlement in the early twentieth century. His brother Arthur was equally prominent. In 1889, Arthur would be elected to the Legislative Assembly of the Northwest Territories, and in 1910 would become the second premier of the Province of Alberta.

On the Dignam side, Deborah Nasmyth had influential artists and social radicals in her family. Her aunt, Mary Ella Dignam, was a feminist and artist whose work was popular in the late nineteenth century. She founded the Women's Art Association of Canada and the International Society of Women Painters and Sculptors and was committed to giving female artists the same opportunities as men, even if it meant scandalizing some people along the way. She organized the first all-female international art exhibition, and was the first Canadian artist and educator to provide nude models for female life-drawing students.[12] It was Mary Ella Dignam's feminism that would one day inspire Beatrice Nasmyth's suffragist sympathies.

Deborah Nasmyth's own life was much more conventional than that of her activist aunt. Her time was spent managing the household and caring for her husband James and their young family. Beatrice was the couple's only daughter. She had four brothers — three older and one younger.[13] In her later years, Beatrice would tell her grandchildren that her mother favoured the male members of the household, while her father "shamelessly spoiled" his only daughter. Later correspondence between Beatrice and her parents bore this out. Her letters to her mother were short and formal and dealt mainly with shopping and social visits. Her letters to her father, however, were long and unrestrained, candidly describing her encounters with men, the challenges of her work, and her often-dangerous adventures in wartime London.

While Beatrice may have been closer to one parent than another, what is not in doubt is that she was a well-cared-for and much-loved child. James and Deborah provided their children with a comfortable, secure life. Their home was spacious, with a large kitchen, parlour, and dining room. Heating was provided by a fireplace in the drawing room and a wood-burning stove in the kitchen. The children all had their own chores, but the heavy work was left for their live-in maid. This freed them up to pursue their own interests, from sledding to hockey to quieter pleasures such as reading and drawing.

During many of her free hours after school and on weekends, Beatrice would stop at her father's drugstore. It was panelled in dark oak, lined with shelves holding the large glass bottles that contained the pungent medications dispensed by their father. But it wasn't the medicines that attracted Bea. Along one wall was a long marble counter with tall stools sitting underneath. At the centre of the counter stood a tall silver soda fountain. At the time, soda was believed to be cure-all for many different kinds of illnesses. Fountain drinks included mixtures of various drugs — sometimes including cocaine and caffeine — that were flavoured, carbonated, and mixed with ice cream. It wasn't the "medicinal" value of the sodas that Beatrice would remember all her life, but the cut glass tumblers which her father filled with carbonated water, strawberry ice cream, whipped cream, chocolate curls, cherries, and nuts.

The Nasmyths were a large, noisy, healthy family. James Nasmyth was a fervent believer that physical fitness was the key to good health and he encouraged all of his children to exercise and participate in sports. Next to their home was a barn that housed not only James's horse and buggy, but a gymnasium equipped with bars, rings, and ropes for the Nasmyth boys to swing on.

During the summer months, the family regularly travelled to Glenwilde, their cottage on Mary Lake in Muskoka. Those were the

Glenwilde, the Nasmyth cottage.

days before Muskoka cottages were associated with six-figure incomes. In the late nineteenth century, middle-class families could still afford low-cost rustic cabins on the three lakes — Joseph, Rosseau, and Muskoka — east of Georgian Bay. The Nasmyths spent summers there, canoeing, visiting, and enjoying the rugged scenery. Sitting in the grass under the shimmering white birch trees, Beatrice would write stories and poems and send them to her father, whose work often kept him in Stratford.[14]

When she returned home from long hot summers at the lake, Beatrice involved herself in more refined pursuits. A large upright piano took pride of place in her family's drawing room. In her teens, she would make a weekly thirty-mile train trip to London, Ontario, for private music lessons. On her return, she would spend hours practising the piano, developing a lifelong passion for the soaring, intense music of Felix Mendelssohn.[15] In many ways, young Bea was temperamentally similar to the composer, a man who liked to play some of his movements "as fast as possible, provided that the notes can be heard."

Beatrice consumed books full tilt, in much the same way as she played the piano. On warm summer afternoons, she would curl up on a rocker on the front porch and drink in novels such as *Little Lord Fauntleroy* by Frances Hodgson Burnett and books about adventurous but virtuous girls, such as the Elsie Dinsmore series. The heroines in these stories were always running pell-mell through life, getting into scrapes and fighting their way out of them again, unscathed.

There were other distractions, too. In a city with a name like Stratford, it was almost a matter of faith that every citizen should have a finely honed appreciation for the theatre. Local public schools bore the names of the playwright's heroes and heroines — Hamlet, Lear, Romeo and Juliet. Beatrice saw her first play at the age of nine. It was *Uncle Tom's Cabin* by abolitionist Harriet Beecher Stowe. It ignited her passion for justice, especially for women. Bea's love of inspiring literature by women such as Stowe may have also given her the idea that she could be a writer, too.

STRATFORD, Ontario, May 1896. Eliza Johnston sat at her desk reading and re-reading the short story assignment submitted by Beatrice. There was nothing for it — she would have to inform the principal. It was simply not possible for a ten-year-old child to have written this story. The prose was far too crisp, the tale far too mature. It was surprising that such a clever girl would plagiarize her assignment, but Beatrice could be a little too self-confident sometimes. Maybe a visit to the principal's office would rein her in. Eliza got up from her desk, the offending story in hand, and stepped into the hall.

The next morning, Beatrice was sitting at her desk, with its polished pine top and cast-iron frame. She liked to run her hands across its soft wooden surface and trace the outlines of ink stains left there by its previous tenants. The Lord's Prayer had already been said and "God Save the Queen" had been sung. Now the group of thirty or so students was waiting for the first lesson of the day. Instead, Miss Johnston quietly walked down the centre aisle and stopped beside Beatrice's desk.

"Miss Nasmyth, report at once to the principal's office."

The other students were as excited as witnesses to a train derailment. What had Beatrice done? A visit to the principal meant the strap — a thick leather belt across the hands — or worse, expulsion and shame. No one was ever sent without a good reason. Beatrice was too shocked to speak. Her palms were sweating and her skirt felt too tight. As she slowly walked down the corridor, she ran through a list of possible sins that might have led her to this place. Nothing added up.

"This story is clearly plagiarized. What have you got to say for yourself?" Seated behind his massive, golden oak desk, Mr. Scott looked stern and forbidding, his white collar stiff and white, his rust-coloured moustache neatly clipped, glasses perched on the edge of his beaky nose. He was not a man to trifle with, but Beatrice could not give him the answer he wanted to hear.

"I wrote the story. It's my work," she said quietly.

"Well, if you won't admit the truth, then you must suffer the consequences." He made Beatrice carry a high-backed chair from classroom to classroom. At each stop, she was made to sit in front of the class while the principal made the day's announcements, including a description of Beatrice's infraction.

After school, Bea tearfully described the incident to her mother. Deborah Nasmyth listened quietly and, without a word, went to her room and changed into her best black taffeta dress, with its crisp no-nonsense pleats and expensive lace inset. She pinned on a small straw hat with black ribbons and pulled on her high leather boots with their double rows of buttons. Beatrice had hoped for sympathy, but the gleam in her mother's eyes reflected more volcanic emotions. "Get your coat. We're going to the school," ordered Deborah.

When they reached the school, her mother ordered Beatrice to sit outside the principal's office. A majestic Deborah Nasmyth swung open Mr. Scott's office door and slammed it shut behind her. For a while, all Beatrice could hear was the sound of raised voices — mostly her mother's. Then the door opened again and Beatrice was invited in by a subdued and white-faced principal.

"I must apologize, Beatrice." He took a deep breath. "I made a mistake regarding the authorship of your excellent story."

Beatrice wasn't given time to respond to this astonishing reversal of fortune. Deborah took her by the arm, nodded curtly, said "Good day, Mr. Scott," and marched Beatrice from the room. They could hear the faint voice of the principal echoing in the distance. "Good day, Mrs. Nasmyth."

When they reached home, Deborah offered to buy Beatrice a special present to make up for the humiliation she had endured. A few days later, Beatrice was handed a red, leather-bound journal.[16]

The Nasmyths moved from Stratford to Woodstock when Beatrice was sixteen. Her father's business had become so successful that he had decided to sell his store and establish a larger one in the town of his birth. The family moved into a large Queen Anne–style home with a wide front porch and three tall, shuttered windows opening from its second storey. The house was surrounded by a vast front lawn and tall spruce trees, with a central sidewalk leading to the street and an arched wrought-iron fence and gate. It was the home of a well-to-do businessman, not too long from retirement.

After graduating from the Woodstock Collegiate, Beatrice boarded and attended Alma College, a private women's finishing school in

St. Thomas. At a time when many universities and colleges barred women's participation, the founders of Alma were dedicated to providing a comprehensive liberal arts program for their female students. The curriculum was represented by the school colours — red for music, gold for art, and blue for literature. Founded by the Methodist Church in 1877, its program of study was designed to help the daughters of Canada's growing middle and upper classes "make their lives useful and happy, and their tastes elevated and refined."[17]

The college's central building was designed in the high Victorian Gothic Revival style. It was a mass of beige stone, green-gray spires, and tall arched windows. Within its wide, high-ceilinged classrooms, Beatrice took courses in modern languages, English literature, elocution, deportment, and history. Alma College also believed in the "promotion of bodily vigour"[18] and every student was expected to participate in a sport of some kind or other. The girl who had enjoyed rough-and-tumble summers at her family's Muskoka cottage had no difficulty excelling in athletics, playing hockey and receiving a prize for being the school's "most graceful runner" (despite the fact she managed to break the nose of an opponent during a hockey game).[19] Beatrice's training in piano also continued. By the time she graduated, she had completed the four-year Toronto Conservatory program.

After graduation, Beatrice studied at the University of Toronto. But in 1907 she abandoned her studies, convinced she had spent enough time in school and was now ready to go out into the world and make a living for herself.[20] Her chosen career was journalism.

WOODSTOCK, Ontario, September 1907. "Miss Nasmyth has been spending the entire summer at the family cottage at Lake Mary and has become quite accomplished in aquatic sports. She was first in the ladies single canoe open, ladies single scull for tourists and second in another single scull event."[21] The *Woodstock Sentinel Review*'s report on Beatrice's summer activities was likely written by Beatrice herself. She was not only a reporter for that newspaper; she was also moonlighting for its competition, the *Gazette*.[22]

Beatrice didn't work for the Woodstock newspapers for long. In 1909, James Nasmyth retired and he and Deborah moved to Washington, where one of their sons now lived. With no family left in Woodstock, Beatrice began to seek out some new adventures of her own. Her brother Hope, a lumberman, had settled in Vancouver and urged his sister to join him. Beatrice agreed and moved to the roaring city in 1910, eventually moving into a hotel on Granville Street. The Vancouver of those days was very different from the sprawling city of today. When Beatrice arrived there, eastern and western investors were pouring money into developing British Columbia's mineral, lumber, and fishing resources. Vancouver was the province's financial, transportation, and trading centre. One hundred thousand people lived there, all hoping to find success in the raw frontier city — and it was very raw, indeed. Stanley Park, the city's version of New York's Central Park, had been established. However, the streets and avenues so familiar to us today were still being cut out of old-growth forest, and houses, mills, schools, hospitals, and factories were being constructed as quickly as land could be cleared to accommodate them.

In Vancouver, Beatrice took up her favourite winter sports — skating and sledding. In January 1911 she described her activities in a letter to her mother. "We all went over to Nelson Street where the coasting was in full swing. Dozens of bobsleds were flying down the hill and the horns and bells and yelling made a great din. The people certainly went crazy and no wonder. There was a path of ice down the middle of the hill and there were hundreds and hundreds joining in the sport. They would start at Jervis and go nearly to Chilco Street, below Denman — over five blocks — at a rate that had the autos beat. Of course there were no horses or autos within blocks and there was a policeman at Denman to stop the cars there. We were offered seats on one fine pair of bobs and made the most of it."

By 1912, Beatrice was working as a staff journalist for the *Vancouver World* and book review editor for the *Saturday Sunset*. Journalist Mabel Durham, senior editor of the women's page at the *Vancouver Province*, also recognized Nasmyth's potential, hiring her as assistant women's editor. The two forged what would become a lifelong friendship.

Whether Beatrice was describing trends in women's fashions or the rising popularity of séances, her feminist views frequently crept into her articles. She had little patience with the limitations that society placed on women and saw no reason why women should not have the vote. According to historian Marjory Lang, "Mabel Durham and Beatrice Nasmyth of the *Province*, Clare Battle of the *World*, and Lily Laverock of the *News-Advertiser*, despite the rivalries of their respective papers, shared a sober-minded fervour that materialized into an unusually marked emphasis on social reform in the women's pages of Vancouver newspapers during the lively decade of female activism before and during the First World War."[23]

Beatrice would sometimes air her views in unconventional ways. Late one morning, her father showed up at the newsroom of the *Vancouver Province*. He was in town for a brief visit and wanted to surprise his daughter and take her out to lunch. Unfortunately, Beatrice had plans of her own for that day, but she changed them and suggested they go to one of the more popular downtown restaurants. As they sat together at a linen-covered table, amid the clinking of china and swell of conversation, she took a deep breath. She stood up, rapped her glass, cleared her throat and launched into a stirring pro-suffrage speech.[24] Her father was seldom surprised by anything his daughter did and her speech was no exception. In her nineties, Beatrice could still remember him beaming at her. "Oh, he was proud of me!"

Beatrice was a charter member of the Vancouver branch of the Canadian Women's Press Club (CWPC), becoming president of the chapter in 1913.[25] One of the members of the CWPC was the poet Pauline Johnson. Pauline had made Vancouver her permanent home in 1909 and quickly made friends in the booming city. Beatrice and Pauline became close, meeting regularly for lunch on the shores of Stanley Park where Pauline beached her canoe. They would also correspond whenever Pauline was on one of her frequent speaking tours. Pauline nicknamed Beatrice "little girl" and confided to her many of Pauline's own challenges as a writer, including scathing comments about publishers who released her books without making necessary corrections. One Christmas, Pauline presented Beatrice with a copy of her book *Flint and Feather*. It was inscribed "to my fellow craftswoman, Beatrice Nasmyth, with my love, E. Pauline Johnson." The close friendship between the two women lasted until 1913, when Johnson became seriously ill, likely with breast cancer. Bea and a small group of female journalists took turns attending Johnson throughout the short months before her untimely death.[26]

In May 1914 another event captured Beatrice's interest. Vancouver's boom had gone bust two years before, the result of overexpansion and a depressed world market for the province's commodities. Vancouver businesses had suffered, and unemployment had grown. One-third of the city's population was British-born, and many looked for scapegoats to blame. They found them among the growing Asian population. In the late nineteenth century, many Indians and Chinese had emigrated to Canada and helped build the railroad and clear the land on which Vancouver now stood.

The contribution of Asian immigrants was quickly forgotten when the jobs of white Canadians were threatened by the recession. Anti-Oriental riots erupted downtown, and the federal government tightened

Beatrice's First World War passport photo.

immigration rules. This included the implementation of a "continuous voyage" regulation that stated that Indians could come to Canada only by continuous passage from India (a British colony) — at a time when there was no direct steamship route between the two countries.[27] Into this tense situation sailed an immigrant ship called the *Komagata Maru*. The ship was owned by Gurdit Singh, a Sikh who wanted to challenge the unfair Canadian legislation. When the ship reached Vancouver's Burard Inlet, its 376 Indian passengers were not allowed to dock and disembark. Food and water ran short, but Canadian officials wouldn't budge.

In the name of protecting British Columbia from illegal immigrants, many Vancouverites — including Beatrice Nasmyth — took turns watching the ship as it lay in the harbour, reporting whenever it looked as though its hungry and exhausted human cargo might make an attempt at disembarking. During this less-than-shining moment in her life, Beatrice's usual tolerance and sense of fair play were absent, and she was part of the intolerant majority that wanted to keep Canada for the English. A few months after the *Komagata Maru* incident, she would be on her way to London to cover the First World War — an experience that would make her reassess such prejudices and redefine what it really meant to be Canadian.

MONTREAL, Quebec, August 10, 1914. Beatrice stood waiting by the gangplank while Guy finished checking in. The Port of Montreal thronged with men who had booked passage for England. Most planned to join the British Expeditionary Force, fearing that the war would be over before the Canadian army made its way overseas. Women were travelling to Britain too, afraid that they might not be able to travel to the old country once hostilities really got underway.

Beatrice had checked in her heavy trunk, but continued to carry her small black Underwood typewriter in its own tough black case. "Do you want help with that, Ma'am?" asked a porter. "No thanks, I'm fine," she replied. She wasn't about to entrust anyone with the most important tool she would need once she reached England.

Chapter 2

Military Daughter

So often, we go through our battles in private. As it was with me and with many of the women in my generation. We were taught and reared and molded to keep that stiff upper lip and to never explain in public how deeply some people have hurt us. I cannot get away from that mold. I am comfortable in it. I derive my sanity from it.

— Psyche Roxas-Mendoza

MONTREAL, Quebec, December 1904. Tobacco smoke hovered over the cluttered desks in the *Montreal Star* newsroom. Back issues of the newspaper were glued to the wall, and calendars showing smiling girls in clinging gowns were hung here and there to add visual interest. Behind one of the desks, a thirty-something man in a baggy suit and grimy collar was pecking away at a black cast-iron typewriter. Next to him sat a balding man scribbling in a small notebook, his lit cigar lying forgotten on the edge of his desk, burning into the oak veneer. Another cluster of men was gathered in the opposite corner of the room, discussing the landslide victory of Theodore Roosevelt in the American presidential election. That conversation stopped abruptly when an elegantly dressed woman stepped into the newsroom.

Mary MacLeod Moore ignored the silence and raised eyebrows and crossed quickly to the managing editor's office, her tailored navy blue skirt swishing across the scuffed wooden floor. She was the only female journalist assigned to the newsroom "reporting, interviewing and writing on every imaginable topic,"[1] and she was well aware her presence was still a novelty.[2] While the *Star* was accustomed to having famous women on its staff — popular writer Sara Jeanette Duncan had been a columnist in the 1880s — over twenty years later, a woman in the newsroom was still a rare sight.

Fortunately for Mary, social prejudice didn't deter the editor of the *Star*. After all, it *was* the twentieth century, and Mary was a popular journalist he'd managed to poach from the *Montreal Herald*, one of his paper's main rivals. He didn't invite her to sit down. He had a breaking story and Mary was just the person to handle it. A young woman had answered an advertisement offering agricultural education to women on a working farm. She had paid the tuition, but when she arrived at the farm it became clear that not only had she been cheated, but her teacher had no intention of allowing her to leave. What his plans were for his student weren't clear, but the woman didn't hang around to find out. She escaped by attracting the attention of a passerby and was now staying with friends who lived outside Montreal.

Mary was to go to where the woman was staying, interview her, return by the night train, write the story, and turn it in the next morning. It was precisely the kind of assignment she had been hoping for — a serious story rather than the frothy society fare she'd been forced to dish up in her former job at the *Herald*: endless stories about the "lovely" wedding of Miss Upper-Crust to Mr. Snob, with detailed descriptions of gowns worn, flowers on display, and famous visitors in attendance. Thankfully, that was in the past. This was *real* journalism.

There was a deep blanket of snow on the ground when Mary started off on her three-hour train journey. She arrived at the station late in the afternoon and walked a mile to the house, where she got her interview and spent the early evening visiting. Her hosts invited her to spend the night, but Mary turned them down, saying she had to return to Montreal on the late-night train.

It was almost eleven o'clock when she finally left the house. Only the moon illuminated the tree-lined road as she walked nervously along, feeling icy cold despite her heavy winter coat. In the dark, everything looked the same, and Mary had no way of knowing if she was going in the right direction. She finally spotted the lights of a train station across a wide white field and started to cross it. Before she had gone a dozen steps, Mary fell face-downward into a deep drift. Her heavy coat was covered in snow; the flowers on her wide-brimmed hat were drooping. By the time she managed to pull herself free, she had stopped being anxious and was stubbornly determined to file her story at all costs. Wet and bedraggled, Mary stumbled across the field to the station and woke the elderly station-master who was asleep by the potbellied stove in the reception room. He wasn't happy, especially since she was at the *wrong station*. He directed her to a spot a few kilometres away and Mary started off yet again. This time she arrived at the proper destination and waited until the midnight train thundered in at last.

Back in Montreal, Mary took a cab to the *Star* office, where she typed out her story, handed it in, and went home to bed. When the paper arrived on her doorstep, she read it from end to end. Her story was nowhere. "The proprietor had decided that the matter was libelous!" Years later she would laugh off the experience. But it was a lesson she would remember — journalists, male and female, existed in a box in which the interests of editors, publishers, and advertisers reigned supreme. Through a combination of persistence, discipline, talent, and determination, Moore would eventually rise above the challenges and become a popular international columnist, covering everything from women's suffrage to two world wars. But it was a long road that took her there, a road that had begun in an isolated outpost of the British Empire.

"My childhood was spent a mile from a French-Canadian village on the St. Lawrence River,"[3] Mary MacLeod Moore would one day write. The village she was describing was La Prairie, Quebec. Fifteen kilometres southeast of Montreal, it was already over 250 years old by the time of Mary's birth in 1871.[4] The site of the village had been "discovered" by the French explorer Samuel de Champlain in 1611 when he sailed up the St. Lawrence River and landed in an area the Native peoples called "Kantake." The explorer translated "Kantake" as "La Prairie" and the name stuck.

By the end of the seventeenth century, Jesuits had established a mission in La Prairie, and French colonists began to settle there. The newcomers didn't enjoy their peaceful life for long. In 1754, war erupted between Britain and France, spilling over into what was then Lower Canada. For seven years, French and English fought a pitched battle in North America, resulting in the surrender of New France to Britain.

The end of the war did not mean the end of French identity and culture in Quebec. In La Prairie, a British garrison was built at the edge of the village, but the community itself — with few exceptions — continued to be made up of French-speaking innkeepers, railway workers, blacksmiths, merchants, shoemakers, tavern-keepers, saddlers, physicians, lawyers, and grocers. The streets were lined with thick-walled houses with deep casement windows and wooden shutters, steep roofs, and stout chimneys. In 1841, the grey stone Roman Catholic Church of the Nativity was built and several French-speaking schools were established in the village and surrounding farming community. By the 1860s, nearly two thousand people lived in La Prairie and its garrison.[5] One of them was Mary's father.

Lieutenant Colonel William MacLeod Moore, a jowly, bearded, middle-aged officer with a high forehead, thinning hair, and a generous waistline, was the descendant of a long line of aristocratic Anglo-Irish soldiers. Born in Kildare, Ireland, in 1810, he was educated in Scotland and then sent to Sandhurst Military College in England. He joined the 69th Regiment in 1831, serving in the West Indies, Ireland, Malta, and Canada. In 1864, he was posted to La Prairie as "Staff Officer of Out-Pensioners,"[6] charged with administering small stipends to military retirees. It was a plum job, a reward for loyal service to the British crown. Yet it was a lonely kind of prize when there was no one to share it with. Moore's wife, Mary, had died in 1840, and their only daughter, Charlotte, had recently married and left home.

By 1868, Moore had found a partner to fill the void. His second wife was Emily Susan Barber, a woman twenty-six years his junior and one year younger than his daughter. She was an intelligent, well-read woman. Her mother, Lucinda Shortiss, was from an old established Toronto family, and her father, George Anthony Barber, was publisher and editor of the conservative *Toronto Commercial Herald* — the very line of work that his future granddaughter Mary would pursue.[7]

LA PRAIRIE, Quebec, December 4, 1871. William MacLeod Moore was relieved. His beloved Emily had survived childbirth yet again. Their second child was a round-faced, dark-haired bundle whom they named after William's first wife, Mary. Their first child, Catherine Elizabeth, had been born in 1869. The Moores would have two more children — Anna, born in 1874, and William in 1877.[8]

All four children spent their childhood years in the La Prairie garrison. Soldiers were allowed to marry and live with their wives and children in the whitewashed barracks, finding privacy behind curtains hung around rough wooden beds. However, William MacLeod Moore and his family were provided with separate and much more elaborate quarters. They lived in a long, low building that housed apartments for officers and their families, with an outside well dedicated to their sole use, along with two outdoor privies located conveniently nearby. There were servants to wash their clothes and cook their meals. It was a simple but comfortable life.

LA PRAIRIE, Quebec, August 1881. It was a scorching-hot afternoon. The air smelled of dust and dry grass. Mary and the other children found shade beneath the drooping leaves of an ancient maple tree in the corner of the church cemetery. Four-year-old William had already fallen asleep in a pile of brown leaves, his chubby hands wrapped around a bedraggled toy horse, while seven-year-old Anna attempted to make a chain from the dandelions growing among the headstones. Mary and Catherine had weightier matters on their minds. Mary had dug a small hole behind a tall marble cross and was putting a small wooden fruit crate into the pit. Inside the box, wrapped in a scrap of purple satin, was a mass of white feathers that had once been a much-loved bantam. Mary stuck a small shingle into the ground at the head of the little grave. On it, written in flowing script (or at least as flowing as a ten-year-old could manage) were the words "Here Lies Lord Bantam." Twelve-year-old Catherine began reading the Church of England's service for the dead.[9]

The story reveals a melancholy and isolated childhood. According to Mary, her family "had no near neighbours and there were only three English families in the village with whom we were intimate."[10] There were few if any other children living at the fort when the Moores' father was stationed there, and they were not encouraged to make friends with French-Canadian children. There was still a deep divide between the two cultures, with La Prairie embodying French history and culture and the military representing the British Empire with its power and sense of racial superiority. Those living in the garrison had little need to interact with locals — the fort provided for all their needs. It had a bakehouse, cookhouse, storehouse, officers' quarters, infirmary, barn, and horses and other domestic animals.

The single mile between the Moores' home and the village might as well have been a hundred for Mary and her siblings. Yet that isolation had its advantages. It made Mary independent and allowed her the space to develop a rich imagination, an imagination actively nurtured by her parents. They "talked of people in books as if they were next-door neighbours (not that we had any) and had the pens of ready writers, albeit not professional ones."[11] William MacLeod Moore had an extensive personal library to which he allowed his daughter ready access. There was also a well-stocked library in the La Prairie garrison, and many of the books her father borrowed found their way into Mary's eager hands. Whether influenced by her parents or by her maternal grandfather's involvement in the newspaper business, by the time she reached her teens, she had begun to dream of becoming a writer. Those were the years when her "aims were high, and nothing but the top of the tree figured in my dreams as a future position for a small girl."[12] This quiet, happy life, however, did not last for long.

LA PRAIRIE, Quebec, March 1882. Catherine MacLeod Moore was the first to get sick. She had a high fever and her entire body ached. Soon, a blistering, flaming rash covered her skin. Catherine died after only a few days' illness, but not before the disease had fatally spread to young Anna.

The loss of the two sisters was not the last disaster to devastate the Moore family. One evening in September 1882, a lightning storm began. Inside the Moores' apartment, everyone was asleep — Mary and young William snug under feather comforters, their parents slumbering in the main bedroom. Lightning struck the officers' quarters and flames spread across and up the tinder-dry walls. Smoke seeped across the floor of the kitchen and wound its poisonous way up the stairs. Then panic, screaming and shouting, children and parents semi-conscious from the smoke. In the morning, only a smoking ruin was left of the home in which Mary had been born and of the prized books that had once nurtured her fertile imagination.

In a brief memoir in *Saturday Night Magazine*, Mary makes no mention of the death of her sisters and only the briefest of references to the fire that destroyed her childhood home. It is no surprise the daughter of a military man would hold a stiff upper lip in the face of such extreme loss. Mary's reticence about sharing intimate family details in print, especially grief, was part of the hardened outer shell with which she would protect herself and her feelings throughout her life and career.

Within two years, William MacLeod Moore was transferred to the British garrison in Prescott, Ontario, and Mary was dispatched to one of the many low-cost, slightly down-at-the-heel Montreal boarding schools operated for the children of Canada's growing middle class. At thirteen, the introspective and solitary child was already beginning to dream of a future career as a writer. She created her own school newspaper, and when "one particularly severe teacher smiled" while reading it, Mary felt her "career was assured."

It was at boarding school that Mary also began to develop an essential skill for freelance journalists — the ability to turn any event into good, saleable copy.[13] "The first time I ever saw anything of mine in print was after a certain thrilling adventure which took place one night when the school had retired to bed," she later wrote. "A gentleman who was not enslaved by the principle of temperance disturbed our peace by pounding on the door demanding admission under the impression he was locked out of his own house. He was routed by our dear Head and we returned to bed. Inspired by this lively affair, I wrote the story of "Mr. Kelly" which ended pompously with the words: 'And so defeated by our teachers, Mr. Kelly faded away like a meteor of the night, shining but to leave more lonely hearts that hailed its transient flight.'" Somehow the story of the drunk and the boarding school was brought to the attention of the editor of *Saturday Night Magazine*, who published the story.[14]

In 1891, Mary's father died.[15] She knew she would need to find a career soon if she were to support herself. Mary graduated from boarding school and managed to pursue further studies at the New York School of Applied Design for Women. The school was the dream of philanthropist Ellen Dunlop. Established in the heart of what is now Manhattan, it championed the Arts and Crafts movement, providing courses in book-cover illustration, stained glass, and textile and wallpaper design. The school enlarged Mary's appreciation of art and modern design, something that would reveal itself again and again in the columns she would one day write.

THOUSAND ISLANDS, Quebec, 1898. A grey-haired man on a dilapidated bicycle drew up to the cabin and dismounted. "Anyone here named M.E. MacLeod Moore?" he asked, waving a telegram. "That's me!" Mary tumbled out of the hammock where she'd been reading the latest issue of *Saturday Night*. She'd run out of money in New York and was back in Canada, visiting friends in the Thousand Islands and planning her next steps. The telegram was from her brother, by then "a youngster with a firm of trade papers in Montreal."[16] The message said there was "something" for her to do if she returned home right away. Mary took the four a.m. train to Montreal, where she learned that her brother's boss had just purchased a weekly newspaper — the short-lived *Montreal Metropolitan*[17] — and didn't have an editor. Mary was promptly hired as "chief cook and bottlewasher at a salary of five dollars per week." Later, a "real" editor was appointed and Mary became his assistant.[18]

For Mary, the opportunity to work as a paid journalist was a coup. It was the height of the Victorian era, a time when society embraced an idealized understanding of home and family. Men were to work in the "public sphere," in the dirty world of business and politics, while middle- and upper-class women were expected to be the queens of the "domestic sphere," to work inside the home as wives, mothers, and obedient daughters — not battle-worn journalists toiling in smoky, noisy offices. Mary, raised in a genteel but relatively poor family, was well aware that Victorian expectations for women were a sham. Women like herself — fatherless and without husbands to support them — were forced by circumstance to earn their own living outside the home, and at a time when few careers were open to women, most of the jobs they were allowed to do were anything but refined.

The new century brought greater opportunities. Newspapers and magazines were moving away from being mouthpieces for political parties to being vehicles for delivering information and entertainment to a broad audience.[19] As publishers became less dependent on political patronage, they became more dependent on advertising revenue. Ads for everything from corsets to washing machines suddenly began to appear. Since women were making most of the buying decisions related to household and personal items, advertisers began to press newspapers to appeal to their female readers. Publishers took the hint, and the "women's department" was born.

The women's pages provided the first major opportunity for women to break into the world of journalism, and many of the women who were featured in the section would become household names. According to historian Marjory Lang, "the editor of the women's page frequently created her own newspaper identity, often earmarked by a catchy pseudonym with which her readers could identify. Her editorial might take the form of an "over-the-fence" chat, projecting the illusion of private communication into a public venue. For isolated rural readers, the editor was a surrogate friend and the women's page a kind of neighbourhood forum. In urban centres, where the communities had grown too large to be cemented by female ties, the women's page carried on the tradition of telling women things about other women whom they did not know but whom they came to recognize as mainstays of the society or clubs column."[20]

Mary MacLeod Moore was one of the pioneers of this form of journalism, written *by* women *for* women. Sometime around 1902 the editor of the *Montreal Herald* offered her the job of editor of the women's page and "reporter of all matters affecting women."[21] She quit her job at the *Metropolitan* and accepted the new one with "alacrity, and flung myself into work which still involved the detested 'personals,' as well as a children's page, which I signed 'Pandora.'"[22]

Mary's choice of pseudonym was prescient. Like the mythological character, she had an insatiable curiosity, and would one day lift the lid off the struggles of women who were living in the shadow of war. However, in the early 1900s, "Pandora" was just another young woman trying to make her way in the world of journalism.

MONTREAL, Quebec, June 1902. The crowd broke into applause as the open-air performance of *As You Like It* came to an end. It was a warm summer evening, and the grounds of McGill University were lush and green. A young couple stayed long after the performance, chatting in their collapsible wooden seats, mulling over the performance for the review the young man was planning to write. The black-haired woman with the blue-grey eyes was Mary MacLeod Moore, and the tall, athletic-looking man in the shabby suit was friend and fellow *Herald* reporter Calvin McQuesten.

Calvin McQuesten was a member of a once-prosperous family from Hamilton, Ontario. His family lived in a grey stone mansion called Whitehern and had once been leaders of Hamilton's political and social scene. In 1888, their status rapidly declined when Calvin's father, Isaac, went bankrupt and died shortly afterwards, possibly as a result of suicide. The family was suddenly unwelcome in many upper-class homes, and Calvin's mother, Mary, had to struggle to keep their house and possessions out of the hands of creditors, re-establish the family's reputation, and educate her children. The crisis meant that Calvin — despite having been born with a "withered hand" and some disability on his left side — had to find his own way in the world. For a while, he turned to journalism, writing a society column under the pseudonym "Nina Vivian" for the *Toronto News*. In 1902 he moved to the *Montreal Herald*, where he covered local events and wrote another column, "The Tatler." It was in the dingy offices of the *Herald* — "where we waded through the dust and muddle of the ages"[23] — that he met Mary MacLeod Moore.

Mary and Calvin had a lot in common. They were roughly the same age (Calvin was born in 1876), and both had been raised in cultured, educated families with modest incomes. According to his biographer, Calvin was a true Renaissance man who had a "broad knowledge of history, politics, religion, art, literature, social issues, poetry and humour."[24]

Despite his deformity, he was attractive, with a square, open face, dark hair, and ready smile. Mary matched him with her own good looks. She was slender, with high cheekbones, coal-coloured wavy hair, large eyes, and a straight nose. They made a striking couple as they chatted in the drab newspaper office,[25] but their relationship didn't evolve into a grand passion, possibly because Calvin's controlling mother wanted him to marry someone more "suitable" than dowerless Mary. Yet it was clear she meant a lot to Calvin. After his death in 1968, many of Mary's early letters were found among his private papers.

The stress of meeting tight deadlines in exchange for meagre pay had opposite effects on the two reporters. In 1903, while covering a violent strike of street railway workers in Montreal, Calvin suffered a nervous breakdown and resigned. He had always been better suited to writing society gossip than headline stories. Mary, however, thrived under pressure. She was ambitious and had more confidence in her own abilities, chafing at the low salary meted out to reporters, especially women. Mary had also become a keen suffragist, believing that women should be given the same opportunities as men in the newsroom. When the editor of the *Montreal Star* offered her a "good salary with a rise in prospect," she jumped ship.

At the *Star*, Mary finally got the chance to write "hard news," but her resolve to move beyond the cloister of the women's page didn't last long. Perhaps it was the disdain of her fellow reporters or the isolation of being one of only a few women on the staff; whatever the case, by 1905 Mary had quit her job and was the assistant editor of the New York fashion magazine *L'art de la Mode,* a "journal of the latest styles."[26] Her tiny office was on bustling East Nineteenth Street, in the heart of the booming city.

The *Star* may have offered Mary the opportunity to work in the newsroom, but *L'art de la Mode* offered her more money — forty dollars per month, an impressive salary for a female journalist at the turn of the century. "Ladies' magazines" in North America and Europe were the first to provide reasonable pay for female writers, along with the opportunity to showcase their abilities. Luminaries such as George Eliot and Harriet Martineau worked on such magazines before becoming leading literary figures.

After only a few months in her new job, Mary took a leave of absence so she and her mother could set off for England to visit her brother, now a member of a London advertising firm. Such a trip demanded a new wardrobe. "What would appear to Montreal and Toronto even more startling is that for the first time in my life I have gone in for swell clothes and have just bought a $90 gown for England," she wrote to Calvin. "It was made to order but the lady went into mourning, so my chief bought it for me at a very swell price for $50. Imagine in the *Herald* days thinking of a gown at $50!"

———

WINNIPEG, Manitoba, June 1906. The train was filled with well-known female journalists from across the country, from veterans such as war correspondent "Kit" Coleman to agricultural reporter Cora Hind and society columnist Katherine Hughes. Together they were on a round-trip train journey across the Prairies to Banff and back to Winnipeg.

The junket, sponsored by the CPR as a way to promote settlement in Western Canada, was the highlight of the first convention of the Canadian Women's Press Club. The convention was a special treat — an opportunity to mix with women who shared similar goals and aspirations — and Mary was thrilled to be among some of the leading women in her profession. It had only been a month since she had returned from England to take up her pen once again for *L'art de la Mode* and already she was chafing at the limitations her job imposed upon her. Being surrounded by ambitious, successful women who were working for major publications made Mary critical of her job at the fashion magazine. "There is nothing literary about it," she wrote to Calvin. "Apart from the actual editing, make up, engravers, etc., I supervise the work of the artists, criticize, change, etc. and keep a watchful eye on the fashion situation. It is good training but even with the prospect of eventually getting $50 per week, I don't want to end my career in a fashion magazine."

After the convention, Mary stayed at her post for one final year before returning overseas, this time permanently.[27] She had been brought up to believe that London was the centre of the imperial universe and, like her brother, Mary knew she could and would make her fortune there.

Military Daughter   49

LONDON, England, 1907. Mary sat in the large bay window, her table set with a white linen cloth, a silver pot of hot tea, and sweet rolls on a china plate. Seated at other tables were women of various social classes — from women in expensive Paris day gowns to brisk young women in high-necked blouses, well-worn skirts, and matching jackets. They were all enjoying their afternoon tea on the second floor of the Lyceum Club, an austere, five-storey white brick building at 128 Piccadilly, in the heart of London. The Lyceum was dedicated to giving professional women — particularly writers and artists — a place where they could conduct business, attend lectures, and meet others who shared their interests. According to its founder, the brilliant writer and actress Constance Smedley, it "was intended to be a corporate social home for educated women, wherein women of small or large incomes could feel part of the aristocracy of intellect, and come into free and helpful contact with men and women from all over the world."[28]

Smedley had founded the Lyceum Club in 1904, partly out of frustration at the limitations she had experienced as a member of another women's organization — the Writers Club. The Writers Club was devoted to female writers, but offered poor accommodation and food to its members. Men's clubs, by comparison, were opulent places where members could entertain clients in style. Fine china, linen tablecloths, and formal service were the hallmarks of those smoke-filled clubs, where men sat in comfortable leather chairs, drank port from crystal glasses, and cemented important business deals. Literary dinners at prestigious men's clubs such as the Savile also offered male writers the opportunity to dine with influential editors, reviewers, agents and publishers.

Smedley felt women deserved and needed similar meeting places if they were to compete with men on a level playing field. She drew on her vast network of social and literary connections and, with the backing of her businessman-father and society suffragists like Lady Balfour, established an organization open to all educated women. The influence of the Lyceum Club soon spread throughout Europe. Sister clubs were formed in several major capitals. As historian Grace Brockington writes, it was "no ordinary social club, for it provided a unique information bureau to advise women about their careers, a permanent art gallery, and, pre-eminently, an international network of club-houses across Europe."

Many of the members of the Lyceum Club were professional journalists. By 1907, in Great Britain as in Canada, women were a well-established part of the fabric of most newspapers and magazines. Three of the best-known columns by women appeared in the weekly *Illustrated London News*, the *Graphic*, and the daily *Pall Mall Gazette*. These publications had a commanding reach. Each boasted a circulation of a quarter of a million copies, and the journalists who wrote for their women's pages enjoyed a vast and loyal following. On the surface, their columns were intended to provide female readers with light gossip, along with fashion and domestic advice. Yet their authors often had very different agendas. At the *Illustrated London News*, ardent suffragist Florence Fenwick-Miller penned a column combining "society, dress, domesticity and charity" with "culture, thought, and public welfare." And over at the rival *Graphic*, Lady Violet Greville was busy writing about art, literature, theatre, and dress while at the same time promoting women in sport. Such columns weren't flashes in the pan — Fenwick-Miller's column would run from 1886 to 1918.

Mary, who had pulled herself up by her own bootstraps, was determined to become every bit as successful as these writers. She and her mother were now living with her brother at 39 Ashley Gardens in fashionable Westminster, a short walk from the Houses of Parliament, Westminster Cathedral, and Buckingham Palace. Mac was now a successful advertising man with a comfortable income, his home a considerable contrast to the isolated wooden outposts of their childhood. Ashley Gardens was a series of tall red brick blocks built in 1890 for affluent Londoners. Within their thickly carpeted rooms with their heavily draped windows and well-upholstered furniture lived some of Britain's most famous sons and daughters. Thomas Hardy had lived there in the 1890s and George Bernard Shaw had made one of the flats the setting for his comedy *The Philanderer*. When Mary and her mother had moved in, Sir Henry Lucy, one of England's most famous parliamentary journalists, was living in the flat on the floor just above theirs.

"We have a very happy time and I do the things and meet the people we used to read about in papers and books and think so wonderful,"

Mary wrote to Calvin. "I am doing some work on 'Canada,' published here. Also free cause work here and some for one Acton Pub. Co., Montreal and Toronto, which is only potboiler fashion, I only work about one-third of the time and do voluntary work gratis and amuse myself the rest! Does that sound like me?" But she was doing much more than she let on. Mary was carrying a heavy load of freelancing (perhaps aided by her brother's Fleet Street contacts), and by 1910 was also writing an occasional column for Canada's *Saturday Night Magazine*. Entitled "London Letter," it was an upbeat feature covering topics as diverse as politics, fashion, the royal family and women's suffrage. Mary's articles revealed she was a staunch feminist, concerned not only with the vote, but the rights of women in general.

"I am frequently surprised and mildly amused at the quite inadequate and sentimental reasons given against women's suffrage by its strong opponents," she wrote in one column, after excoriating a prominent anti-suffrage campaigner. In other columns, she profiled prominent women who had broken down obstacles in the fight for their rights: "Miss Edith Campbell, said to be the first woman candidate in the United States to have received a vote of a President, has just been elected member of the Board of Education of Cincinnati," she wrote in the January 1912 issue of *Saturday Night*.

At first, Mary's "London Letters" were in the news section of *Saturday Night*, signed "M. E. McL. M." The signature was an attempt to disguise her gender from readers — old prejudices against women on the news side would take decades to disappear. However, after writing a highly successful series on the coronation of King George V, "much admired" by the Canadian public, her column was moved to the women's section of the magazine and became a weekly feature, with her byline signed in full.

Mary was also hired to write a regular feature for the London *Sunday Times* under her old pseudonym "Pandora." Her new boss was editor Leonard Rees, a short, monocled martinet who wore baggy suits and cross-examined reporters with his "hands thrust into his pockets, leaning back against a table, illuminating the discussion with a quip and a wink of the eye."[29] Leonard demanded loyalty and hard work from all of his staff, and usually got it. "He made all who did work for him feel the dignity of their craft," writer Herbert Sidebotham would recall years later. "You felt in writing for Rees that you were doing more than earning your living, you were discharging an honourable public office."[30]

Editor of the newspaper since 1901, Rees had a reputation for knowing talent when he saw it, hiring gifted writers such as Desmond MacCarthy, Ernest Newman, and Gerald Barry. He treated Mary in the same demanding, professional way that he treated all his staff — but as subsequent events would prove, his feelings for her went much deeper.

"I have been elected to the council of the Society of Women Journalists with Beatrise Hanadan et al, and I do a good bit of work at the Lyceum Club, the largest professional women's Club in the world," Mary wrote to Calvin. Gone was the breathless girl, amazed at her own audacity in purchasing a fifty-dollar gown. She had been replaced by a self-assured professional who was now working for major newspapers and covering stories about the comings and goings of Britain's wealthiest and most prominent citizens. In 1912 she was one of only a few women listed in *Canadian Men and Women of the Time*, a "Who's Who" of prominent personalities. But her best stories were yet to come. Within just two short years, Britain and her colonies would be facing the first "war to end all wars," and Mary would be in a perfect position to cover it for the folks back home.

Chapter 3

The Aristocrat

I believe in aristocracy, though — if that is the right word, and if a democrat may use it. Not an aristocracy of power, based upon rank and influence, but an aristocracy of the sensitive, the considerate and the plucky. Its members are to be found in all nations and classes.... They represent the true human tradition, the one permanent victory of our queer race over cruelty and chaos. Thousands of them perish in obscurity, a few are great names. They are sensitive for others as well as themselves, they are considerate without being fussy, their pluck is not swankiness but power to endure, and they can take a joke.
— E.M. Forster, *Two Cheers for Democracy*

PARIS, France, August 18, 1914. Elizabeth Montizambert sat at her usual table at a café on the Boulevard Sebastopol, sipping espresso and munching a sliced baguette covered in creamy butter. She was a tiny woman with a long oval face and large nose, curly brown hair, and intelligent hazel eyes. A bell-shaped silk tunic and lavender hobble skirt clung to her figure, an outfit that would make any other woman look like a mauve lampshade, but that on Elizabeth seemed the height of elegance. In her right hand she held a long silver pen that she tapped absentmindedly on the table as she watched shoppers gather in front of the grocery store on the opposite side of the road. The shop wasn't due to open for another half hour, but already at least twenty women were waiting outside.

In between bites of crisp bread, Elizabeth jotted notes for her upcoming column for the *Montreal Gazette* — descriptions of the tumultuous events of the past few weeks. France was now living in the shadow of war, and everyone was on edge. Only a few days before, there had been a run on the Caisse d'Epargne, a bank catering to small-account holders. The police had been called in to restore calm and enforce the new rule of paying out only ten francs per customer every two weeks. Then, on July 30, the Banque de France was forced to pay out thirteen million francs in five-franc pieces in exchange for banknotes. With the Germans marching towards Paris, no one trusted paper currency any longer.

When she looked up from her copy, Elizabeth was astonished to see that there were now over a hundred women waiting for the grocery store to open. Seamstresses, housewives, and servants jostled together, each struggling to hold on to her place on the pavement. More and more women were joining the throng, and within minutes over a thousand were crowded down the sidewalks on both sides of the store.

To Elizabeth, they resembled a theatre queue waiting to get in for a sold-out performance. But there was no happy anticipation in this crowd — only desperation and fear. Across Paris, women were laying in heavy stores of flour, sugar, and other provisions against the threat of future hunger. Most were familiar enough with French history to remember the Franco-Prussian War. From 1870 to 1871, Paris had been surrounded by invading Prussian forces. Food ran out and people were forced to eat dogs and horses, even rats. After enduring terrible bombardment by long-range siege guns, the city finally capitulated. Now the Germans were on the march again, and Parisians were preparing for the worst.

Outside the grocery store, patience was wearing thin. Women began to push and shove, struggling to force themselves as close to the front of the line as possible. The crowd surged over the curb and backward into the busy road — horse-drawn carriages and cars struggled to avoid driving into the mob of women. Elizabeth gathered her purse and notebook and began to edge her way along the storefronts, fearful that the violence was going to overflow to her side of the street. As tempers frayed, women began to punch and kick one another. Others were knocked to the ground and trampled as women struggled to get out of harm's way. Whistles rang out and the police arrived, breaking up fights and forcing the crowd back.

The story of the grocery store fracas would appear in Elizabeth's next column. "No one dreams of buying anything but food," she wrote. "The sidewalks outside the big department shops like the Gallerie [sic] Lafayette and the Printemps are desolate, and the open air counters with their ribbons and remnants piled up as usual look oddly arresting without the accustomed fringe of buyers. At the big grocers there is another tale, for the long line of would-be customers takes its stand as soon as the shop is opened…."

Only a few months before, few would have dreamed that France would soon be facing such deprivations. But a complicated pattern of alliances and dreams of imperial expansion had triggered what some were already calling a "world war." It had all begun with the murder of an Austrian archduke by a Serbian nationalist. Austria had used the assassination as the excuse it needed to invade Serbia, a country that had once been under Austria's thumb. Germany, ready to extend its own power across Europe, had jumped to the aid of its Austrian ally while casting a wary eye on Russia, Serbia's ally. Russia was mobilizing its army, and Germany demanded that this be stopped. It also handed France, Russia's other ally, an ultimatum — declare neutrality or face the consequences. When Russia did not respond and France replied that it would act only according to its own interests, Germany declared war on both. Now German troops were in Belgium, en route to Paris.

No one seeing the fashionable, aristocratic-looking woman edging her way along the Boulevard Sebastopol would have guessed that she was a journalist, intent on reporting on this new, "great" war. Had they known her family — her mother, Alice Gibb, and father, Charles Montizambert — they would not have been surprised.

QUEBEC CITY, Quebec, December 1866. It was a bitterly cold evening outside, but inside the ballroom, colour swirled across the dance floor like a handful of handkerchiefs drawn from a magician's pocket. The blue and scarlet of military uniforms mingled with the pale pastel shades of ruffled silk gowns and gold, brown, and auburn hair cascading in ringlets.[1]

The elderly widows presiding over the silver punch bowls at the back of the room couldn't help but notice the attention being paid to pretty sixteen-year-old Alice Gibb at this, her debutante ball. It was the event of the season, and the daughters and sons of most of Quebec City's wealthiest families were there. Many of the city's finest young officers were vying for the opportunity to dance with the young heiress, who was taking her first tentative steps into high society.

Alice was the youngest daughter in a Quebec family distinguished by its vast wealth. Her late father, James Lawson Gibb, had been an influential Scottish-born entrepreneur whose businesses included lumbering, banking, real estate, and transportation. James had come to Canada in 1814, a penniless immigrant who went to work as a clerk for William Torrance, a dealer who traded in "foodstuffs, wines, and spirits."[2] The Torrances were an affluent family, part of a network of Scottish Canadian immigrants who had become hugely successful businessmen. William took young James under his wing, providing him with a wage, food, and lodging, and teaching him the trading business. In the process, he fell in love with James's sister Isabella, and eventually married her. A few years later, James cemented the ties between the two families by marrying William's sister Marion.

By the end of the 1830s, with the help of his Torrance relatives, James established his own successful import-export business. There was a shortage of agricultural products in Lower Canada at that time, so Gibb made his money by importing large quantities of wheat, flour, and meat from New York.[3] By 1840, James was president of the Bank of Quebec and the richest man in the province.

The Gibbs moved to a sprawling country estate known as Woodfield, a mansion set high on the banks of the St. Lawrence, within a mile of the spot where General Wolfe was rumoured to have landed.[4] Away from the smoke and grime of Quebec City, the area was popular with the anglophone upper class. Like his neighbours, James had his property landscaped in the manner of an English country estate. The results were impressive. Following a visit to Woodfield in 1857, the American travel writer J. Jay Smith wrote, "Here is everything in the way of well-kept lawns, graperies and greenhouses, outhouses for every possible contingency of weather, gardens, redolent of the finest flowers in which bulbs of the best lilies make a conspicuous figure, and every species of fruit that can be grown. The traveller who does not see Woodfield has not seen Canada in its best trim."[5]

At a time when most people in Quebec were working hard to eke out a basic living (the average work week for factory labourers was sixty hours), Alice Gibb and her eight brothers and sisters were raised in a sheltered, privileged environment — a home glowing with mahogany furniture, thick rugs, and a troop of servants to look after them. There were nursery maids and governesses, the finest clothes, and the best food. In winter, there were sleigh excursions through the frosty white countryside surrounding Quebec City. Spring and summer were spent riding, going on picnics, visiting, and giving and attending parties.

James and Marion Gibb were enthusiastic travellers, touring Europe and visiting relatives in Scotland. At home, they were social leaders — holding huge balls at Woodfield in which local military officers and the cream of Quebec society dined and danced until the early hours of the morning. James was also a patron of the arts whose favourite painter was Cornelius Krieghoff, a friend whose work he liked so much he had it reproduced on his calling cards.

There was a serious side to the sophisticated, high-society Gibb family, too. During the 1820s and early '30s, they attended St. Andrews Presbyterian Church in Quebec City. Quebec Presbyterians were famous for their habit of "walking out" and joining or starting new congregations. James was no exception. Following a disagreement with the minister, he left St. Andrews and eventually bankrolled the building of Chalmers Presbyterian — a larger church in a more affluent part of the city.

QUEBEC CITY, Quebec, October 10, 1858. After attending Sunday worship, James Gibb began to feel ill. He stopped briefly to visit his brother-in-law and then returned home. Pain began to course through his chest. Within an hour, the Scottish immigrant who had risen from clerk to millionaire was dead. He left thousands of pounds to various local charities and, surprisingly, given the widespread religious intolerance of the time, large bequests to both Protestant and Roman Catholic cathedrals.[6]

James's death dealt an unexpected and devastating blow to his family. While they were left in good financial circumstances (Marion received a life interest in Woodfield and each child received fifteen thousand pounds — a fortune by the day's standards), the patriarch who had once directed all their lives was gone. Alice was just ten years old when her father passed away. She would soon lose her mother, as well. Overwhelmed by the loss of her husband, Marion left her children in the capable hands of governesses and relatives and travelled to France. She died in Tours just five years later.

So it was that an orphaned Alice Gibb took her first steps into high society without the benefit of either parent's guidance. Fortunately, her chief suitor seemed like the perfect match. Charles Montizambert was a slender, handsome officer with wide sideburns and a thick, bushy moustache. He was descended from one of the province's most respected families — his great-great grandfather, Pierre Boucher, had arrived in New France early in the seventeenth century, and in 1622 became the first governor of Trois Rivières. After the loss on the Plains of Abraham, his descendants made their peace with the English. In the 1860s, Charles's father, Edward, was law clerk of the Senate and his younger brother Frederick was a prominent physician who would one day become Canada's first surgeon general. Legal and military blood also flowed on his Anglo-Canadian mother's side. Lucy Bowen Montizambert was the daughter of a chief justice and the descendant of several decorated English officers.[7] The wedding of Charles and Alice would unite two powerful and influential Quebec families, but it would be anything but a calm and happy marriage.

QUEBEC CITY, Quebec, May 21, 1867. The spring flowers that decorated the gardens of Woodfield were in full bloom on the spring day when Alice and Charles were married in a quiet ceremony at the home of the bride's late parents.[8] After their honeymoon, the couple moved into a spacious townhouse on Saint-Geneviève Avenue, in the exclusive Upper Town area of Quebec City. From the wrought-iron balcony of their bedroom, the couple could look out at the St. Lawrence River, a view similar to the one Alice had enjoyed at Woodfield. Their first child, Edith Constance, was born in July 1868.

Charles supported his family, not through his volunteer soldiering (which paid very little), but by working as a broker in the lumber and shipping business.[9] He worked with one of his closest friends, George Tudor Pemberton, a young and ambitious entrepreneur whose offices were in St. Peter Street, a rabbit's warren of brick buildings housing merchants, wholesalers, and banks, near some of the busiest wharves that lined the St. Lawrence River.[10]

Charles's military ambitions quickly outstripped his business interests. In 1871, the British army withdrew most of its forces from Canada. The Canadian government decided to establish two artillery batteries that could take care of the artillery and materials left by the departing British army and to run artillery schools for the militia (which up until this time had few training opportunities). These formed the foundation of Canada's first permanent force. Battery A was stationed in Kingston, while Battery B was assigned to Quebec City under the command of British-born Major-General Thomas Bland Strange. With the establishment of a professional army, Charles abandoned his work with George Pemberton and transferred into Strange's company. He quickly grew to admire his commanding officer. When the Montizambert's second daughter was born in 1873, they named her Beatrice Bland in his honour. Charles rose quickly in the ranks, promoted to major in 1871 and lieutenant colonel in 1877.

Charles lived a good life as a high-ranking officer. He joined the Garrison Club, an officer's group with roughly equal numbers of French and English members. Hard drinking and a common social class bound the men together. The club's other major concern was maintaining its members' reputations and honour. "One member was expelled for failing to take legal action to quash malicious rumours that were circulating about him," writes historian Louisa Blair.[11] Charles would one day find his own reputation in tatters — but that time was still a long way off.

In the 1870s, Quebec City was enduring a recession. With the withdrawal of three thousand British troops from the city, local businesses were facing difficult economic times. The lumber and ship-building industries were being replaced by industrial manufacturing and the rise of the steamship. While businessmen worried about their diminishing profits, immigrant Irish labourers were beginning to protest inhumane labour practices and calling for better wages and treatment. When rioting and looting broke out after contractors tried to cut the wages of labourers working on the new Quebec legislature, Charles and his men were called in to quash the protest and defend the interests of commerce.[12]

QUEBEC CITY, Quebec, February 1875. Inside the thick stone walls of the Citadel, Alice Montizambert prepared to give birth to her third and last child. As an officer, Charles was entitled to free medical care for himself and his family, so on that chilly afternoon the fortress's military hospital had been transformed into a temporary maternity ward. It was a rough delivery, and the baby girl was not expected to live. She was baptized at home on March 11, her health too fragile to risk the drafts of the Anglican cathedral that the couple was now attending. But tiny Elizabeth rallied and eventually thrived. She would one day look back on her birth in the Citadel as an appropriate beginning for a future war correspondent.

With three children and a large household to manage, Alice led a busy life. The wives of Canadian officers in the late nineteenth century were expected to be modest, reserved, and attractive, but also to raise families, supervise servants, entertain large groups, and most importantly, support their husbands' careers. It was Alice's responsibility to train their young Irish maids, such as pretty, black-haired Elizabeth Murphy, to care properly for the marble fireplace and the heavy, ornate furniture in the front parlour. For her part, Murphy would have been expected to work sixteen-hour days, seven days a week (with one afternoon off a month), and do all the heavy lifting necessary to keep the large townhouse spotless.

While the life of the "downstairs" staff was an endless round of cleaning and cooking, the "upstairs" world was occupied with securing and nurturing the place of the Montizamberts in Quebec society. During the many dinner parties Alice organized for officers and members of the city's elite, fine silver cutlery and thin gilt-edged china gleamed on her dining-room table. Savoury roast beef, lamb and pork, pies and puddings, thick soups, creamed vegetables, and crisp golden potatoes were prepared by their capable Irish cook, Annie Doolan. Elizabeth and her sisters were not included in the guest list at such parties, and instead took their simpler meals in the upstairs nursery. But through the stairs they caught glimpses of soldiers and ladies laughing in the foyer and heard the piano playing in the front parlour. The smells of gravy and mincemeat pie wafted upwards and sweetened the creamy milk, cheese, and bread of their usual nursery tea.[13]

LONDON, England, 1881. Like her parents, Alice believed in the importance of travel in the education of upper-class children. In 1881, she and her daughters travelled to London, staying with their maid in a boarding house at 26 Eastbourne Terrace.[14] The comfortable stone mansion was located near Paddington Station, the terminal for both the Great Western Railway and the London underground rail service. From this central spot, Alice and the girls could easily visit friends and relatives and explore the city's many shops, museums, and galleries.

It was six-year-old Elizabeth's first trip abroad. She would one day come to know and love London so much that it would be the subject of three travel books, two of which would be written for children. In *Michael's London*, she described a governess named Maretta taking a little boy named Michael out to see the sights of the city. "You can find almost anything you want to find in London if you only know where to look for it, and there are any number of stories hidden in the streets and games you can play there," Maretta tells Michael. One can imagine a tiny Elizabeth playing hide and seek around the lions in Trafalgar Square or in the shadow of Cleopatra's Needle on the Thames Embankment.

The trip overseas was just the beginning of the social education of Elizabeth and her sisters. As the children of a high-ranking officer and as the descendants of two distinguished Canadian families, the girls were expected to act in a manner that reflected their social status. This became even more important in 1882, when Charles became commandant of the Citadel and moved his family into the officers' quarters. During the summer, Canada's governor general, the Marquis of Lorne, and his wife, Princess Louise (daughter of Queen Victoria), also lived at the fortress. As commandant, Charles was expected to attend social functions and receptions sponsored by the vice-regal couple. Early one evening, Elizabeth and her sisters stood awkwardly in the Citadel's grand reception hall as the Princess bent down and talked to each girl as if she were just as important as any of the adults standing stiffly nearby.[15]

For the Montizamberts, 1882 was an auspicious year for other reasons as well. Late in the year, Charles's battery was transferred from Quebec to Kingston. Alice and the children continued to live at the Citadel while Charles spent most of his time with his men at Kingston's Fort Frontenac. As commandant of the battery and its artillery school, he was now more than ready to have his military leadership tested. That opportunity would come in 1884. Trouble was brewing in the West. The First Nations peoples of what are now Saskatchewan and Manitoba were close to starvation due to the disappearance of the buffalo. The Métis — descendants of French voyageurs and First Nations women — were also desperate. They had been forced to shift their livelihoods from hunting to farming, and many were finding the transition difficult. In 1884, Métis leader Louis Riel returned to Canada from the United States to help them defend their rights in the Saskatchewan Valley.

Not everyone was happy with Riel's return. Many remembered that in 1869, he and a group of settlers had proclaimed a provisional government in northern Manitoba. In the ensuing upheaval, a group led by a man named Thomas Scott attempted to overthrow this government. The effort failed, and Scott was executed. When troops came west to fight the Métis, Riel fled to the United States, and federal forces took control of Manitoba without firing a shot. Now, with a new rebellion brewing in the West, old memories of Thomas Scott began to surface, and across English Canada came calls that Riel be arrested for the "murder" of Scott.

On March 19, Riel formed a government at Batoche and demanded the surrender of the North-West Mounted Police headquarters at nearby Fort Carlton. Duck Lake was a small settlement half-way between the Fort and the Métis headquarters at Batoche. When a group of nearly one hundred Mounties and volunteers tangled with Métis and First Nations forces near Duck Lake, they were soon surrounded. Twelve Mounties were killed and the remainder forced to retreat. Five of Riel's men had also been shot dead, but instead of allowing his followers to finish the Mounties off, Riel ordered his men to let them to return to Fort Carlton with their lives.

News of the battle swept across Canada. Men rushed to volunteer in order to "punish" the First Nations and Métis peoples for their supposed arrogance and to ensure that European settlement of the West would go forward without obstacle. Soldiers in Kingston and Quebec City spent hours polishing their equipment and cleaning their uniforms. They were finally going to participate in a real war, and many were eager for the blood sport.

KINGSTON, Ontario, March 28, 1884. Charles was in Kingston when the call came to prepare his men to leave for the northwest. Eight officers, 108 non-commissioned men, two cannons, nine wagons, and eighteen horses gathered at Fort Frontenac. A bugle was sounded and ranks were formed quickly. Charles gave the signal, and a military band began to play. As he marched his men out of the fort, the column was met by cheering crowds. On the avenue to the railway station, women waved from windows, and on the street below wives and children cried and waved handkerchiefs and the military band played "God Save the Queen" and "The Girl I Left Behind Me."

Alice Montizambert was not among the women cheering and crying in Kingston. She was in Quebec City, where opinion was divided about the righteousness of Riel's cause. Across town there were Riel sympathy meetings as well as noisy discussions denouncing him as a traitor. Opinion didn't follow strictly ethnic lines in Quebec City, as it did in the rest of Canada. Francophone Adolphe Caron, minister of militia in the federal government, was responsible for sending troops to put down the rebellion.

The Irish-born Quebec lawyer Charles Fitzpatrick would later defend Riel in court.[16] And the Montizambert family, despite its long French history, was clear about where its loyalties lay. Now Charles and his troops were on their way to clash with Riel in bloody battles in the bush and prairie grass at Fish Creek and Batoche.

While Charles was campaigning in the West, Elizabeth and Beatrice had begun their studies at an exclusive boarding school on the outskirts of Toronto. Bishop Strachan School had been established by the Anglican Church to provide "the practical training and instruction of young ladies in the various branches of a liberal education, including Christian doctrine, as contained in the Bible and the Book of Common Prayer."[17] Its principal was Rose Grier, daughter of a clergyman and descendant of United Empire Loyalists. Classes were held in Wykeham Hall, a solid, three-storey brick mansion on College Street, a quiet mud road lined with wooden sidewalks and bordered by farmers' fields.

The two girls were not confronted with a particularly rigorous academic program.[18] Courses were designed to prepare them to be socially refined wives and mothers. They were taught scripture, liturgy and catechism, reading and elocution, writing, orthography, needlework, grammar, arithmetic, composition, history, geography, English literature, languages, drawing, algebra, elementary science, class-singing, and calisthenics. Optional courses in music, art, harmony, and painting were also offered. Skating, croquet, and bat-and-ball were the main physical activities, with calisthenics offered to enable students to develop "poise and good carriage."[19] Despite the school's lack of academic expectations, it left a lasting impression on the Montizambert girls. Beatrice developed a lifelong passion for painting, while Elizabeth embraced art, literature, and writing — the foundation of her future career.

QUEBEC CITY, Quebec, May 5, 1894. Alice Montizambert opened the latest issue of the *Quebec Chronicle* and silently noted the abrupt announcement that "Major Montizambert, of the Eighth Royal Rifles, is leaving Quebec, having accepted a position with a well-known lumber firm in Rockland, Ontario."[20]

Alice knew the wrenching truth behind the simple announcement. According to a descendant of Frederick Montizambert, "Alice caught her husband with the maid and left him."[21] At least that was the story passed down in the family. But in the late nineteenth century, would such an incident result in the dissolution of a marriage? Social position was extremely important to upper-class Victorians. Many women chose to overlook their husbands' infidelities, preferring a sham marriage to a potential scandal. The maid would have been blamed for the incident and summarily dismissed, while the husband would have been forgiven. Why, then, did Alice choose a permanent separation?

The answer may have been that it was not a servant with whom her husband was involved. Was Charles having an affair with a woman of his own social status? If so, this would have been a great affront to a socially conscious, privileged woman like Alice. Or perhaps Charles had become involved with a man. Under either circumstance, Alice would have been much more likely to have "walked out" of her marriage, just as her upright father once "walked out" of a church when it no longer reflected his values. Material concerns would have posed no problem — Alice's substantial legacies from her parents would allow her to live a comfortable and independent life without her husband's support.

As for Charles, his new job in the Rockland firm was fortuitous for him, an escape from the inevitable disgrace that would have tainted his career and undermined his social standing among his peers at the Garrison Club. His absence from the military was short-lived. By 1897, he had accepted a new post as a DOC (district officer commanding) and inspector of artillery in Kingston. His reputation in tatters, by 1901 he was living in a rooming house with his "wife" Hellen, although there was no record of a divorce between Charles and Alice.

While their parents' marriage was falling apart, Elizabeth and Beatrice were getting on with their own lives. Beatrice was in New York, studying art, while Elizabeth had moved to Toronto to attend St. Hilda's College at Trinity University. Established in 1851, Trinity was one of the most important degree-granting institutions in Canada. By the time Elizabeth entered its wide stone hallways, the university had been admitting women for less than ten years, and many people argued their presence was inappropriate at best.[22] None of this seems to have fazed Elizabeth.

She graduated with a bachelor of arts degree in 1896. A photograph taken around the time of her graduation reveals a confident, smiling young woman with a Roman nose, thick hair drawn back into a French braid, and kiss curls framing her face.

Normally, Elizabeth would have expected to return home to celebrate, ready for the inevitable "coming out" parties in which her parents would pair her with eligible men of her own social class. But there were to be no balls or parlour room romances. So shattered was Alice by her husband's infidelity, she would make it nearly impossible for them to have normal relationships with men their own age. In 1897, she took her three daughters on a grand tour of European capitals. They would never stay in one place very long. According to one Montizambert descendant, "As soon as a man got interested in one of them, she'd move again."[23]

Eventually, Alice's daughters convinced her that they needed to settle down. Some time around the turn of the century, the four women took a chic apartment in London and began to build a network of influential friends and social contacts. The sisters were no longer children, and their mother's influence had finally begun to wane. Elizabeth had yet to decide on a career, but Beatrice had already decided what path she wanted to pursue, enrolling as a student of painter Frank Brangwyn. Brangwyn, a former apprentice to William Morris and well known for his designs for furniture, jewelry, and textiles, and glass,[24] supported his art through tutoring wealthy young students. Under his guidance, Beatrice became a gifted painter and miniaturist, her work displayed at important galleries in Britain and North America.

In the summer of 1902, Elizabeth and Edith travelled home to Canada to visit their old friend Marjorie Howard, the daughter of the former dean of medicine at McGill University. Marjorie lived with her family in a sprawling mansion in Métis-sur-Mer, Quebec. The three women spent their time in long walks or boating off Boule Rock, a local landmark. Elizabeth was now an accomplished photographer and took many pictures of the women socializing with Marjorie's friends. She and Edith were finally able to meet freely with men of their own class, but nothing more than friendship emerged from these encounters. It was as though the fiery destruction of their parents' marriage had dissuaded them (and perhaps some of their potential suitors) from pursuing romance.

KINGSTON, Ontario, 1905. Charles Montizambert had died. Her parents' separation had been devastating for Elizabeth, and her father's sudden death left a scar that would not heal. Over fifty years later, in a hospital in Gloucestershire, a doctor would note that the breakdown of her parents' marriage remained one of the most painful events of her life.

Fortunately, turn-of-the-century London offered many distractions. The London social season was an all-consuming preoccupation for privileged women such as the Montizamberts. Around February, the upper class began returning to the city from their country homes and opened their urban mansions to parties, dinners, dances, and charitable events. Elegant women promenaded in Hyde Park or hosted five o'clock teas in luxuriously decorated parlours. There were theatre parties, the annual opening of Covent Garden, and visits to the opera. Private viewings at the Royal Academy (a prestigious art school in Piccadilly) were held, with wealthy women in the latest fashions browsing paintings by talented young artists.

Some would call this the "golden age," a time when old-fashioned values reigned supreme and everyone knew their place in the social hierarchy. But it was not such a golden time for the great majority of Britons at the bottom of the heap. Nowhere was this clearer than in London. Before the Great War, seven million people lived in the capital, over one-third of whom were under the age of twenty. The majority spent their lives working ten- and twelve-hour days, seven days a week. Working-class men found jobs on the busy docks that lined the Thames or in factories, especially in the food and printing industries. Middle-class men found their way into offices and shops.[25]

One-third of London's women also worked, and this statistic would grow during the war years. Most were domestics, working sixteen hour days, seven days a week, cleaning and caring for the homes of the upper middle class and the mansions of the wealthy. When other options were offered, as they would be when hordes of men left to fight for king and country, these women would exit domestic service rapidly, leaving behind scores of unprepared and slightly bewildered aristocrats.

Elizabeth, whose grandfather Gibb had managed to pull himself up by his own bootstraps, may have sensed that change was on the horizon.

British class-stratified society was not an eternal, immutable structure, and the lives of people at all levels of society would soon be shaken up by forces beyond their control. For now, Elizabeth entertained and attended parties, gliding through London's social scene like a glittering fish in a small, privileged school. Her social circle included brilliant and well-connected women such as Lady Balfour, Lady Northcote, and Lady Margaret Boscawen.[26]

Elizabeth also began to build relationships with artists and writers, particularly women. Some of her new friends were lesbians, including the playwright and prominent suffragist Cicely Hamilton. Hamilton was a short, slender, raw-boned woman with soft fair hair and a no-nonsense attitude. The two women met often for coffee, Elizabeth dressed as though she had just walked out of a couturier's studio while Cicely, the rebel, wore comfortable, tailored clothes that allowed her maximum freedom of movement. Despite the difference in clothing, both were non-conformists whose early years had been marked by upheavals in their families. Like Elizabeth, Cicely was the daughter of a military officer and had grown up in and around army barracks. Her mother had disappeared from her life by the time she was ten years old and there was some suggestion she may have been institutionalized for a mental illness. When Cicely was just nineteen, her father died, leaving her with few financial resources. Forced to make her own living, she began work as an actress and playwright. Galvanized by her struggle to survive, she became an ardent feminist, writing plays about the hard life and difficult choices faced by working women.

Perhaps encouraged by Cicely, around this time Elizabeth began to embark quietly on her own career as a writer. Few of her peers expected a woman born into wealth to have a career at all, other than as a wife and mother. Some would have even viewed any foray into money-making as rather disreputable. That didn't stop Elizabeth. By 1912 she had moved from London to Paris to embark on a career as a journalist for Montreal's *Gazette*, charged with covering arts and culture, high society, and the fashion runways of that most fashionable city. She was the perfect choice for the job, well educated both academically and culturally. Her hours at the theatre and London's great art galleries made her well qualified for her new position. Together with her fluent French and her intimate knowledge of the upper crust, she fulfilled all the requirements for a fashion columnist in the city of haute couture. Elizabeth's columns were entitled "Causerie de Paris" and appropriately enough, given her upbringing, were signed with the pseudonym "Antoinette."

PARIS, France, April 6, 1912. "I suppose a fashion writer is more convinced than anyone else of the profound truth that there is nothing new under the sun!" Elizabeth was describing the latest outfits on the Paris runways — coral-and-white-checked dresses, filmy gowns with tiny embroidered "pompadour flowers," and heavier garments in mustard, blue, and green brocades. In 1912, Paris fashions were drawing from the same palette used by post-impressionists such as Matisse and Marquet, who had painted colour-drenched street scenes from the windows of their Paris apartments.[27]

In Elizabeth's columns for the *Gazette*, art, culture, and fashion flowed together. She particularly featured the work of female artists such as Jane Poupelet, the only woman to be admitted to the prestigious Société Nouvelle. "Her work is so full of virile strength that it is difficult to believe it has been done by a feminine hand. The bronze statuette, 'Devant la vague,' and the 'Après le Bain,' in plaster are worthy of their place near the terrible bronze hand sent by Rodin, which shows all the mighty power of the great sculptor's best work."[28] Elizabeth knew what she was talking about, having met the aging Rodin at the cluttered studio of artist and composer Yvonne Serruys, whose sculptures were exhibited at Paris's Beaux Arts salon.

The Paris of Serruys, Poupelet, and Rodin was an earthy city, one that unfolded in its bedrooms, tiny apartments, and cafés. Historian Jean-Louis Robert points out that in the Paris of 1912, food, fashion, and sex were part of the air its citizens breathed.[29] The tiny, voluptuous actress and writer Colette — she of the exotic dance costumes and intimate memoirs — was in her heyday, scandalizing Paris with her public romances with both men and women. Sensuality was everywhere, even in music. This was reflected in Elizabeth's own coverage of the ballet of Nijinsky, the "weird" music of Reynaldo Hahn, and the "silver-clad" form of dancer

Mlle Nelidoff. As the journalist proudly declared, even Canadians had become part of the avant garde Paris scene, with Canadian contralto Edith Miller taking the "risk" of appearing in the still-controversial Bizet opera *Carmen*.

Parisians were fiercely proud of their history. Just a decade and a half earlier, the city had hosted the Universal Exposition. Held on the one hundredth anniversary of the storming of the Bastille, it recalled the revolution and celebrated France's achievements in arts, literature, architecture, exploration, science, and music. The entrance arch to the fair was the newly built engineering marvel la tour Eiffel, and included within the exposition were some of Paris's great historical structures — the Grand Palais, Gare d'Orsay and Les Invalides.

Yet underneath the glittering monuments and proud martial history was another Paris — a city in which tuberculosis and alcoholism were widespread and prostitution and poverty were common. One-third of all births in Paris were illegitimate, and prostitution was widespread. Fifty-eight percent of women aged fifteen or older were employed outside the home. Forty percent of these workers had jobs in the textile, flower, and millinery trades — labouring hard to produce the very gowns, hats, and ornaments on which Paris's reputation as a fashion centre was built. Among them were well-paid seamstresses and furriers, but the bulk were those who did "sweat" labour in tiny apartments for sub-poverty wages.[30] Yet some women were breaking new ground. "Napoleon's idea that a woman is as much the property of her husband as an apple tree is of the gardener has gone out of fashion long ago," wrote Elizabeth in March 1912. "In fact, the casual stranger passing through Paris is often struck by the enormous amount of the business of daily life that is carried on by the women of France. They sell you your railway ticket, your newspaper and your magazines; they keep the box offices at the theatres. They sell in the markets and most of the smaller shops are entirely directed by them."[31]

It was in this city of contradictions, of beauty and harsh struggle, that Elizabeth began her thirty-two-year career with the *Gazette*. Her apartment at 52 Rue Vaneau was in the heart of the seventh arrondissement, one of Paris's most elite neighbourhoods. Embassies, ministries, and government offices stood alongside aristocratic mansions. Here was

Napoleon's final resting place under the cupola of Hôtel des Invalides, not far from one of the city's most famous department stores, Au Bon Marché. More importantly for Elizabeth, however, was that her apartment was only steps away from the homes of artists such as writer Edith Wharton, sculptor Auguste Rodin, painter Walter Gay, and numerous others. It would be the work of gifted individuals such as these that would sustain her and others during the harsh days of war that lay just ahead.

PARIS, France, August 28, 1914. "No one really expects the Germans will be able to get as far as Paris, yet the fortifications are being examined and put in order, as if they were timed to arrive tomorrow. The preparations made for the reception of the wounded are on a colossal scale, although of course it is hoped that they will not all be needed."[32] The content of Elizabeth's columns had begun a rapid transition from haute couture to grim descriptions of Paris under siege. The change was surprisingly easy. From her father Elizabeth had inherited an understanding of the meaning of war and the challenges of fighting it; from her mother she had gained courage and a belief in her own convictions. She would draw on all these qualities as she made the transformation from fashion columnist to war correspondent.

Elizabeth Montizambert.

Part II
Behind the Lines

War is not two great armies meeting in the clash and frenzy of battle. War is a boy being carried on a stretcher, looking up at God's blue sky with bewildered eyes that are soon to close; war is a woman carrying a child that has been injured by a shell; war is spirited horses tied in burning buildings and waiting for death; war is the flower of a race, battered, hungry, bleeding, up to its knees in filthy water; war is an old woman burning a candle before the Mater Dolorosa for the son she has given.

— Mary Roberts Rinehart

Chapter 4

Called to the Colours

There wasn't a crowd at the station,
to riot and make a fuss.
That may be the way with others.
It isn't the way with us.

Scarcely a word to the missus,
and the missus was well-content;
not even a line to the Kaiser
to tell him the way that we went.
— "Business as Usual," Anonymous

LONDON, England, August 1914. A crowd gathered in the shadow of the giant sculpted lions of Trafalgar Square to watch an anti-war demonstration led by labour activist and member of Parliament Keir Hardie. Mary MacLeod Moore was in the crowd, struggling to see above the sea of caps and wide-brimmed ladies' hats. Despite the humid weather, the elderly Hardie strode across the platform, his white moustache and beard bristling. He begged the crowd to prevent England from going to war with Germany. "Down with the rule of brute force! Down with war! Up with the peaceful rule of the people!" he shouted.

To Mary, it was almost incomprehensible that the murder of Archduke Francis Ferdinand, only a footnote in most newspapers a month ago, had led England to this point. Yet the facts were clear. The murder of the Austrian Archduke had started a chain reaction that had led Germany to declare war on Serbia, France, and Russia. Some years before, Britain — concerned about the growth of the German empire — had made a complicated set of treaties, including a promise to protect Belgium's neutrality. Now German troops were in Belgium, en route to France. Britain demanded that Germany withdraw from the tiny country. Germany refused to respond. All eyes were now on Parliament. Would the government lead the country into war?

Keir Hardie was adamant that it should not. He believed that the impact of a European conflict would fall hardest on the poorest of the poor. The illegitimate son of a servant from Lanarkshire, Hardie had helped support his family when he was only eight years old, working as a delivery boy. He never attended school, but was taught to read by his mother. By seventeen, he was working twelve-hour days in the mines. Later, he established a union at the colliery and in 1880 led the first strike of Lanarkshire miners. Dismissed after the strike, Hardie became a journalist and fought for miners' rights. In 1892, he was elected to Parliament as the country's first socialist MP. The saint of unpopular causes, he promoted self-rule in India and women's and workers' rights.

Mary MacLeod Moore agreed with Hardie's support for women's suffrage and his compassion for the poor. However, as a soldier's daughter and avid imperialist, she parted ways with pacifists. "All parties have forgotten their differences, if one accepts the Socialists of the Labour party who are ready to beg for peace with dishonour rather than war," she would later write. "They speak with the only alien voice, and fortunately, the unity existing in the House of Commons makes their illogical and unpatriotic demands of none effect."[1] As far as Mary was concerned, Hardie was a traitor and "had no business to be an M.P."[2]

Most of the crowd at Trafalgar Square shared her distrust of the labour leader. "[E]ven those in the gathering who were opposed to the speakers gave them fair play and listened to their speeches until patience could stand no more, when there was a counter-demonstration,"[3] she observed. As punches flew, the police moved in. At that moment, a thunder storm broke. The rain bucketed down, dispersing the crowd and leaving the pro- and anti-war forces to fight another time.

The next day was a bank holiday, that strange British tradition in which banks are closed and a public holiday declared. Bank holidays usually provided working-class people with a rare opportunity to relax with their families — but not this time. "As a rule, the people are merry-making. On Monday they walked the streets in quiet anxiety. Outside the House of Commons where Sir Edward Grey was making his wonderful speech, the crowd gathered and peered through the iron railings watching with painful interest as the Members and the journalists and District Messengers came and went through Palace Yard. When [Prime Minister] Asquith drove through the gates at six o'clock there was a rush to cheer him," wrote Mary. "It was a glorious day of sunshine and warmth, and it was strange to see the people who are usually away enjoying the country or the sea, strolling up and down, reading the 'extras,' as they appeared, and waiting, waiting, waiting, for news of what was to happen next."[4] Crowds had also gathered outside the German embassy, where only a few weeks before, the King and Queen of England had been guests of honour. Now the embassy was empty, the ambassador and his wife recalled to Germany.

At midnight, the waiting was over. The British government announced that it had declared war on Germany. Mary's friend, the poet Alfred Noyes, described the strange, pervasive calm with which the news was received, not "in a riot of flags and bands," but "in silence with a mustering of men."[5] The silence didn't last long — by evening, crowds of men and women were gathered on street corners, singing patriotic songs and waving flags as if cheering on invisible troops.

"In all the rush and clamor of this crowded week, the terrible tension, and the dark shadow of coming mourning and privation, two facts stand out, so clearly and brilliantly that they should illumine the pages of the history that is to be written," wrote Mary. "They are the magnificent unity of the whole British race in the face of adversity, and the calm and freedom from hysteria of people and Press alike."[6]

Unfortunately, the "calm and freedom from hysteria" Mary described was more bravado than bravery. Few Britons had ever directly experienced of war. The only conflict in recent memory had been the Boer War, which had been fought successfully by a force of approximately four hundred and fifty thousand (of whom twenty-two thousand died, mostly of disease). Many still remembered the triumphal parades and celebrations that accompanied the relief of Mafeking, a minor battle but one that had instilled national confidence in British military superiority. Britain was destined for victory, at least according to the tens of thousands of young men who were already overwhelming recruiting stations across the country. They would quickly teach the Germans a lesson and be home for Christmas.

According to Dick Barron, an early recruit: "We were all patriotic in those days. I mean, most of the colonial wars had been very successful, a third of the whole landmass of the earth belonged to the British Empire. We knew nothing about wars of course, not the sordid side. I'd seen pictures of the Zulu War where we just captured them — after all they were natives and they were fighting with spears. We didn't see the poor buggers that were wounded and lying there, or bodies stripped of anything worthwhile. No, soldiers were glamorous."[7]

Mary echoed Dick Barron's early sentiments. As she would write to her friend Calvin, "My brother is in the Army, the last of 260 years of soldiers, of which we are proud, and his sister would like to go too if they took women!"[8] A combination of war fever and intense patriotism gripped Mary. It would take a long time before she would see the war as anything less than a heroic venture in which British knights in khaki were fighting valiantly for King and Empire.

PARIS, France, August 1914. To Elizabeth, the three days following Germany's declaration of war against France had completely transformed Paris. "Events have moved so rapidly that it is difficult to realize that this time last week the autobuses were still running, the boulevards were still blazing with electric lights every evening, while the cafes were black with people eagerly discussing the news of the war declared by Austria against Serbia," she wrote.

> On Saturday came the announcement that France would mobilize at once. Instantly the aspect of the city changed. The private motors disappeared off the streets like magic,

every vehicle being requisitioned by the government for transport purposes. Those still seen flew about at lightning speed conveying soldiers, officers and officials of all sorts to the different stations. Deep and prolonged cheering greeted the appearance of four Red Cross nurses en route to the front. Apart from the enthusiasm displayed by bands of youths under the enlistment age of nineteen, who paraded the streets waving flags and singing the Marseillaise, the quiet orderly demeanor of the crowds was remarkable. It is difficult to find words in which to do justice to the extraordinary courage and devotion shown by the women of France in this terrible crisis.... They are quiet, composed, sometimes even submitting a brave smile to the children, and if there were no heavy eyelids telling of sleepless, anxious nights, one could hardly realize that practically nearly every household has lost the husband, father or brothers."[9]

Three hundred thousand soldiers had responded to the compulsory military draft and left Paris for the front. Soon, there would be an exodus of another kind. As German forces marched towards the capital, the French government would move to Bordeaux,[10] and over three hundred thousand women, two hundred thousand children, and two hundred thousand men would desert Paris.[11] Those flooding out of the city came from the ranks of the middle and upper classes and could afford to move to safer lodgings on the coast. The people who remained behind were openly contemptuous of those who had left. Yet it was perfectly understandable that any who could escape would choose to do so. Many could still remember the Franco-Prussian War of 1870, in which the city was encircled by invading forces and the citizens had been forced to eat rats in order to survive.[12] It would be hard to begrudge anyone who was attempting to avoid a similar fate.

Parisians weren't the only ones leaving the capital. Paris was the centre of fashion, art, and culture, and wealthy North Americans almost always included the city on their European jaunts. Now those with foreign passports surged out of the capital as quickly as their first-class train tickets could take them. Some were fleeing the German invasion, while others were returning home to enlist. Elizabeth's lanky blond cousin Harold Gibb had been visiting her when war was declared. A chaplain with the Royal Irish Dragoon Guards, he was en route home to England to rejoin his regiment.[13]

"Paris is like a house where the casual guests have gone and left the home to its real owners," wrote Elizabeth. "One hears French spoken in the streets — a thing to be remarked in the month of August in ordinary years — and Paris is 'chez elle.' And as soon as the foreigners had fled, all those places of entertainment which exist solely for their benefit, and are usually run with foreign capital, were obliged to close. In the shock of very real events the city shook off the pose of showing her worst side to the world as if there were no other. There is no posing now. Parisians are showing what they are and what they always have been underneath a mask of more or less flippant indifference as to what is thought of them."[14]

The disappearance of tourists and well-to-do Parisians had a tsunami-like effect on the local economy. Before they left the city, many business owners closed their companies and dismissed their employees. The ones that remained open suddenly had no customers. The result was mass unemployment. Within a few weeks of the outbreak of war, six-hundred thousand Parisians were out of work, approximately one-third of the city's remaining population.[15] The fashion industry was one of the hardest-hit sectors. "It is a difficult enough task to write about fashions when everyone's mind is filled with sterner realities than chiffons," observed Elizabeth.[16] "Yet it has been pointed out that unless some of the big industrial centres, where work is given to thousands of people in the fabrication of feminine garments can be kept open, the misery of the working classes will be even greater than it is at present. Many of the big dressmakers are keeping open at a loss and [have] given their employees half pay to keep them from starving, so the woman who economizes by not ordering her Paris frocks this year in order to have more money to give to charity may really be defeating her own ends." As German troops drew ever-nearer to the city, however, even the few women who could afford them were losing their taste for evening dresses of "gauze exquisitely decorated with colored silk butterflies" or bridal gowns covered in "tiny circles of deftly embroidered swallows." For many, black was the colour of the day, and dressing extravagantly was in poor taste while French soldiers were risking their lives.

Now thousands of female clothing workers — from well-paid Parisian seamstresses and furriers to sweat-shop workers — were out of work. To make matters worse, in the absence of male breadwinners, many women had suddenly become the main providers for their families. French soldiers could contribute little to their families' budgets. They were paid only one franc a day, at a time when a pack of cigarettes cost nearly half a franc.[17] New solutions had to be found to meet the problem of female unemployment, if families were not to starve.

In late August, Elizabeth interviewed a woman who had some answers to that problem. Dr. Madeleine Pelletier was a well-known physician, psychiatrist and social activist. In the open society of France, she was one of many avant-garde lesbian intellectuals who freely explored new ideas in the bohemian cafes of Montparnasse. The two women were a study in contrasts — slender, sophisticated Elizabeth in her short-waisted ankle-length afternoon dress and the round, short-haired Pelletier in her man's suit and bowler hat. Yet despite outward appearances, they were remarkably similar — both were single, independent, passionately curious individuals who were unafraid of exploring new ideas. Madeline was also the type of woman to whom Elizabeth was often attracted. Like her other unorthodox friend Cicely Hamilton, Pelletier was a radical thinker who campaigned for women's rights. "Dr. Pelletier is an ardent feministe and she points out to the authorities the many ways in which women may be used to fill the posts left vacant," wrote Elizabeth. "Among the occupations quoted by this valiant lady are bread making, cooking, the transport of food and its distribution, laundry work, the cleaning and repairing of military uniforms, so important for the health of the troops, and the transport of ammunition which was partly confided to women during the Balkan war. Dr. Pelletier also thinks that women could be employed in the auxiliary army so as to allow of the men now used for this purpose being sent to the front. She estimates that it would not be difficult to recruit 200,000 women for this purpose."[18]

What women like Pelletier proposed was called "dilution," a system in which women took jobs formerly held by men, freeing those men for military service. During the early days of the war, this idea was rejected by governments and military leaders in all the warring nations. But when the first wave of casualties began to appear, dilution would be taken much more seriously, and journalists such as Elizabeth would eagerly promote it.

LONDON, England, August 20, 1914. Mary was trying to finish her weekly column, but it was difficult to concentrate with all the activity on the street outside her window. She could see a hawker, selling tiny British lapel flags to whomever he could collar. A group of soldiers was marching down the street and transport trucks were rumbling by in the opposite direction. "We accept the soldiers marching through the streets as if they represented the most natural of conditions," she typed. "Those beautiful lawns that slope to the Embankment are given up to earnest young men doing the goose-step and watching the instructor demonstrating flag-wagging. They are wearing their ordinary clothes at the moment, these young recruits, but one sees them sometimes carrying rifles as well."

At this early stage in the war, not everyone was welcome to join the colours — with so many volunteers, recruiters could afford to be fussy about just whom they would allow to join in the great adventure. One of those who didn't quite meet requirements was Mary's brother William, who went by "Mac." He quit his publishing job when war was declared and returned home to Canada to enlist. But despite a three-year stint with the Victoria Rifles in Montreal, he was rejected by the military because he was too old (thirty-seven) and because his health had been compromised years before by a botched appendicitis operation. Still determined, he returned to Britain and finagled a job as "honorary captain" in the British Red Cross. He was assigned to be the administrator of the Queen's Military Hospital in London. Mac accepted, all the while looking for a chance to play a role as a "real" soldier.

To Mary, it seemed as though everyone had "war work" of some kind or another, including women. "Naturally there is a great rush of offers to take short courses in nursing; to make bandages, to attend ambulance classes; to do something towards protecting the country, and even if later — provided the war drags on for some time — there be people who weary of steady duties, there will still [be] many reliable, capable ones to carry on the necessary work and keep the machinery well oiled," she wrote. "Thousands of women all over the British Isles are holding working parties in order to send supplies of flannel shirts, socks, sweaters, cardigan jackets, etc., to the hospitals while clothing for women and children is also much needed. Many of the families are in want, as the men were called out so suddenly that there was no possibility of making any provision."[19]

Like their French sisters, many British women didn't want just to sew and knit for the war effort. As their brothers, friends, fathers, and sons left for the front, they looked for concrete ways to contribute. Before the war, suffragettes such as Emmeline Pankhurst and groups such as the Women's Social and Political Union took radical action to fight for women's suffrage — breaking windows, blowing up buildings, and mounting prison hunger strikes. But when Britain declared war on Germany, they changed course. "It is pleasing to be able to record that the Women's Social and Political Union has suspended activities and the National Union of Women's Suffrage Societies, absolutely constitutional, has placed its powerful organization of five hundred branches at the services of those in authority," Mary reported. Feminists — including Mary — were now ready to channel their passion for women's rights into an equally strong passion for the British Empire, its allies, and the cause of the war. They didn't see themselves as abandoning their feminist commitment, simply believing that the war would give them the opportunity to prove that women not only deserved but had earned the vote and a much greater recognition of their human rights.

At first, military and political authorities were simply relieved that they wouldn't have to contend with feminist militancy at a time of national emergency. They accepted the women's decision and then promptly ignored their offers of support. This was only temporary. As the war ground on, the government would be forced to accept and even welcome women's contributions to the war effort.

In the interim, feminists began to create their own organizations, ready to answer what they believed would be an inevitable call for their services. "A number of well-known actresses have organized a Women's Emergency Corps, with headquarters at the Little Theatre, where they find voluntary work for women as cooks, interpreters, and drivers of motor cars," wrote Mary.[20] Efforts like these would be just the beginning — fully equipped hospitals, funded and staffed by British women, would be in France before Christmas.

The one service offered by women that the government *was* more than prepared to accept was that of nursing. Britain already had a professional military nursing service. The Queen Alexandra's Imperial Military Nursing Service (QAIMNS) was founded in 1902 and had been deployed in the Boer War. The peacetime strength of the QAIMNS was only three hundred, but there were nearly two thousand military nurses attached to the British Territorial Force and thousands more working for civilian hospitals who could be called up later, as needed. Until then, nurses had their hands full, since there was an outbreak of infectious diseases just as the war began. This experience would be good practice for many of the women, who would face horrific conditions when they were finally called into action.

"So many nurses will be needed for the sick and wounded that other women are taking short courses in nursing to be able to relieve the regular nurses when they are in need of rest," observed Mary. Many of the women taking "short courses" belonged to "voluntary aid detachments." These were groups of unpaid nursing assistants (later known as "VADs") who wanted to do "their bit" for the wounded. Roughly thirty-eight thousand would serve on the home front during the war, while about two thousand would serve abroad.

In newspapers and magazines, VADs were often portrayed in a more noble light than professional nurses, since they were unpaid volunteers. Such views often overlooked the fact that these girls often came from middle- and upper-class families that provided for them, while professional nurses were often women dependent on a paycheque for their survival. Mary, accustomed to earning her own living, didn't make such distinctions. Women of many backgrounds and experiences would make their way into her wartime columns.

Like all journalists based in Britain, Mary was now operating under new rules. Britain's war chief, Lord Kitchener, had made it clear that journalists — male or female — were a security risk. Correspondents were banned from entering a military zone around the British Expeditionary Force, and any dispatches from France had to be submitted to the War

Office before publication. The War Office established its own Press Bureau, and this bureau censored news and reports sent from the British army and then chose what to release to the waiting press in London and around the world.[21] More importantly — from Mary's point of view — was the Defence of the Realm Act (DORA), passed in 1914. This Act made it illegal to publish anything that directly or indirectly aided the enemy. As historian Martin Farrar points out, this included "information on any troop or naval movement, any description of war and any news that was likely to cause a rift between the public and military authorities."[22] In other words, Mary couldn't write anything that could be interpreted as bad for public morale. Even the landing of the British Expeditionary Force in France in mid-August wasn't mentioned in her column — or anywhere else — until early September.

Mary didn't seem to mind the interventions of the censor — nor, it seemed, did many in the press. "The newspapers are very steady and very loyal. Not a scrap of news that might be useful to the enemy is published," she wrote. "Many things are known that never appear in print. Besides acting in this spirit as regards the news, the papers daily tell how to help the country. It is not only by fighting, attending classes for first aid, or by sewing or by contributing to the great funds for the people who will need help; it is also by refraining from various acts likely to hamper the authorities and to agitate others."[23]

It seemed that censorship and propaganda were already bedmates. At first, the general public didn't object. Initial acceptance of censorship was so widespread, according to Mary, that "little comment was heard except upon the loyalty of the press in keeping absolutely silent about facts which were known to a great many people."[24] Public support of censorship would change as casualties mounted and people wanted to know about what was really happening to their fathers, sons, and sweethearts on the battlefront.

As busy as she was writing for *Saturday Night* and the *Sunday Times*, Mary still managed to do her own "war work." At least once a week, looking matronly in her high-necked white blouse, tailored wool jacket, and ankle-length skirt, she visited the slums of Southwark and Lambeth as a volunteer for the Soldiers' and Sailors' Families Association. The SSFA supported those military families that were finding it hard to manage until those servicemen received their first pay. With the help of other volunteers, Mary distributed money, clothing, coal, and food to those in need.

"One woman confided to her visitor [Mary] her expenses for one week. Her husband has gone to the war and she is drawing a guinea per week, separation allowance for herself and two children and allotment from husband. His late employers allow her a quart of milk per day as a gift. 'We'd be very comfortable indeed,' she said, 'me and Myrtle (aged three) if it weren't that there is so much to pay off, you see. Me havin' that long illness and a doctor and a nurse, I 'ad to borrow money from the Club (there is always a Club of sorts in these accounts), then there's insurance to pay and what with one thing and another I'd only three and six this week for food besides the children's milk.'"[25] Helping such women was natural to Mary, who had grown up among soldiers and had observed her father seeing to the welfare of the elderly soldiers whose pensions he administered.

PARIS, France, August 20, 1914. Anticipation hung in the air of the French capital as everyone looked for news of the fortunes of the French army. The Germans had invaded Belgium on August 4 and were marching in a semicircular arc, the aim of which was to overrun Paris on both sides and sweep northwards to divide the French army in half and deliver a quick and decisive German victory. "No one really expects that the Germans will be able to get as far as Paris, yet the fortifications are being examined and put in order, as if they were timed to arrive tomorrow," wrote Elizabeth. Despite her brave words, most Parisians knew that their city and country were at grave risk — 358 battalions of German infantry were bearing down on them, and the piles of paving stones and crossed spikes placed at the entrances to the city would provide very little protection should the French army fail to stop the enemy's advance.

What was known with certainty was that there would soon be an influx of wounded men. "The preparations made for the reception of the wounded are on a colossal scale, although of course it is hoped that they will not all be needed," wrote Elizabeth. "The same thing may be said of the arrangements in aid of the wives and children of the soldiers at the front, though there, alas, it is almost impossible to do too much to replace the many breadwinners who have left their families in dire want."

Hunger was stalking the French capital, but efforts were being made to prevent starvation among the poorest of the poor. "A marvelous network of charities has sprung up under the direction of the 'Assistance Publique' comprising workrooms for the women, crèches and kindergartens for the children, soup kitchens and employment bureau etc. As usual it is the class above the very poor who suffer most and the number of people who find themselves suddenly deprived of a comfortable income and with no immediate prospect of replacing it is a serious problem which can only be met by the splendid solidarity of which the French people are now giving so many instances."[26]

If life was difficult in Paris, it was a thousand times worse on the front lines. Since August 14, the French army had been advancing into the former French territories of Alsace-Lorraine (an area lost by the French during the Franco-Prussian War), while German troops retreated eastward until they were ready to counterattack. On August 20, they turned and faced the French, pushing them back to where they had begun. It was only the beginning of the bloodletting. Between August 20 and 25, French troops, trying to stem the German advance through Belgium, soon came face-to-face with the enemy and ended up retreating to the Meuse River, where they formed a line running southwest from the town of Verdun.

On August 21, German troops reached the Sambre River and crossed two undefended bridges across the river. The French counterattacked, but could not stem the German tide. The next day, the Germans attacked on the French right, crossing the Meuse where it met the Sambre. There was now a gap between the French Fifth Army and the Fourth, retreating after defeat in the Ardennes. On August 23, the French army was forced to retreat once again.

The French weren't fighting alone. By mid-August, eighty thousand British soldiers were marching on the cobbled streets of Boulogne, Rouen, and Le Havre, most on their way to what would become known as the First Battle of Mons. Mons was a small, sleepy Belgian hilltop town located near the French border and about fifty kilometres southwest of Brussels. As a base for military operations, it posed a number of challenges. According to historian Holger Herwig, Mons's main industry was coal, and the town was surrounded by "polluted ditches, swamps, watercourses and canals,"[27] along with pitheads and slag heaps.

The Battle of Mons began when British commander Sir John French moved seventy thousand of his troops forward from the coast of Belgium, en route to meeting French General Lanrezac's Fifth Army near Charleroi on the Sambre River. Before reaching Lanrezac's forces, a cavalry patrol belonging to the 4th Royal Irish Dragoon Guards came in contact with a German cavalry patrol. It was August 22. Elizabeth's cousin Harold Gibb (back in France with his regiment) would later recount what happened: "The main road was struck at the little village of Casteau, where the Squadron halted in concealment, while scouts were sent on. They reported a German patrol in sight coming down the road; our patrol was directed by signal to move straight back towards the south, to draw on the Germans. Two Troops were dismounted, ready to open fire, the other two Troops drew swords ready to pursue. About six German Dragoons were seen coming cautiously down the road. At about five hundred yards from the ambush, they apparently smelt a rat, stopped and consulted, and then turned round and slowly went away. At this moment the first shot by the British Army in the war was fired by Corporal Thomas 'C' Squadron."[28] There was a short skirmish, and when it was over, the British had captured a small number of prisoners.

Realizing that German troops were pounding towards them in large numbers, Sir John French ordered his five divisions to establish defensive positions over a forty-kilometre front east and west of Mons. On the morning of August 23, seventy thousand British troops faced one hundred and sixty thousand German troops. At first, the British held their own, inflicting heavy casualties, their rapid rifle fire convincing German officers that the British were using machine guns. Five thousand German troops were lost in the battle, while the British had 1,600 casualties. Soldiers fought in the rain, amid brick buildings, under a constant barrage of shellfire, shrapnel, and bullets.

By mid-day on August 24, the unequal distribution of power, together with the decision of France's forces to retreat, led Sir John to instruct his outnumbered forces to withdraw, slipping and sliding down damp cobbled roads, climbing over fences, and struggling to avoid falling into ditches, all the while trying to avoid German shells and gunfire. Forced to withdraw hastily, they left behind guns, ammunition, and equipment. Even the wounded were sometimes abandoned. Progress was slow; the British were often accompanied on their way by Belgian and French villagers, attempting to put as much distance as possible between themselves and the invaders.

Strangely enough, the defeat at Mons was actually a kind of success. The Germans had wanted to sweep through France and into Paris and claim a speedy victory, but the tough resistance in Belgium and the fighting at Mons had slowed them down. As they neared Paris, the French (with help from the BEF) turned and attacked the weakened German forces in the Marne Valley and pushed them back. When the dust cleared, the Germans were dug in along the Aisne River's high northern banks, and both sides got their first taste of trench warfare.

PARIS, France, September 25, 1914. Elizabeth had spent the previous three weeks in Britain. It isn't clear why she had chosen to leave Paris — she may have been persuaded to return to England by her cousin Harold, or perhaps she had taken a flying trip back to London to reassure her worried family and newspaper that she had a necessary role to play in France. Whatever the case, she didn't stay away long. She returned to a changed city. "After a three-week absence I came back to a very different Paris. Leaving a cold windy autumnal London with its crowded streets, open shops and theatres and few signs of the war beyond the occasional companies of recruits and the scarlet lettered notice posted on all the taxi-cabs: 'A call to arms! Enlistment for war only,' I crossed a sunny channel on the now tri-weekly boat and after a twelve hour journey arrived in the Paris, which as a Frenchman said to me yesterday is no longer Paris."

Although German troops were only thirty-seven kilometres from the city,[29] the capital was "a place of indescribable beauty with its strange, silent, deserted spaces shimmering in the warm sunshine. Everything seems to have fallen under a spell. Where there were few closed shops before there are now whole streets of grey shuttered windows with perhaps a few scattered grocers or provision shops giving an air of almost impertinent activity."[30] With so many vehicles commandeered by the military, there was little traffic in the streets. However, as she walked home one quiet evening, Elizabeth was comforted to see that the lace-curtained cafés were still filled with gossiping crowds, discussing the lack of war news and arguing about how they thought things should be done.

The absence of information, so lamented in Paris cafés, was due to the imposition of censorship. From the start of the war, the French government had been opening citizens' mail and had limited what could be said about the war in newspapers and other publications. "Everyone is waiting, waiting, and the lack of news from the front makes the suspense the harder to bear though the reason for the press censorship is so obvious that there is no grumbling. Everyone reads what news there is three times a day, repeated by the midday editions from the morning, and in the evening papers from midday. The streets are full of women and girls selling them," wrote Elizabeth. The arrival of wounded soldiers helped meet some of the hunger for news. "Now that the wounded are coming back from the front all sorts of interesting and unofficial anecdotes are leaking out." The stories told by the men were sprinkled liberally with accounts of atrocities. The censor seemed to tolerate publication of these, and in the absence of hard news, even Elizabeth — whose European travels had given her a keen appreciation of German culture — was not immune to their lure.

"There is a general confirmation of most of the tales of German atrocities which are being circulated. One of the most ghastly, which I heard from an authentic source, was of an English doctor who was attending to a wounded German on the field when a German officer came up and as soon as the doctor had finished his ministrations his hands were slashed off at the wrists. Such horrors seem incredible." Fantastic stories such as these, reported by many war correspondents, made it difficult for readers to sort out fact from fiction. Yet some of the stories were true. During the German push into Belgium, thousands of villagers (including women and children) had been rounded up and shot to death in retaliation for the deaths of German soldiers at the hands of Belgian snipers. One of the most famous atrocities occurred at the City of Louvain. After shots were fired at German troops by unknown assailants, the town of university professors, nuns, and retirees was looted and its citizens terrorized. Roughly forty thousand were deported to Germany, 248 were killed, and 2,100 buildings destroyed by fire. In one library, two hundred and thirty thousand books (including a thousand books printed before 1500) were lost in the flames,[31] a tragedy that Elizabeth would have grieved, if only privately.

LONDON, England, September 1914. Beatrice Nasmyth sank her teeth into the soft, buttery scone. She was glad she had accepted her friends' invitation to tea. It was a welcome break. London now had a one percent vacancy rate, and Beatrice was spending every waking hour looking for accommodation. Today, she had left that worry behind, although she wasn't able to enjoy the peace and quiet for long. Others had also been invited to tea, and she found herself "pushed forward as the latest thing from the colonies," and the target of many questions. "Do you know my relatives in Memphis?" asked one. "How did they disguise your ship when you came to England?" asked an elderly man, tea cup shaking in his hand. "I heard that the navy had made them look like icebergs.... And from a tall, angular woman who had relatives in "Manito-baw" came the question, "Is it true that Canada is sending a tribe of wild Indians against the Kaiser?"

It was excruciatingly hard for shoot-from-the-lip Beatrice to prevent herself from replying: "Quite true, Madame. The first flotilla of war canoes overtook us a few hours before we entered the Mersey. The war whoop of the painted savages as they bore down upon us, mistaking us at first for the enemy, was blood-curdling. I tremble to think of its effect on the Kaiser when his turn comes." Instead, she simply suggested that the information her questioner had received most likely referred to East Indians.[32] However, Beatrice didn't just leave it there. She filed away the conversation and shared it again a few months later, in a feature article entitled "Visiting England in Wartime."

That article reflected the wartime mood. Many Canadians — especially soldiers — were travelling abroad for the first time and learning, to their dismay, that most Britons had little understanding of life in the "colonies" and had a paternal attitude to the newcomers. Encounters between Brits and Canucks could be funny, frustrating, and occasionally full of bitter anger and conflict — all grist for Beatrice's journalistic mill. "[T]he Canadian and English elements are forever at war," she later wrote to her father. "Really, I sometimes wonder why we should be over here fighting for the English at all. We understand each other about as well as the Turks and the Armenians."[33]

In November, Beatrice picked up the theme again in a half-page feature article entitled "Canadian Soldier Lads See World's Metropolis." Its humorous, slightly cynical tone would characterize much of her wartime output. "The Khaki-clad Canadian has come to London to see the sights. And to the Canadian abroad he looks just a little bit taller and straighter and more efficient than any of the other thousands of other uniformed figures which throng the streets of the metropolis. Up from his huge camp at Salisbury Plain he comes with a merry eye and a cheerful air, and one meets him at every turn. He flits about in taxis, he parades the street with eye alert for novel sights, he threads the traffic to put a dozen questions to the policeman, he even penetrates to the churches, galleries and museums, but for the most part he appears to have found his element in the front seat on the motor bus top and from this elevation he views the scene about him with an expression of the frankest interest."[34]

Shortly after the outbreak of war, Canada had offered to contribute an infantry division to the war effort. Minister of Militia Sam Hughes saw that this promise was more than fulfilled. More than thirty thousand volunteers from across the country poured into the military training camp that Hughes quickly established at Valcartier, Quebec. Under Hughes's slapdash leadership, training had been quick and cursory at best. Men spent time shooting, riding, and visiting in the heat of the Canadian summer. For many it was a kind of summer camp; few had any idea about what real warfare was like. They were finally shipped overseas in October, only to be stationed at Salisbury Plain. There they trained again, this time in cold, rainy, muddy conditions. The British government was not yet sure what to do with them, and Bea summed up the situation in her usual tongue-in-cheek style.

"Prophecies as to what is to be done with the Canadian troops vary so widely that one can gather no more idea of what is likely to befall them, than of what is going on from day to day in the war area," she wrote. "One man declares they will eat Christmas dinner either on Salisbury Plain or en route to Canada again; the next that they will be at the front in three weeks at the farthest."[35]

While the Canadians cooled their heels on Salisbury Plain, fresh British territorial troops were preparing to go overseas. "One cannot ride any distance in this city without being held up by long lines of Territorials on their daily marches. They swing along singing and whistling, some companies of a thousand looking very strange and new, others fine and fit; some in civilian dress, some in uniform. As one rides past, bits of various songs are heard as the different groups break into the Marsellaise, Rule Britannia, or the old standby, 'It's a Long Way to Tipperary,'" wrote Beatrice. "Occasionally a long line of motor busses whiz past. They have been painted in the khaki color, even with windows being made opaque with paint and they are driven by men in uniform. Sometimes they are inscribed in white letters with such legends as "Follow this for the shortest route to Germany," or "Khaki express. Non-stop to Berlin!" They are on their way to France, where already thousands have gone before. The khaki covered vans, with their huge red cross on top and sides, are also a familiar sight and frequently a white bandaged arm or leg protrudes from the side coverings."

Although the "khaki covered vans" with the red crosses painted on their tops were becoming familiar, few — including Beatrice — realized the depth of the devastation they represented. By the time Beatrice was typing her first story for the *Province*, deadlock had set in between the Allied and German forces, and two parallel lines of trenches extended from Switzerland to the North Sea.

Only one gap existed in those lines, and both sides wanted to exploit it. It was located at the ancient Belgian city of Ypres, located in a bulge of land or "salient" that protruded into what was now German territory. It was the one small piece of Belgium that wasn't in German hands. What's more, Ypres was also near vital Channel ports that the Allies were determined not to give it up — if the German army, which now controlled most of Belgium, could reach the ports of Boulogne-sur-Mer and Calais, the war would be over, and the Germans would have won.

In early October, the British Expeditionary Force (BEF) had retreated to Ypres after Antwerp had fallen to the Germans. They held a fifty-six-kilometre line in the centre of the salient, while the French Army held the flanks to the south of the city. The Germans first began their attempt to break through the Allied lines by striking Belgian defences on the Yser River between Dixmude and Nieuport. The Belgian army fought courageously, but at the end of October was forced to fall back. But they left the Germans a parting gift. On October 27, they opened the sluices that held back the sea from their fertile fields. This effectively flooded the land between their positions and those of the Germans, creating a barrier that slowed the enemy's forces.

Undaunted, the Germans assaulted the city of Ypres itself. The attacks began on October 31, when German cavalry successfully attacked a smaller British cavalry unit on the Messines Ridge at the southern end of the bulge. The British counterattacked. Despite the fact that the Germans had more troops at their disposal than did the British, British troops were able to keep them at bay with superior rifle fire. Later accounts by German survivors would claim that Allied troops had "machine guns," when in reality the British guns were simply faster and more accurate than those of the Germans.

On November 11, two German divisions attempted to break the British lines just north of the Menin Road a mere six and a half kilometres from Ypres. German and British troops pushed each other back and forth at the Town of Hooge, but a motley collection of British troops, including medical orderlies, clerks, and engineers, managed to stave off the enemy.

On November 22, the dust finally settled on the First Battle of Ypres. After three weeks of shelling and attacks, sixty thousand British soldiers were dead or wounded along with fifty thousand French troops and approximately one hundred and thirty thousand Germans. Yet the Allies were still holding on to the ruined city that was now a symbol of British and French tenaciousness in the face of overwhelming odds. Unfortunately, as Canadian troops would soon learn, the battles surrounding Ypres were only just beginning.

LONDON, England, December 5, 1914. As the first Christmas of the war approached, few Londoners held any illusions that the war would be over any time soon. Most of the first wave of British soldiers — the cream of the British army — were now dead, wounded, or captured. For those who were still at the front or convalescing in hospital, Mary and her mother — like thousands of other British women — were carefully wrapping dark, rich Christmas puddings in brown paper and packing them in parcels loaded with "socks and mufflers and mittens and wristlets and shirts and belts." For those at home, the omnipresent reminders of war made it hard to celebrate the season, especially if there were loved ones at the front. "I sat on a bus top the other day listening to a conversation between a soldier who had been invalided home after Mons and a civilian who had a son at the front," wrote Mary. "The soldier was perfectly unself-conscious and willing to talk about the war. 'What do you feel most when you are actually under fire?' asked the other man. 'Why you see, it's like this,' said Tommie. 'When you've time to think you 'ope the grub is 'olding out well, and the other thing you have in yer mind is; perhaps the next turn will be mine as you see the chaps falling. Then another one drops and you say to yerself 'e got mine that time and maybe I'll get another fellow's bullet.'"[36]

PARIS, France, December 24, 1914. In Paris, toy shops were filled with tin soldiers and tiny nurse and soldier costumes, along with chocolates shaped to look like cannons. Unfortunately, few parents could afford to make such extravagant purchases. Families were struggling to survive, while out on the battlefront French soldiers huddled in the cold with little to celebrate. "With their pitiful pay of one sou a day, of course, they buy nothing for themselves if they happen to be poor and their families either have enough to do in keeping off starvation these hard times or else they dispatch parcels that never arrive. In either case, the *piou-piou* freeze,"[37] wrote Elizabeth.

Yet, out on the Western Front, a few happy stories were emerging. "One hears many quaint tales of the modus Vivendi between these enemies who are forced by their underground mode of warfare to live so close together. I remember some weeks ago when the apple trees still bore their fruit there was a fine tree within tantalizing reach of the trenches, but of course neither side dared to so much as put their noses above ground. The temptation grew too strong for a British Tommy and he opened negotiations by carefully wrapping up a cigarette and tossing it with skill into the enemy's quarters. In a few minutes came back the retort courteous with a bar of chocolate. After these preliminaries the rest was easy. A notice was hoisted on two bayonets to the effect that if the English soldiers could rely on the Germans not to fire while they filled their pockets with apples, the Germans would be allowed to do the same. The consent of the latter was received with cheers and after both sides had rifled the apple tree with impunity they began to kill each other again with renewed vigour."[38]

Holiday tales like this one — reported by Elizabeth — had begun to make the rounds. They would include the famous "Christmas truce," in which German and Allied soldiers up and down the long line of trenches would spontaneously put down their guns and meet in no man's land to share gifts and food in honour of the season. In the New Year, generals on both sides of the conflict would ensure that such peaceful gestures were not repeated. Yet for the cosmopolitan Elizabeth, such stories proved that a finer humanity was still alive and well among men of all nations.

From the outset of the war, Mary, Elizabeth, and Beatrice had used their columns to cheer on the troops, damn their enemies, and vicariously mourn the loss of so many husbands, sons, and fathers. But the war had not yet arrived on their own doorsteps. That would change in 1915.

Chapter 5

Total War

Air-raid: (n. 1914) an attack by hostile aircraft, especially with bombs.
— John Ayto, *20th Century Words*, London: Oxford University Press, 1999

PARIS, January 15, 1915. "Everyone is so accustomed to abnormal conditions of life by this time that when anything happens as it used to, in those faraway days before the war, there is a slight sensation of shock," wrote Elizabeth. She had been strolling along the Boulevard de la Madeleine when she noticed a small crowd gathered around the window of the art dealer Bernheim-Jeune. She pushed her way to the window, expecting to see the usual collection of war pictures. Instead, she was confronted with a Monet painting of Notre Dame, as well as several Breton scenes by Lucien Simon. Looking into the excited faces of the crowd, Elizabeth thought that this was a particularly French way to respond to the emotional desolation caused by the war. Perhaps that was why the government had recently revoked its ban on the fancy breads she loved so much — after all, Paris wasn't Paris without hot croissants any more than it was without the art of Monet or Simon.

Yet even croissants and canvases couldn't make one forget the war for long. Travelling to Dinard later that week to visit the wounded in a

Canadian military hospital, she observed that "Every station is full of soldiers coming and going. They are very fine, sturdy men, these Norman and Breton peasants, and the women who come down to see them off are curiously like them in their stoic calm." In towns like Dinard, the big hotels had been transformed into hospitals, with sentries instead of doormen. White-capped nurses and ambulances burdened with wounded men were now familiar sights in places that had once been known more for their ancient cobblestones and twelfth-century cathedrals.

An upper-class tourist hot-spot before the war, Dinard was itself a military hospital depot with several facilities treating more than two thousand patients at any one time. Elizabeth learned that the "'Hospital Canadien'" was in the "Hôtel Crystal, the largest of the most luxurious hotels in the town."[1] Like all Canadian military hospitals, it was open to all Allied soldiers, and its beds were filled with Belgians, French, and Senegalese. Any wounded soldier fortunate enough to end up within its walls received treatment fit for a millionaire, since the hospital was staffed by one of France's most famous and expensive surgeons, Dr. Pierre Duval. Since the hospital had opened in November, seven hundred patients had come through its doors. Only four had died, due in no small part to Duval's talents and hard work.

As she stood in the hospital's wide front entranceway, Elizabeth's interest was caught by a sign that had been glued to a gilt-edged mirror. She peered up through her feather-trimmed hat at what seemed to be a page from the *Echo de Paris*, outlining the conditions that Germany would impose on France if the country capitulated. "It is an astonishing document enough to make the most peace-loving man take up his arms again rather than submit to its brutal demands."[2] Given France's past history with Germany, the publication was an excellent "incentive to a quick recovery."

LONDON, England, January 1915. "It is a khaki winter. One has been long accustomed to it," wrote Mary MacLeod Moore. "The soldiers pass in and out of shops, where they are getting outfits, or escorting friends on leave or you see them in restaurants or in the street. All intent, quiet and efficient. They march past you in the dark, singing as they come back from drill, or a long line of very new recruits looms through the trees and mist in the dark. Silently the khaki men slip away, without bands or flags or loud farewells, and the women who have been seeing them off at the station, either on their return to the front after leave, or on their first journey to the horrors raised by Germany, smile to the last and wave as the train pulls out."[3]

The bands and hoopla of 1914 were gone. Thousands had already heard the knock on the door and seen the face of the telegraph boy as he delivered the message that no one wanted. Those who hadn't lost a husband, son, or sweetheart weren't immune to the impact of the war, either. Price increases and shortages of basic foods meant that the poor and working class were fighting silent and bloodless battles against malnutrition, exhaustion, and poverty.

Mary, now supporting her mother on her meagre journalist's salary, turned her own struggle to survive to her advantage, writing a series for *Saturday Night* about the cost of living in London. "The question of how to live on a pound a week may seem a purely academic one," she wrote. "Life and death, health and weakness, respectability and lost caste, hang on making a pound a week, or a little more, cover the expenses of several persons and something that can be called a home possible."[4] She listed the necessities that the majority of Londoners had to eke out of meagre budgets — "Bread, which is the great standby, costs about five pence the quartern loaf, and potatoes a penny for two pounds. Milk is expensive for poor people, and many babies have to go without this necessity." Suet puddings were used to fill empty bellies. Butter was a luxury even for the middle class, and margarine, an oil-based spread once promoted by Napoleon to his hungry troops, had become commonplace in British kitchens.

The series ran for four weeks, augmenting Mary's own income and allowing her to put some real butter on her own table. Life had become a little less comfortable lately. Mac had sublet his apartment while he was on service with the Red Cross, and Mary and her mother had moved into "apartments with attendance — a delightful English arrangement which gratifies the national taste for privacy which I entirely share. We have a sitting room and two bedrooms and the people cook and do the housework etc, but we need not see the other tenants unless they go in and out under our noses."[5] It cost Mary a guinea a week, was comfortable and met their needs, but with the smell of boiled cabbage hanging in its corridors, it was a long way from Ashley Gardens.

Circumstances were just as bad, if not worse, for Mary's fellow Londoners, especially women. Poor and working-class women had always worked — as domestics and casual labourers. But now, with male wage earners off to the front, middle-class women were finding their grasp on respectability a little harder to maintain. Many were looking for work to augment the family income. "Half a million women between the ages of fifteen — poor, inexperienced little wage-earners — and thirty-five are engaged in London in paid occupations," Mary wrote in the third installment of her series. "Some of these women are well-paid; some are so badly paid that the woman who is not well-trained and is not young lives from hand to mouth with the awful shadow creeping towards her of the day when she no longer has anything to carry from one to the other." The number of those living "from hand to mouth" had risen sharply after the outbreak of war — when upper-class women began "patriotically" to cut back on purchasing new clothing, many women were thrown out of work, laid off from traditional female jobs as milliners and seamstresses.

Educated and employed women workers also faced challenges — "for them accommodation of a suitable kind does not nearly equal the demand." Few could afford "apartments with attendance," and safe lodging houses catering to women were almost impossible to find — and almost always full.

LONDON, England, February 1915. During her first year in London, Bea's solution to the housing problem was an Edwardian form of couch-surfing. Until she could find a permanent job and a room of her own, she stayed with well-to-do acquaintances and wrote stories about their wartime experiences. "If you don't come soon you will have to take pot luck with the refugees," declared one of her many hostesses. She and her husband had turned part of their imposing mansion into a twelve-bed military hospital and refugee reception centre. They were glad to welcome the young and vivacious Beatrice to the party, especially if she might be able to use their example to promote the war effort.

Visiting the family gave Bea a bird's-eye view of what life was like for the upper class early in the war. In some ways, their experience was the same as that of any other family in Britain. "The two eldest sons had gone to France with the first British Expeditionary Force and had been at the front since the very beginning of hostilities; the third was with his regiment in Egypt, the fourth still in training at a camp pitched in Hyde Park, likely to be ordered abroad at any time," wrote Beatrice. "As we rode home I heard the latest news from the sons at the front. So far they had been able to write fairly regularly but details of time and place were deleted from their letters and their people knew only that they were well, that this or that little packet from home had reached them safely."[6]

What did differentiate the family from most others in Britain at the time were the immense financial and physical resources it could dedicate to the war effort. In one cavernous wing of the house, Beatrice watched a small army of servants lift large landscapes and portraits down from the high walls, which were then repainted a light green. Later, the floor was covered in a soft pad of green linoleum and the windows were "hung with daintily shirred white muslin curtains." A dozen gleaming white hospital beds were arranged around the room, and a few of the paintings were brought back, "adding pleasing touches of colour." Other rooms were converted into hospital kitchens, a storeroom, and nurses' quarters.

During Bea's visit, a refugee family from Antwerp arrived. The father had once been a prosperous businessman, but the war had swept all that away. As he huddled near the fire in the drawing room, he described how his youngest child had been born during the bombing of the Belgian capital. With buildings shattering all around them, he made the terrible decision to leave his ill wife and their newborn temporarily behind with her parents while he and their four older children escaped the city by car.

"Fleeing inhabitants were pouring from the doomed city in tens of thousands towards Holland," wrote Bea. "So thronged with trudging refugees was the road he had to travel, that it was impossible to urge his car at a higher rate of speed than that at which the slowest could move. Hour after hour, they drove in the centre of this congestion of fleeing men, women and children, the road black with people as far as the eye could see, both before and behind. Many of the scenes through which they passed were so harrowing he could not remain unmoved. Old, old men and old, old women and crying, hungry children shared the terrific heat and dust of the roadway and the awful miseries of their common lot."

The youngest child became sick on the fourth day. The father tried desperately to find a doctor, but gave up and made the child as comfortable as he could on the back seat of the car. On the fifth day they reached the town where he had arranged to meet his wife, baby, and in-laws. It was no longer a town. There were only blackened timbers "several days cold."[7] With no sign of the rest of his family, he made the difficult decision to continue the journey. Since the roads were so badly clogged, they finally had to abandon their car and carry on by foot. When at last they arrived in Holland, the family was miraculously reunited.

It was the kind of dramatic, happy-ending story that Bea liked — the triumph of one family against all odds. That it described a Belgian family made it even better. Like most people in Canada and Britain, she had been appalled by the stories coming out of Belgium after the German invasion. Whole towns and villages in the small country had been laid waste. Thousands of refugees poured into Britain and France, arousing sympathy and acts of kindness from normally reserved Britons. Bea would capitalize on that, writing many stories of heroism even as Belgium crumbled and the Germans turned their attentions toward Paris.

PARIS, France, March 20, 1915. Elizabeth was lying in bed reading her daily copy of *Le Temps* and sipping a glass of Bordeaux when suddenly the bugles of the fire brigade blared out a warning. Her wine spilled, her newspaper forgotten, she rushed to her window. The night was perfect, starlit, clear, and cold. Then she spotted the first Zeppelin. To Elizabeth, it looked like a huge cigar lit from within, with fireballs falling from it in a zigzagging circular motion. The force of bombs hitting the ground a few blocks from her building made her lose her balance. Clutching the window frame, she stared skyward, unwilling to miss any of the spectacle. "Soon the French aeroplanes in chase made their appearance, travelling at a tremendous rate. They carried headlights too, which made them look like shooting stars. All this while enormous searchlights from the Tour Eiffel and the different Paris forts circled the sky and the loud buzzing of the Zeppelin's engines sounded as if they were much nearer than they were."[8]

It was like scene out of an aerial operetta, but the cost was much higher. The next morning, she learned that twenty-three people had been killed and thirty injured in the raid. Elizabeth and the rest of Paris would soon become accustomed to the sight of the silver "cigar." There would be many more attacks on the capital and hundreds would die. The raids reflected the belief of German military commanders that "acts of frightfulness" against civilians would create terror and bring about a speedy end to the war. But while public morale did suffer, the bombing stiffened military resolve and damaged Germany's international reputation. "The Germans never seem to gain any military advantage when they take to the air," wrote Elizabeth, "while the Allies keep their bombs to gain them some strategical advantage instead of wasting them on women and children."[9]

PARIS, France, April 1915. Thoughts of bombs and destruction were far away as Elizabeth stepped onto the red-velvet-covered staircase leading to the art gallery. She was wearing one of the new "war crinolines" — a tunic and skirt ensemble with a full skirt that stopped daringly above her ankles. A light fox stole hung around her slightly plump shoulders. All around her were women in rustling silk gowns and soft, sweeping capes, chatting in groups or rushing up the steps, leaving a trail of perfumed air behind them. A few elderly men and a few military officers were scattered about in the crowd. "Tout Paris" — what was left of it — had come together for a special art lottery sponsored by George Petit, one of the most influential art dealers in Paris. For two francs, participants bought a chance to win one of the many paintings covering the high walls of the gallery. There were works donated by Claude Monet, Leon L'hermitte, Henri Le Sidaner, and Jean-Paul Laurens, as well as sculptures and glassware signed by Lalique.

Elizabeth was glad that the money raised from the art lottery would go to four charities supporting impoverished artists and writers. Even so, for just a few seconds she hoped that her two-franc ticket might bring her a Monet canvas. She thrust the thought away just as quickly, knowing full well that before the war, Paris's artists had lived hand-to-mouth. Now, fewer people were buying art, and those artists who weren't already fighting or doing war work were having an even harder time.

Just a few weeks earlier, she had visited an artists' soup kitchen of sorts. It was held in one of the most popular and colourful cafés in Montmartre. La Feria was decorated in a style that was more reminiscent of Casablanca than Paris, with arched doorways, ornate pillars, mirrored walls, and mysterious screened-off areas. On the day of her visit, the café was filled with cigarette smoke and crowds of people gathered around circular tables covered in shiny red-and-white oilcloth.

"The smudgy Spanish paintings still adorn the walls, but the tawdry hangings — the stage and the brightly shawled dancers of the night café have vanished," she wrote, breathing in the smell of cigars and uncorked wine. "Round the tables sit about two hundred members of the artistic world of Paris. Some of them are true 'cigales' who enjoyed large incomes before the war, but now have nothing left and are glad to come to this well-served meal where they find themselves among their own kind. Each guest has to produce papers to certify that he or she is really a member of one of the artistic professions — otherwise the big hall would never be large enough to hold the crowd. Two hundred people are catered for daily, and for the modest sum of ten cents they have an excellent meal of meat and vegetables — *salade*, pudding, red wine, and coffee."

It was "guest day," when the top layer of Parisian society came to lunch with the artists who regularly used the soup kitchen. She spotted the director of a big Parisian bank across the room, sitting next to a well-known dancer from the opera. Nearby was a journalist from one of Paris's most famous daily papers. One or two actresses from the Comédie Française and the Police Commissioner completed the group, making "the illusion of ante-bellum days more real."[10] Yet illusion it was. Already, tens of thousands of men on both sides of the conflict would never return home to their families. Now, in the blood-soaked city of Ypres, Canadians were about to make their own sacrifice to the god of war.

YPRES, Belgium, April 1915. Ypres was a ghostly mass of rubble. For the past six months, combat over the salient surrounding the town had gradually simmered down and it seemed like a good place for untried Canadian troops to learn the art of war. They had arrived in France in March, and in mid-April replaced a French division near the city. The Canadians had little expectation that they would see major action any time soon. They were wrong. Within five days the Germans launched a sweeping offensive with a frightening new weapon. It was the beginning of what would become known as the "Second Battle of Ypres."

It began on Thursday, April 22. At five o'clock on that clear spring afternoon, two greenish-yellow clouds slowly rose from the German lines and began to roll towards the Algerian troops stationed to the left of the Canadians. The clouds were chlorine gas, spewed out of 5,730 cylinders behind the German lines. French-Algerian troops poured out of their trenches, grasping their throats, their eyes streaming. Just ten minutes after the gas attack was launched, five thousand men were dead of asphyxiation.

Four heavy guns belonging to the British were captured by the Germans at the southwest corner of Kitchener's Wood, a forest crammed with ammunition and dugouts. The capture of the heavy guns and the collapse of the French lines meant that the inexperienced Canadians stationed on the west side of the salient were left to stop the Germans from marching through the seven-kilometre gap and on to Ypres.

Fifteen hundred troops from Alberta's 10th Battalion and 16th Canadian Scottish confronted the enemy's machine-gun fire at Kitchener's Wood. Only five hundred would return from the fray, but they would manage to slow the German advance. Over the next twenty-four hours British and Canadian troops struggled to prevent the enemy from pushing through the remaining lines. Reserve companies stationed at St. Julien, a village northeast of Ypres, heroically kept the invaders at bay. More gas was turned on the two Canadian brigades that still held out in the salient. Despite covering their mouths in urine-soaked cotton, scores died, while survivors continued to fire on the advancing Germans. Somehow, despite the odds against them, by the end of the battle the Allies still held

Ypres. The salient had taken high casualties. Over thirty-five thousand German, fifty-three thousand British, six thousand Canadian, and ten thousand French troops were dead or wounded. And somewhere in the midst of it all, a famous Canadian poem was written by a doctor treating the gassed and wounded. Overwhelmed by the human wreckage scattered around him, Lieutenant Colonel John McCrae scribbled down the poem "In Flanders Fields."

LONDON, England, April 1915. Far from the destruction, Mary MacLeod Moore — in typically bellicose language — celebrated the Second Battle of Ypres as proof of Canada's military prowess. "The English newspapers continue to express the general feeling of admiration for the Canadian troops who fought and many of them died so gallantly," she wrote. "Day after day one reads with pride the comments and the appreciation. The loyalty of Canada was not in question but her sons have proved their splendid courage, their endurance, their enterprise." In the next breath, she reported that the War Office had gathered 570 respirators to be sent to the front "as a protection against the gases with which our civilized enemy poisons our soldiers."[11]

In May, the war came to the home front again. The passenger ship *Lusitania*, en route to Liverpool from New York, had been torpedoed by a German U-boat. Of the 1,959 people aboard, only 761 survived. The tragedy had a personal connection for Mary. Her brother, Mac, had been touring France with Canadian Red Cross leader George Sterling Ryerson when the ocean liner was struck. Ryerson had recently lost a son in the Second Battle of Ypres and was visiting another son who had been wounded in the same battle. His wife and daughter, travelling to England to be with him, had been on the *Lusitania*. Only the daughter survived.

It didn't take Mac's angry accounts of Ryerson's grief to enrage Mary. For her, the sinking of the *Lusitania* was not only a crime against one family but a crime against humanity. It confirmed all the prejudices she harboured about German deceit. "There is only one topic now in England and in Ireland and that is the crime of murder committed by the Germans in sinking the Lusitania," she wrote. "War is war and even those whose sons and husbands have been killed in action make no moan of injustice. They were killed in battle — except in the case of those who were poisoned by gas. But the deliberate murder of hundreds of innocent women and children and non-combatants, men over military age, or neutrals is something that cries to heaven for retribution."[12]

Mary wasn't alone in calling for retribution. In London, anti-German feeling was being expressed with the destruction of German shops, dismissal of employees with German-sounding names, and the bullying of anyone who wasn't "English" enough. But despite the calls for the bombing of German cities, Allied commanders kept their powder dry. In this war, at least, the Allies would not bomb "soft" targets, preferring to reserve their ammunition for military ones.

PARIS, France, May 1915. Undeterred by the threat of Zeppelins, Elizabeth slipped on her smart navy skirt and jacket, pinned on her matching cloche hat and set out for Paris's Latin Quarter. She was in pursuit of a story about a weekly gathering of avant-garde Russian artists. "When you have tripped over the greasy cobble stones in the darkness and saved yourself from an untimely step in a steep flight of stairs, you arrive at a fairly large studio. The walls are hung with cubist pictures that have a curious démodé look, like everything else we used to do and see 'before the war.' There are also some interesting Russian designs in color used as wall hangings, for the owner of the studio is a Russian. She welcomes all comers clad in a wonderful cubist garment and conveys by her welcoming smile that you are an old friend instead of a casual visitor." The woman in question was Russian-born Marie Vassilieff, a thirty-one-year-old journalist and artist. Vassilieff had lived in Paris since 1905, studying under Henri Matisse, and establishing her own Academy. Her studio had become a meeting place for many on the cutting edge of art, including Chagall, Picasso, and Modigliani, and her walls were covered with their painting and sketches. When war came, she volunteered as a Red Cross nurse and became aware of how difficult the war was for her fellow artists. Marie established a canteen where they could gather with fellow artists and get a meal for a few centimes.

"The origin of the cheery entertainment offered you lies in the hard times that came to so many of the artists in the Latin Quarter when war broke out. One of them used to struggle with his evening cooking over a demoralized spirit lamp till a confrere offered to join him and put their sous together to market to better advantage. It was the cooperative spirit of these two genial souls that appealed to the lady of the cubist blouse, who occupied the studio across the way and she finally offered to join the brotherhood and do their cooking for them. The fragrant odor attracted other artists, and so the Russian cantine [sic] became a recognized institution." On this particular evening, Marie's apartment was crowded with tables surrounded by Russians, Poles, French, Americans, English, and Italians, "all chattering and discussing the one and only subject." After dinner, the group poured across the hall and crowded inside another studio to listen to a concert. A group of Russians sang several unaccompanied choruses while "an English colonel, an American attaché, three or four Canadians, a Scotch journalist, a Russian violinist and women of every nationality under the sun" listened attentively.[13]

LONDON, England, July 17, 1915. Mary MacLeod Moore stood on the edge of the crowded pavement, watching as Emmeline Pankhurst led her procession of over thirty thousand women through the streets of London to the Houses of Parliament. There was a drizzling rain, but it did little to dampen the excitement of the marchers. Wearing gowns in the colours of the warring nations, they carried banners reading "The Situation is Serious, Women Must Help to Save It," "Mobilize Brains and Energy of Women!" and "Shells Made by a Wife May Save a Soldier's Life."[14]

"One would say off-hand that all women are helping in the war work, but the thousands were offering themselves to the Government to be used as was most necessary and urgent," observed Mary. The women were also motivated by economic need. Female employment had stagnated since the war began. Jobs in munitions factories and other war industries would allow women to support themselves and their families.

By now, the government was more than willing to acquiesce. The military needed to increase production of shells, and that meant hiring many more new workers. However, with more men needed at the front, it would be women who would have to do that work. In August, a compulsory national registry scheme was established, and all women were required to register and provide information about their skills. Mary sincerely hoped that this would lead to women being matched with the right kinds of jobs. "Few can give all their time to one definite work, but a great readjustment would place the square peg in the square hole and not hold the woman whose organizing ability or other special qualifications made her of definite value to make munitions that a woman of less faculty could do as well."[15]

Whether or not every woman found the job that best suited her, the government's scheme was fast and effective. Within a year, the number of women working in war industries would double from two hundred and fifty-six thousand to five hundred and twenty thousand.[16] The women would receive more pay than they had before the war, but not the same as their male counterparts. While this was frustrating, Mary hoped it was a small concession on the road to something even greater — the vote and full human rights.

PARIS, France, July 1915. Everyone in France now seemed to be pressed into war service, including journalists. When she wasn't writing, Elizabeth spent most of her time travelling to the front as a volunteer with the Paris Press Syndicate. The union of writers and journalists was funding a special boxcar attached to one of the hospital trains that cut through the countryside collecting the wounded. The car had a fully stocked kitchen complete with counter, stove, urns of coffee and soup, and much-needed gifts for the men. Female volunteers distributed food, along with cigarettes, scarves, socks, gloves, handkerchiefs, and countless other items.

"This Causerie will be posted in Paris, but as a matter of fact, we have left the 'arriere zone' behind us and are now nearer the front than ever, so near that the firing of the canon makes the window of our box car shake. It is true that the bombardment we are promised every night has not yet occurred, but a Taube [Zeppelin] paid us a visit two days ago and dropped three bombs quite close to us, so we felt as if we were back in Paris again," wrote Elizabeth, tongue firmly in cheek. This time, her boxcar was parked on a siding near an evacuation hospital. Each day, she and her colleagues waited at the station, dressed in their crisp blue uniforms and white aprons, their pockets stuffed with supplies, carrying tall blue pitchers filled with steaming coffee and tea, ready to serve the arriving or departing wounded. Over one three-week period, they would give food and drink to more than five thousand wounded men.

"The men are brought down from the front, a distance of only a few kilometres, in motor ambulances and taken to the evacuation hospital overlooking the railway station. Here they are sorted out and typhoid, infections and dysentery cases as well as the badly wounded, who can only travel for three hours at a time, are put into our morning train. As soon as we have seen that they are provided with milk, tea and coffee, they are taken off to a hospital centre three hours away."

Loading the hospital trains was an arduous process. "The stretcher cases come first and are carefully lifted up the inhuman height a French train thinks it necessary to rear itself up above the station platform. Each stretcher is at once linked on its iron frame with three tiers without disturbing the patient. A wagon can hold eighteen stretchers when necessary — one nurse orderly is attached to each wagon and as a rule they are very gentle and sympathetic though they make no claim to special skill. One of the greatest trials we have had to combat were the flies which swarmed in thousands over every train, harassing the wounded and adding to the discomfort of the heat. Luckily some friends had sent me a supply of little paper fans from Paris and they were the delight of all the men who had arms available to use them. Of course, the nearer one is to the trenches the worse they become so what to us seems a veritable plague is a comparative relief to the men."

French soldiers were the most poorly paid and fed among the Allies, and were deeply grateful for anything the volunteers could do for them. "Fresh pillows, stuffed with weed or sweet smelling dried grasses, evoke a sigh of content and a heartfelt 'la va mieux' that would greatly please the sixteen-year-old in Paris who sent me so many pillow slips for this purpose. Squares of gauze for putting over badly wounded faces to prevent the maddening attentions of the flies are our own invention and has had the unlooked-for honour of commendation from the medicine chef." Over the next few years, Elizabeth would spend many days criss-crossing France with her squares of gauze and pots of steaming coffee, desperate to help her beloved *poilu* in any way she could.

LONDON, England, September 1915. Beatrice had finally found a job. She was a clerk for the estates branch of Canadian Pay and Records, the London-based office charged with administering soldiers' pay, overseeing the military postal service, compiling war statistics, registering the location of graves, and processing the estates of dead soldiers.[17] She worked from nine-thirty until six on weekdays, and nine-thirty in the morning until one on Saturdays,[18] typing letters, answering the phone, and operating the copper tea trolley that was the mainstay of so many London offices. She was paid thirty shillings per week for the privilege. It wasn't a bad wage at the time, given the fact that a milliner would make about seventeen shillings and a machinist roughly thirty-nine.[19] Her job also gave her an intimate view of the administrative superstructure that oversaw the Canadian war effort. In a pattern she would follow throughout the war, she would mine her workplace and her own day-to-day experiences for stories. In an article that appeared in the *Daily Province* a few months after her job began, she described the processing of wills.

"Thousands of wills made by men in the field and extracted from pay books after their death are on file and every one of the thousands has its own individuality. There is one that says: 'In the event of my death (loud cheers) I give all my property and effects (loud and prolonged cheers!!!) to etc. etc.' Another man 'leaves all to my beloved sweetheart provided she can hit it off with her would-be brother-in-law,' another adds to his, after a detailed statement of property and heirs, 'I want my mother to know not to try to sell my homestead now, it would cost her more than she'd get out of it.' The great majority of wills leave everything to 'my mother,' and an equal majority of the letters from the front that are sent to the estates branch to be tested for their testamentary value are written to the mothers of the writers."[20]

Many of the men who worked in the office were soldiers who were no longer fit for active duty. "In one corner sits a young Toronto lad. He has just been returned from France and has just come into the office from a long siege of hospital treatment. He is still pale and coughs a good deal but his spirits are bright and nothing he can do to help someone else is any trouble to him. He is known in his department as 'The Night Before Christmas,' but you would never guess the reason. It is because he sits all day long at a huge table and makes up little bundles of worthless articles, just as so many hundreds of people do on the night before Christmas. Sometimes the parcel includes an old cigarette tin, soiled letters, odd-shaped stones, some twisted bullets or a foreign coin, sometimes a rosary, a testament, some photographs and mementoes of home. Worthless indeed to the uninterested onlooker, but full of tender memories and association for the people to whom they are addressed. For these are the personal effects found on dead soldiers in the field and returned to their relatives through this office."[21]

Not all of Beatrice's experiences at the Pay and Record Office made their way into her articles. Her father, as always, was her confidant:

> Dearest ... I am the only Canadian girl in a civilian staff of nearly a hundred and being Canadian I am made the unwilling confidante of all the Canadian men in the department, from the corporal who tells me in lurid detail all about the bar room brawls in which he comes out victor and other wise, to the Lieutenant who doesn't want to be sent back to the trenches and who relates his past experiences with tears in his eyes and touching references to his wife and child. Then there is a PPCLI man who was a practicing solicitor in Edmonton and has a fearful fit of blues to work off every day or so and hangs round waiting to pin me into a corner.... They all want to get back to Canada. Most of them tell me how they are hitting the booze, that they don't know a soul in London and they all fight with the English they do know and so and so on, till my head fairly buzzes.[22]

Lovely, independent, and forthright, Beatrice was the object of more than one man's speculation. Some even offered to set Beatrice up in an apartment as their mistress, but she declined all offers. If she was going to have an affair, it would be on her own terms, not someone else's.

Unwanted male attention was not Bea's only problem. London was experiencing the repercussions of war first-hand. On Thursday, September 7, Beatrice left her office at six and struggled to find her way home. It wasn't an easy task, since each night the city was as dark as the inside of a sealed envelope. Street lights no longer illuminated the streets, and all citizens were warned to cover their windows lest the light provide a target for the hulking grey German Zeppelins that patrolled the skies above. In January, the first German bombs had been dropped on the coast of Britain. On May 31, the Zeppelins reached London. They dropped eighty-seven incendiary and twenty-five high-explosive projectiles. Thirty-five people were injured and seven were killed, including four young children.[23] As she walked home, Beatrice couldn't help but recall the May attack. It had happened on a night as clear as this one. Her steps quickened, despite the very real danger of bumping into someone in the inky darkness. She was relieved when she finally reached St. George's House in Vincent Square, a few blocks from the Pay and Records Office.

St. George's was her latest temporary home. The women's residence had been opened in 1905 for "ladies engaged in training or professional work." For a modest rent, each of its fifty residents got a small bed-sitting room with its own gas metered fire, a double bed, tall wardrobe, and elegant inlaid desk. For Beatrice, who had searched high and low for accommodation, it was a palace.[24] After eating dinner in the communal dining room, she went to her room, shut her curtains, and worked away on a story until nearly 10:00, when she finally fell into bed. She wasn't allowed to sleep for long.

> At 11 o'clock I came back most unwillingly to consciousness from what optimists call a "beauty sleep," struggling hard against my awakening. Subconsciously I had been hearing distant reports and reverberations, just a little louder and a little different from the thousand other night noises of the city. Then, before my eyes were fully

open, there came an explosion that seemed to lift me bodily and set me in a perpendicular position on the floor. "Zepps!" I said, and reached for my slippers and gown. As I did this I remembered standing two days before in front of a window of one of the big shops on Oxford Street laughing merrily at the air raid display set forth within. The window was furnished as a bedroom. At the head of the bed a small reading table was topped with a motley collection of the last things one would be likely to think of in an emergency — an electric torch, an illuminating clock, a bottle of smelling salts, etc etc. A chemical fire extinguisher was on the floor nearby and a couple of respirators were close to hand. By the side of the bed was a pair of house slippers and close to them a pail of water (the reader is here given two guesses as to which the panic-stricken civilian would put his feet into first on leaping from the bed), while sumptuous dressing gowns, presumably for receiving the special constable when he knocks at your door and tremblingly commands you to retreat to your own cellars, were draped over a chair placed conveniently in the line of exit. Manifestly you could not get out of the room in any direction without stubbing your toe against at least three corners.

Now the details of this window display came back to me vividly and made me smile a bit ruefully. But I was to have a "window display" all to myself tonight. A reflection from a sweeping searchlight lit up the room momentarily and enabled me to negotiate without accident the knobby route from bed to window. As I leaned out there was a still louder explosion followed by the rapid reports of an anti-aircraft gun coming at the rate of five or six to a second with a harsh barking, penetrating sound....

The bomb explosions continued, closer now. I imagined I could hear a distressing noise of shattering buildings after each, but this was probably only the sounds of reverberation. The firing of the anti-aircraft guns fascinated me and I found myself counting the quick reports as they came in series. The sky was lit up by rigid white bands of light, pivoting and crossing. And somewhere up in the great expanse of night were the "hostile" airships making a perfectly "satisfactory" attack.... It is difficult to convey in words an idea of the sensation of absolute unprotectedness that one feels with bombs dropping on all sides. You wonder how many Zeppelins are aloft, how many bombs each craft can carry and when they will have all been dropped and the murder and devastation cease. And the time seems very long.

It didn't occur to Beatrice that a bomb might drop in her vicinity, and nothing was farther from her mind than the idea of going downstairs. She had been at the window less than ten minutes when there was a lull in the firing. It dawned on her that she was cold, and she became conscious of noises in the outer hallway. One of her fellow boarders burst into her room, shouting, "You must come down at once" before rushing to the next room. At that moment, seven shells from anti-aircraft guns made sweeping curves of light across the sky. Beatrice was held spellbound at the window. Then a terrific explosion came, and she turned away and joined her housemates on the ground floor.

"The Zeppelins seemed to have passed over and the explosions grew more distant. I looked round and realized that so far as my companions of the house were concerned, the Oxford Street window display had been without avail," she recalled later. "No one wore a respirator nor carried a chemical fire-extinguisher or electric torch; no one appeared to require smelling salts. The gowns and slippers were not all that had been prescribed by Oxford Street and in a few cases were altogether missing...."

Beatrice spent the next night with friends who lived on the edge of the city, close to the open country. They were just about to go to bed when they heard the unmistakable sound of aerial engines. They switched off the lights, and once again, she rushed for the windows.

"The night was starry and there was no moon. As we strained our eyes upward there was a sound as of fifty motorcycles each with the exhaust open, rounding the home stretch on a heavenly race course. Then two dazzling lights struck, full of different angles, on the two foremost marauders and touched them into mammoth glow worms of shimmering silver. It was an unforgettable sight. Simultaneously there was a hoarse, hollow coughing from the stationary guns and an accompanying volley of explosions and two bombs fell and burst about half a mile away — fortunately quite in the open fields where no damage was caused," wrote Beatrice. "There was something wonderfully enthralling in the vision of these silver ships of the sky, their great aluminum bodies gleaming like the surface of a placid sea in a full moon.... In the vivifying light from the great search lamps we could see the shrapnel from the anti-aircraft guns burst and fall back in a shower of gold. It was like looking on at some dream of a future century and when the pageant was over we came back to the present with a shudder that such horrors could really be in our own day (and night)."[25]

Beatrice wrote her account of the raids immediately after they occurred. They had inflicted extraordinary damage on London, causing more than half-a-million pounds' worth of damage and leaving twenty-two people dead.[26] Knowing that the censors would block any stories describing the success of the German attacks (stories of the May raid had been suppressed by the government), Beatrice didn't send her story to the *Province* via transatlantic cable. Nor did she mail it, as she had heard that "all mail to newspaper offices was censored at four centres in Canada."[27] Instead, she sent it to Vancouver via her brother Hope, now returning home from a business trip in Britain. The article appeared — uncut — just three weeks after the event. Unlike her colleague Mary MacLeod Moore, who believed that loyalty to the Allied cause involved the sacrifice of freedom of the press, Beatrice would work hard throughout the war to avoid the heavy hand of the British censor whenever possible.[28]

FOLKESTONE, England, October 1, 1915. "Between you and me, I don't know what we should have done without the Canadians this year," the grizzled shopkeeper told Beatrice. "They've kept us alive — in more ways than one, sure enough they have." He wasn't describing the soldiers' feats on the battlefield, but their contribution to his economic well-being. A constantly changing population of roughly forty-five thousand Canadians had been camping and training at coastal towns such as Folkestone over the previous eight months, and local entrepreneurs were amassing big profits by selling them cigarettes, fruit, postcards, souvenirs, and restaurant food at hugely inflated prices. "One shop even flaunts a printed sign: No Extra Charge to Canadians — and under this 'too-much-protesting' guise carries on a lively trade in which Canadians are fleeced," wrote Beatrice.

In town to document the experience of Canadians en route to the front, Beatrice watched as Canadian recruits trained for the horrors of trench warfare. "At intervals you come across bogey-looking rows of sacks strung man-high on long wooden frames. They dangle in a most dejected way and the straw filling oozes from their many wounds. For these are Germans and they have been the objects of many bayonet charges. Sometimes there are several rows of these straw men and in between them a couple of deep trenches, and at the command to charge, the recruits dash through the trenches in rows and on occasion one filled with rotting straw bags, for it seems that to bayonet a man in a trench requires quite a different twist to the wrist to running him through in the open and so for practice there must be entrenched Germans and Germans 'on the level.'" Within a month they would be in France facing real Germans in situations much less ideal.

LONDON, England, November 1915. Despite the heavy load of work and writing, Beatrice still managed to socialize with friends such as fellow journalist Katherine Hughes. The two often met for lunch or took cheap seats in the popular theatres in the Strand. Katherine, a tall, blond Irish Canadian, was working as publicity secretary at the Alberta Agent General's office at 1 Charing Cross Road. The office had been established to promote settlement and investment in Alberta. With the onset of war, it had also become a reception centre for Alberta soldiers passing through London en route to the Western Front.

In November, Katherine was offered a large writing commission and resigned from her job.[29] Beatrice, fed up with the unwanted attentions of many of the men in the Pay and Records Office, applied to replace her and was quickly hired. Not only did she have the journalistic qualifications for the position, but her Sifton family connections eased her way into the job (her second cousin Arthur was now Premier of Alberta).[30]

From the window in her fourth-floor office overlooking Trafalgar Square, Bea could watch the comings and goings of the weak and the powerful — from office clerks to politicians. In the square below, suffragettes led stirring enlistment rallies and workers rushed to their jobs at munitions factories. Stories could be found everywhere. Charing Cross Station, only a stone's throw away from her office, was the site of farewells and reunions as soldiers left for the front, returned home on short leaves, or were disgorged on stretchers from the omnipresent hospital trains. A few blocks farther along was Whitehall, with its government offices, Admiralty headquarters, and home of the prime minister. The Houses of Parliament sprawled along the Thames River, and to the southwest sat Buckingham Palace.

The job was demanding, but there were humorous moments. "It would take a century to learn all I am expected to known in this office," she wrote to her mother. "A man rings up one morning to know where Bottle Ridge is and all about it. I spend the morning finding out from various maps what sort of country it is in, what the taxes are, the class of people who have settled there, the amount of rainfall, the condition of the land etc. etc. and think I am all ready for any similar questions and may take it easy till the next one comes. But the next man wants to know the name and address of the official dog catcher in Bog Gulch and the third whether his third cousin who lived in Lethbridge for six years and cashed in suddenly about four months ago, died intestate or not."[31] Unlike the Pay and Records Office, there was little chance for her to get bored.

Her journalism didn't suffer either. In November, she managed to write a half-page feature article called "Rambles in Dark but Interesting London." One of the stories she told was of a visit to a club for the wives of soldiers and sailors. The club provided tasty meals — "sausage and mashed" for "tuppence ha'penny a plate" — and an opportunity to socialize. Beatrice doesn't name the woman who took her on the tour of the club, but it may well have been Mary MacLeod Moore, a volunteer with the group and a journalist she would come to know better as the war progressed.

VERDUN, France, November 1915. "After an hour's wait we tucked ourselves and the bulky parcels of comforts for the wounded into the only vacant places left in a train crowded with officers and men returning to the front and began a midnight journey under war conditions. Every light in the train was turned out and the voices of our fellow travelers exchanging war stories in the darkness added to the weirdness."[32]

Elizabeth was travelling to Verdun to take "comforts" to the wounded on behalf of the Paris Press Syndicate. The special boxcar used for this work was attached to the train on which she was travelling and would be left at the Verdun train station as a home base for Elizabeth and the other volunteers.

When the stuffy train finally drew into Verdun at 5:00 a.m. Elizabeth was amused to see that the station platform was lined with mounds of sandbags. Across the road was a dugout similarly reinforced "where the cantine [sic] staff are supposed to run for shelter if a bombardment takes place." Such precautions seemed futile, since "no self-respecting shell would be in the least daunted by those inert sacks."[33]

Located on the Meuse River and surrounded by a ring of forts, Verdun was both a stronghold and a salient that projected into the German lines. It had suffered intense bombardment at the beginning of the war, but had somehow survived. It was also home to a vital railway link to Paris. Here, in the shadow of ruined buildings, the wounded were loaded onto trains and sent on to hospitals, away from the front lines.

Elizabeth and her fellow volunteers spent their days going back and forth on these special hospital trains. "On an average we travel every four days and we feed a hundred wounded on each trip. One of us takes the badly wounded on the stretchers to attend to, and the other the semi-invalids who can sit up in the ordinary railway carriages," she wrote. "It seems sometimes as one looks at them that no amount of spoiling could possibly be too much. In front of those mangled limbs and brave faces we have only one thought — to make the few hours we are with them as bearable as possible."[34] In addition to steaming bowls of soup, the women distributed grey wool socks, cigarettes, and handkerchiefs scented with eau de cologne.

Each time she returned to Verdun, Elizabeth was struck by the signs of normalcy in the ravaged city. "Most of the houses are built in grey stone, and one comes upon picturesque windings of the River Meuse at every turn. Even in this icy weather the washer women are bending over the running water, kneeling on their funny wooden trays and slapping vigorously at the linen with the flat, round wooden spoons, whose efficacy always remains a mystery to the uninitiated. Their chattering is punctuated by the booming of the cannon, heard with extraordinary distinctness, and now and then, we see the little white puffs in the air following a flash of light which tells of an aerial battle, whose issue is too far away to be seen by our unaided eyes."[35]

One Sunday morning, Elizabeth took a much-needed break and attended Mass in the city's grand cathedral. For a short while, its vaulted ceilings and the music of its magnificent organ provided a reprieve from the wreckage of war. But the break didn't last for long. "The service was nearly over when the organ was interrupted by an appalling crash that made the stained glass windows rattle. No one paid the least attention. I suppose the Verdunoise scorn to notice anything smaller than long-distance guns. The little acolyte serving the mass looked round and grinned broadly at some of his pals in the congregation, but no one else stirred. As soon as the service was over we hurried back to the station, certain that it had been the centre of attraction. We had missed seeing a bomb fall only fifty yards from our car...."

The Germans had not given up on Verdun.

LONDON, England, December 24, 1915. Beatrice was lonely for home — the maple leaves her father had sent her, pressed between pages of an issue of the *Province*, only made her melancholy worse. London in December 1915 was bleak, foggy, and pitch-black at night to protect against air raids, making it dangerous for anyone on foot. Bea imagined writing a book about "London by Dark," that might contain chapters such as "Peerings in Picadilly," "Stumblings in the Strand," "Curb-leapings in Chelsea," "Pitching in Pimlico," and "Tumbling into the Thames." "There will be special sections devoted to such timely information as 'how to get home on a twisted ankle,' 'the correct form of address on running into a strange house when surprised by an air raid,' 'how to distinguish between a policeman and a pillar box at two paces,' and 'the development of the sense of smell as a guide to nearest underground station.'"[36]

Yet despite her bravado, the darkness had a depressing effect and made Bea long for the big sky and bright lights of home. She may not have been able to go home, but in the end, home came to her. Her old Vancouver friend Sybil Chaloner invited Bea to a holiday dinner party at the Bloomsbury flat she shared with her brother Ernest, a reporter for the *Journal of Commerce*. Ernest had sprung into fame early in the war by writing that the port of London authority was giving a half-a-million pounds a year to a big Hamburg firm to construct docks on the Thames.[37] But it wasn't Ernest who caught Beatrice's eye at the party.

"It was a happy circumstance that placed me opposite a Vancouver officer at a little Christmas dinner a few nights ago — not to mention the luck that placed me at the Christmas dinner!" she later wrote. The officer in question was twenty-four-year-old Charles Adams, a six-foot-tall, chestnut-haired lieutenant in the kilted uniform of the 16th Canadian Scottish. As their eyes met across the table, for once Beatrice was not "fed up with uniforms."

Charles had the disoriented look peculiar to men who had spent the previous eight months in lice-ridden clothes in cold, wet trenches and now found themselves seated in warm dining rooms at linen-covered tables with the only sounds being polite conversation and the clinking of fine china. As her coffee got cold, she listened as he described the trench he had recently vacated as having three feet of water in it. "There will be more than that when I get back," he said with a deep laugh and a queer, sloping smile. But when Beatrice asked him about his battle experiences, the smile disappeared entirely and a kind of grey look took its place.

"A while ago, our company was ordered to make a feint attack on the opposite trenches to cover a real attack in another section a few kilometres away. This brought on a three-day bombardment from the Germans. The shells were falling in a shower. From the whizzing overhead and the sound of the bursting I could calculate the distance between our section of the trench and the place where the shells were landing. I began to realize that each shell was coming a few yards closer with each shot. There was nothing I could do but sit and wait and count, wondering if the next one would fall on our trench or beside it."

When it was all over, hundreds of Canadian troops in neighbouring trenches were dead or wounded. Charles, however, hadn't lost a single man. His luck didn't hold. "I sent five men out to reconnoiter. They were heard at nightfall by the man at the listening post and mistaken for enemies. He gave the alarm and all five were shot dead."

As he finished the story, Charles looked grim and Bea quickly changed the subject, drawing him back to his childhood on Broughton Street and his work as a surveyor before the war. Earnest put on some music, the table was pushed back, and Bea and Charles were dancing, his muscular arms holding her close. For once, Bea forgot that she was a reporter and Charles a soldier. They were just two young people homesick for Vancouver, sick of war, and glad to have found each other.

Chapter 6

Who Dies If England Lives?

There is but one task for all —
One life for each to give.
What stands if Freedom fall?
Who dies if England live?
— From *For All We Have and Are*, Rudyard Kipling

LONDON, England, January 1916. An icy wind swirled along the station platform, chilling the crowds waiting for the next train. Where it would come from was anyone's guess, since a dozen rows of tracks stretched off in various directions. Finally, a winding, huffing giant roared in with a great burst of steam. Doors slammed open and there were scenes of distracting bustle and confusion, as one group of passengers was disgorged and another struggled to board.

Bea rushed through the crowd, her red wool scarf pulled up over her mouth as a protection against the cold and sooty air. She wasn't at the station to meet someone or start a journey. Instead, she was volunteering for one of the hundreds of "soldiers and sailors railway buffets" scattered across England. Beatrice planned to "do four solid hours from eight to 12 of *real* war work" and report on the experience for the *Province.*

The buffet was in an old railway carriage tucked away on a siding. It had been fitted out as a diner, with a gleaming white kitchen and a long counter with a giant coffee urn at each end. At first, Bea stood self-consciously behind the counter with volunteers dressed in tweeds and white-bibbed aprons with blue armbands marked S&SB. It seemed awfully quiet — where were all the soldiers who were supposed to be flooding into the buffet? The manager had warned her that there would be several troop trains coming in that evening, since the New Year's leave had expired and several thousand men would be travelling back to their posts in France.

Just as she was beginning to wonder if she'd have anything to report, there was a boom and a roar and a long troop train rushed into the station and came to a standstill on the main track just across the platform

Beatrice and her favourite correspondent, her father, James Nasmyth.

from the buffet. As the doors flew open, Bea saw something vaguely resembling a disturbed hornet's nest. A cloud of men was rushing en masse toward the canteen and in seconds she found herself handing out hundreds of steaming mugs of coffee, slices of fruitcake, and slabs of bread and butter. The smell of sweat and damp wool hung in the air as the men crowded into the buffet, while others overflowed onto the platform.

Within ten minutes came the "All aboard!" The men popped out of the crowded canteen like corks from a bottle, calling back "G'bye girls!" or "Any message for the Kaiser?" There was no time for the workers to catch their breath. A Scottish express carrying several hundred troops was due in fifteen minutes and they had to refill the urns, wash up the mugs, slice cake, and butter mountains of bread. When the train finally arrived, it was clear that the Scots had enjoyed Christmas a bit too much. Green-faced and queasy, many were too sick to leave their carriages. Those who were still sober carried their coffee to them, while offers of fruitcake were summarily rejected.

By the time Bea's shift was over, twenty trains had come and gone. She left the station more slowly than when she had first arrived, her muscles and back aching. At home, taking off her uniform and setting her armband on her desk, Bea's mind was filled with memories of the men to whom she had handed mugs of coffee, a last touch of home before their return to the trenches. They reminded her of Guy Furniss, the handsome stranger she had met at the beginning of the war, and Charles Adams, the tall British Columbian she had danced with at Christmas. Both were now in the firing line. How many of those she served at the buffet would never return home? And if they did, would they be altered beyond recognition, like the disfigured veterans she had visited in London's military hospitals? The war had already gone on for over a year and half. She wondered when and how was it all going to end.[1]

LONDON, England, January 1916. Just a few weeks after her buffet experience, Bea was boarding a train herself, en route to friends who lived north of London. The carriages were packed with weekend travellers, mostly women and children and a few officers home on leave. She finally found an empty seat next to a tanned, haggard-looking woman with a bandaged foot whose only luggage was a worn wicker basket with a battered granite cup tied to its handle. Bea set her bag on the vacant seat and before the train pulled out, stepped out onto the platform to buy a newspaper. By the time she returned, her seatmate had spread a bedraggled raincoat over her knees to conceal the fact that she had taken off one of her boots.

When Bea asked if her foot hurt much, the woman replied "not very" in a rich Scottish voice. After agreeing it was a fine sunny day to be travelling, they lapsed into a companionable silence and Bea turned to her newspaper. On the front page was a graphic story about the flight of a Scottish women's medical unit from Serbia. Established by suffragist Mabel Stobart in 1915, its staff had treated wounded soldiers and thousands of Serbians during a typhus epidemic. When the Austrians invaded Serbia, the unit was forced to close, and its eighteen nurses were forced into a two hundred-mile journey to safety. They travelled eighty days by foot, ox cart, and pack horse across the Albanian mountains.

As she looked at the newspaper image of the besieged nurses, Bea suddenly recognized the woman sitting next to her. "I was wondering if I could pick you out in the group," she casually remarked. The woman smiled and with a little encouragement was soon describing her recent adventures. She had arrived in London the day before with her fellow nurses, all wearing the same clothes they had worn in their trek through the mountains. "All but the boots," she told Beatrice. "They had literally neither heels nor soles and so I exchanged them in London for this pair."[2]

"What happened to your foot?" asked Bea.

"Frostbite. It is almost better now but while we were trekking through the mountains it was often very painful and several times I thought I would have to drop behind and take my chances with other stragglers. This is my basket I carried every step of the way with me and this is the only cup we drank from and I have nothing else. Everything had to be left."[3] The nurses slogged through knee-deep snow and mud and slept in the open at night, soaked to the skin by torrential rainstorms.[4]

Although the women's situation was desperate, that of the Serbs was worse. Bea's companion described the tens of thousands of Serbians — soldiers, women, and children — and the German and Austrian prisoners forced to walk in front of them. "Our lives were a mixture of misery and desperate effort," she recalled. Hunger haunted all the marchers. Whenever one of the horses in the procession fell at the side of the road, there was a scramble for its flesh.[5] Up in the mountains they faced additional dangers — the muddy trails were often along narrow shelves. Although none of her party died on the journey, others were not so lucky. Caroline Tufnel, a British volunteer with another unit, died when her truck went over a cliff.[6]

In the valleys, the nurses helped themselves to apples in roadside farmyards while young officers stole the occasional pig, which they roasted and shared with the women. Prisoners had a much tougher time. "When we peeled the apples as we walked, often the prisoners would come along behind us and silently hold out their hands to catch the peelings as they fell. We were all sorry for the Austrians because we had nursed many of them in our hospitals and had always liked them for their patience and consideration and other good qualities."[7]

As the woman's story drew to a close, Bea heard her station called. She stepped gingerly over her new friend's bandaged foot and stepped into the corridor, envying — as only someone who hadn't shared the experience could — "her old wicker basket, her battered granite mug, and her frost-bite because they represented a finer heroism and a brave and loyal spirit untouched by hardship and peril."[8]

LONDON, England, February 1916. Mary flung her newspaper down in disgust. The classified section of the newspaper contained column after column of advertisements for cooks, nurses, and maids — all for people who needed little help but had lots of money to pay for it. Mary, having moved from the luxury of Ashley Gardens to a tiny apartment on Warwick Square, wondered if those born with silver spoons in their mouths would ever realize that war meant sacrifices for everyone.

"There is a good deal of talk about economy," she later wrote, "but it is taking people a long time to learn that really to be economical, will mean ceasing to live as they have been accustomed all their lives. Ceasing to have six or eight servants in a small family and managing with two or three. Ceasing to spend money easily and buying all they fancied or thought was necessary to their position. Ceasing, in fact, to regard their position before the war as a standard and realizing that to help the country they must start afresh so far as a manner of living is concerned. No young woman need be long without work, so there is no question of the maids suffering if they are discharged. On the contrary, there is immense difficulty in getting good servants, for so many have been attracted into other fields of labour. Only very high wages will induce them to give up the positions and the independence the war has placed in their way."[9]

Mary knew where those parlour maids had gone, and applauded them for it. "There are 660,000 women in the United Kingdom working on munitions, where just before the war there were about 180,000 engaged in war industries. These women, many of whom never saw machinery, so to speak, before the war, are employed on 471 different processes. They work on aeroplanes, the manufacture of howitzer bombs, shells, fuses, machine tools, marine mines, filling bombs, making bullets and cartridges, and many other branches of the great work of supporting our armies."

Within a few months, the minister of munitions would give Mary permission to tour one of those munitions plants. On the day of her visit, the noise in the factory was deafening, the air stiflingly hot from equipment that operated twenty-four hours a day, seven days a week. Women dressed in caps and sweaty overalls stood side-by-side, bent over long rows of whirring machines. Mary watched intently as one turned copper bands on high-explosive shells. Another tapped and assembled fuse parts. Still others were lubricating bullets and tying cordite. Outside, across a narrow path, women in the "danger building" were handling "explosives enough to blow us all sky high."

Later, over tea and scrambled eggs in the dusty factory canteen, she asked a few of the women why they had signed up for munitions work. "I work in the danger building and every shell I help with I know I'm making it easier for my Dad in the Navy to fight the Germans," answered one young woman.

"Me?" said another girl, "my husband left the week we were married. I'm doing my best to help him here. I'd go wild sitting at home wondering about things, you know. Here I feel I'm fighting too, and I'll go on as long as he wants me to help."

Another motivation, stronger than patriotism, was the desire for a decent wage and the independence that it brought. "The girl of sixteen near us, in one shop started with 12s weekly six months ago and is now making 38s while a quiet young woman who had been a maid before the war told us she was a senior overlooker making £3 10s weekly with overtime and bonus," a far cry from the £28 pounds a year still on offer for parlour maids.

"How will it be after the war?" Mary wondered. "Many of the women are tasting the joys of an independent income to be spent or saved as one chooses for the first time. How will they settle down to the old life when the men return?"[10]

LONDON, England, February 1916. Florence Riddell walked into Charing Cross Station as though in a trance. Bea led her along, carrying the older woman's bag, tickets, and all the paperwork she would need when she reached Folkestone. Less than two weeks earlier, Florence's chief preoccupation in life had been hosting teas for returning students at Edmonton's Alberta College, where her husband John was principal. That work was abandoned when she received the cable saying that her twenty-two-year-old son, Private Harold Riddell, was "dangerously ill in France." Unlike most women, Florence had the means to rush to her son's side in Europe. She wired ahead to the Alberta Agent General's Office, asking them to arrange her crossing to France, and then left for England, a ten-day journey by train and ship.

Beatrice met Florence's ship in Liverpool and travelled with her to London, where she booked her into a comfortable hotel. Riddell was clearly exhausted, but not willing to abandon hope for her son's survival. "[She's] very strung up but won't give in to tears," Bea wrote in a long letter home. "Nobody seems to think there is any hope for the boy. He has cerebro spinal meningitis and the cable yesterday said 'prognosis very bad.'"[11]

The next day, Florence travelled by train to Folkestone, where she was met by a Red Cross official and put on a packed troop ship to France. The channel crossing was rough, but she couldn't think of anything but her son and the European tour they had made together before the war. On the quay at Boulogne, an awkward young Canadian lieutenant was waiting to take her to her billet in St. Omer. As the French countryside whirred past their train window, he told her that the war was going well and that victory was just around the corner. It was cold comfort.

Just as night was starting to fall, they reached the small stone house in St. Omer where Florence would stay. As he said his goodbyes, the lieutenant handed her a special pass allowing her to travel on to the casualty clearing station where Harold was being nursed. As soon as dawn broke the next morning, Florence set out on the muddy forty-minute walk. She was stopped by sentries four times before finally arriving. A nurse took her to the area where her son was sleeping, but despite coming all that way, she could only speak to him through a small opening in a glass partition. According to the medical officer, Harold was "holding his own."

"Three days were granted them, an hour a day, to be thus together. Always the glass barrier was between them. But the boy was rational and liked to talk and tell her things, and he wanted to know all about home," she would later tell Bea. On the fourth day, her son's condition deteriorated and he could no longer speak. Florence watched helplessly as Harold lost consciousness. He would not survive the night.

In the morning, Florence brought armfuls of daffodils and daisies to the nurse to put on her son's grave. The funeral would be the next day, but she wouldn't be allowed to attend. The military was sending her in a car to Boulogne with a group of nurses going home on leave. During the forty-mile trip through the white countryside, the car stopped briefly to watch an encounter between an Allied plane and a Zeppelin. Florence could hear bombs falling behind them and covered her eyes. She wondered why she had brought her son into the world in the first place. "Was it all for this?"

Once Florence was back in London, Bea took her shopping for clothes to wear on the journey home — her suitcase having gone astray during the voyage to England. Florence's composure was now completely gone. She wandered the aisles of store after store, hardly noticing the shirtwaists and skirts that Bea found for her, muttering "We've lost our boy" or "They're burying him today."

"It was a good deal of a strain for me so I don't know what it was for her," Bea wrote in a letter home.[12] Her sympathy didn't stop her from telling Florence's story to readers back in Vancouver. For Bea, it was the perfect illustration of the terrible loss experienced by every mother who lost her soldier son. Each of these men was important to someone, and that fact needed to be remembered in the face of the endless, impersonal lists of casualties.

"Only one in millions! The lists say fifteen million casualties. This means three million men dead and gone in all the areas of war. The statistics show that for every man who dies there are six people to mourn. So this little mother is one of a band of mourners eighteen million strong circling the earth."[13]

LONDON, England, March 1916. "Dear Mr. McQuesten, I was awfully glad to get your letter, which reached me for the New Year, and as a proof of friendship I write on the typewriter. My writing gets worse and worse as times goes on. Did you do it for a bet or was it chance that you wrote a whole letter without mentioning the war? I wonder.

"I loved reading about the peaceful life in the village or town rather, and about the pines and the rapids etc. When I go to Canada again in the days when the war is over and the Germans are outcast and cease from troubling us, I shall certainly go to see you, regardless of the proprieties! Thank you for the picture of your pretty manse."[14]

Journalism had never held the same allure for Calvin McQuesten as it had for Mary, and he was now happily settled as a minister in a rural parish. Calvin was clearly ambivalent about the war. He was working in Quebec, where support for the war was, at best, lukewarm. His mother, always a dominant force in his life, also opposed the war and had prevented his brother Tom from enlisting. In her hastily written letter, Mary tried to persuade her old "socialist" friend of the war's necessity:

> I wonder if you can realize what war is like to us who are in the centre of it. The millions of men who have enlisted, and khaki to be seen everywhere, the wounded in blue, so

cheery and jolly. The few slackers and so-called "conscientious objectors" (the objection, I gather, is to risking their lives, not to having other people do it) count for very little compared to the great rush of men who have given up all their prospects etc. to go. Since the war began I have been one of the committee and a visitor for the Soldiers and Sailors Families Assn., which I love. Also I am a Canadian Red Cross visitor and have been going every week for many months to see wounded Canadians and keep my eye on them till they rejoin. They are such splendid dears.

For many weeks I have been visiting exchanged prisoners, the men who were wounded in April and have been in Germany until lately. If anyone tells you rubbish about the German neglect and cruelty being exaggerated just refer them to me for facts! The men are so moderate and reasonable that when they do say anything you know they mean it and more too. They are quite matter-of-fact about the way the Germans neglected their wounds and left it to chance that they recovered, and one man, who was not at all bitter, told me about the orderlies spitting on a man who was not able to move in bed! Also that a man died in one ward and his body was left there for three days!

England and the whole Empire is magnificent, and much good will come out of this welter including closer relations between the various parts of the Empire, but how long oh Lord, how long?

My mother is well and as young as ever, very busy and always packing parcels for soldiers and doing useful things. Just now she is knitting washcloths. Do write to me soon, and I am going to send you an occasional London paper. Oh! We escaped the Zepps so far, though both times the bombardment was well in view of the windows and we watched with rage! All good wishes, from your friend,

M.E. MacLeod Moore.[15]

Mary's anti-German virulence must have shocked her more tolerant friend Calvin. Her columns now frequently included mentions of the brutality of the "huns" and the chivalry and heroism of British soldiers. She was the kind of woman whom soldier-poets such as Siegfried Sassoon loved to pillory. "You listen with delight, / By tales of dirt and danger fondly thrilled," Sassoon wrote.

> You crown our distant ardours while we fight,
> And mourn our laurelled memories when we're killed.
> You can't believe that British troops "retire"
> When hell's last horror breaks them, and they run,
> Trampling the terrible corpses — blind with blood.

Yet Mary was more complex than that — she was deeply moved by the stories she heard in hospital wards, and she felt a depth of empathy for the men in the trenches. Leonard Rees, her boss at the *Sunday Times*, had two sons in the firing line. And as a frequent visitor to the families of soldiers and sailors, she knew that Sassoon's "laurelled memories" could hardly begin to describe the terrible wrenching grief and economic hardship that families endured when they lost a father, son, or brother.

"A day or two ago there was mention in the papers of an elderly woman whose eight sons joined," wrote Mary. "Four are dead, two wounded, two fighting. She has one left, but when someone, not knowing the circumstances, spoke of this boy joining the army, she said, "I have given the others, but if the King wants him he must go too, even if I have to live in the workhouse."

Perhaps it was the memory of that woman that made Mary so angry on a chill afternoon in February. She had stopped for a moment in front of Selfridge's department store to look at its "war window" with its campaign maps, war news, and photographs. Then, remembering that her mother needed some hairpins, she stepped inside. The store was a shrine to Edwardian elegance, with polished wooden floors, glass cases filled with French perfume, white calfskin gloves, and chic hats. Mary was just considering whether she had time to wander the aisles when a brisk young man walked up to her and asked if he could help. With his handsome self-assurance, he reminded her of her own brother. But

Mac was at least ten years older and had given up a successful career to serve with the Red Cross and was lobbying hard to be transferred to the front in a combat role.

The floor walker smiled as he delivered her to the appropriate counter and called out "Forward Miss Jones, hairpins." When Miss Jones arrived, Mary asked her why the young man was working at the store "when he might be better employed forming fours."

"No one knows why he hasn't enlisted," answered Miss Jones.

"Well, unless he's got a bedridden father and mother and six little brothers and sisters to be supported, the military conscription act will take care of him," Mary replied grimly.[16] The government was about to pass a bill to conscript any man from eighteen to forty-one years old unless he was married, widowed with children, serving in the Royal Navy, a minister of religion, or working in a reserved occupation. Britain needed to replace the hundreds of thousands of soldiers it had lost in less than two years of fighting.

It was that insatiable hunger for more soldiers that would finally allow William MacLeod Moore — thirty-nine and in questionable health — to be taken on strength as a lieutenant in the 46th Battalion "somewhere in France." There, as Sassoon could have predicted, Mary's beloved brother would soon find himself "blind with blood" in some of the worst battles of the war.

PARIS, France, March 1916. A bucketing rain had cleared the dust away from the streets of Paris, and spring had finally arrived. In the woods surrounding the capital, nightingales were flooding the air with song, hyacinths were everywhere, and in the grounds of the Tuileries, Elizabeth watched an elderly gardener "stuffing in his red and white double daisies as if the war were non-existent." Yet even here there were signs of war — from the sandbags that surrounded the statues along the walkways to the leaders gathered at the nearby Hôtel de Crillon for the Inter-Allied Conference. During their intense three-day meeting, a Declaration of Unity had been drawn up among Belgium, France, Great Britain, Italy, Japan, Portugal, Russia, and Serbia regarding military, economic, and diplomatic affairs. Yet, for the average Parisian, it was the newly blossoming chestnut trees in the Champs Élysées, not the declarations of politicians, that renewed their strength and encouraged them.

The winter had also brought some good news to Elizabeth. In February, her cousin Harold Gibb, blinded early in the war, married the VAD who had nursed him back to health. Adria "Noel" Smith-Ryland was the daughter of Charles Smith-Ryland, owner of a large estate in Sherbourne, Warwickshire. The Smith-Rylands owned the "advowson" for Sherbourne Church, meaning they could recommend a nominee for appointment to any vacancies there. With his marriage to Noel, Harold — an ordained Anglican priest — was given that nomination and he would serve the congregation for the next fifteen years.

As she walked across the Square Édouard VII off the Boulevard des Capucines, Elizabeth stopped for a moment in front of the bronze equestrian statue of that king. At the base of the statue someone had placed a bunch of red roses and maple leaves. She knelt down to look at the card attached to the bouquet — it was dedicated to the memory of the Canadians' action at Ypres. Had it already been a year since they had faced those first terrible clouds of gas?

Her countrymen were seldom far from Elizabeth's mind. Only a few weeks before, she had visited the new Canadian hospital at St. Cloud. It was located on the grounds of a popular racetrack. The operating room was in the well-lit bar, the refreshment stand was now a hospital kitchen, and the wards were big yellow tents set up on the tracks where horses had once raced neck-and-neck. One hundred and twenty-six doctors and thirty Canadian nurses were all on hand, ready to care for the wounded who continued to pour into Paris.

Today, however, Elizabeth was en route to a French military hospital, this time to visit the victims of a different weapon of war — flame throwers. Primitive flame throwers using coal had been around since ancient times, but the German military had refined them, creating a small, portable model that used pressurized air and carbon dioxide or nitrogen. It could project a stream of burning oil for up to eighteen metres. In July 1915, German troops had used their new weapon against the British at Hooge, in Flanders. Now Elizabeth was about to see for herself the wreckage that these flamethrowers had left behind, and "a very successful treatment for burns, gangrened feet and hands, and all wounds where the flesh was much lacerated, and the surgeons showed me as triumphs of their skill the men who had been injured by jets of tar on fire."[17]

The visit was harder than she expected. She watched, willing her stomach to stay calm, as doctors painted a man's wrecked face with a composition of hot melted wax, paraffin and resin designed to protect his wounds from germs and leave nature to do its work. Then they showed her another patient, from whom the wax was peeled off like a glove. Underneath, new skin had begun to grow, but the contours of the face were distorted and there were no eyes to meet hers. She tried hard to listen as the surgeons glowingly described the benefits of their new treatments, but couldn't draw her gaze away from the once handsome man, now forever changed. "I wished ardently that every pro-German in the world could see those sightless eyes that no treatment, alas, will ever restore and there ask themselves what should be done with men who fight with such a devil-fired weapon as liquefied tar on fire."[18]

LONDON, England, July 1916. "The great offensive fills the columns of the newspapers and ordinary news is regarded with but faint interest. The leader writers continue to point out that to be too cheerful and optimistic is a mistake, but there is no need to warn the public against boasting for there is none. The thought of the cost of this success is ever present, and the lists of casualties in the daily papers, the names of those who have gone, saying by their deeds, 'Who dies if England lives?' would be sad reading if it were not for the realization of the wonderful spirit that has prompted men from the ends of the British possessions to fight that the traditions of the Empire may be maintained, regardless of the individual."[19]

"The great offensive" that Mary was writing about in such veiled terms would become famously known as the Battle of the Somme. As the public would soon learn, it would provide little reason for "cheer" or "optimism." Designed to draw German strength away from the struggle at Verdun, it was to become one of the most costly battles of the war.

Twenty-seven Allied divisions — a total of seven hundred and fifty thousand troops (80 percent of whom were British) — were to battle sixteen German divisions. The week before it started, preparations were made to stack the deck in favour of the Allies. German lines were heavily shelled, and the British returned the favour inflicted on them at Hooge — putting two new British flamethrowers into action to clear the German defences. Then, on July 1, the first day of the battle, seventeen British mines were detonated. As they stood in their trenches waiting to go "over the top," British troops had every reason to expect that German forces would prove decimated, their barbed wire destroyed and their trenches in disarray. Nothing could have been farther from the truth.

Not only had German barbed wire not been destroyed, many Allied bombs had turned out to be duds — falling to the ground without exploding — and the well-constructed concrete bunkers of the Germans had weathered the bombardment, their occupants surviving to operate the guns that now raked the heavily laden British troops as they struggled to cross no man's land.

Instead of providing a much-anticipated breakthrough, the first day of the Battle of the Somme would forever be remembered for holding the record for the largest number of British casualties — sixty thousand (including twenty thousand killed) — lost in a single day in any war. Any optimism that might have prevailed at the beginning of the battle would soon be wiped away as the news slowly trickled out that the war was anything but won.[20]

LONDON, England, July 1916. Military hospitals were full to overflowing, and crowds of men limping along in sky-blue hospital uniforms were now a familiar sight on the grounds of London hospitals. With their arrival came new opportunities for Bea to tell the stories of the Somme to her readers. Packed into a crowded London bus at the end of a long day at the office, she was en route to interview a wounded Canadian airman who had recently been on duty in France.

When she arrived, she found Fred Sutton sitting outside in the waning summer sunshine, his head swathed in bandages, a cane leaning against the bench where he sat. He pulled himself up and stretched out his hand.

Airman Fred Sutton on his motorcycle.

"Captain Sutton?"

"Just call me Fred." His voice was deep and his blue eyes sparkled through the bandages. The twenty-one-year-old Sutton was wearing the gold-and-white wings of the Royal Flying Corps on the lapels of his blue hospital tunic. His plane had been shot down on the second day of the battle.

"After waiting for it so long I got only two days of it," he said in a disgusted tone. "But they were the two greatest days of my life, and I've come through it alive so I shouldn't complain. We had been in the air since before daylight the second day watching the advance of the British. There are no words in the language to tell of the experiences and sensations of those days. We were the target of the German aircraft guns, the German stationary anti-aircraft guns, the flying shrapnel from our own shells and for anything else that chanced to come our way." Bea was well aware of the low survival rate for flyers — they didn't wear parachutes, their machines were extremely unreliable, and they faced bombardment on all sides. That Sutton had survived at all was miraculous.

"During the morning, our planes were shot through in eight places. We could see the huge shells of the German howitzers pointing at us in their flight, their noses gleaming in the sun. One of these, had it hit us, would have blown us to pieces. Yet luck was so with us that one of them actually flew between our planes on its downward course and left us unscathed. The continuous patter of bullets on our wings was like the sound of a snare drum. Young Ross of Toronto was my pilot — a wonder at the engine." Sutton had been stationed in the forward seat of the plane, manning the gun and the wireless, sending messages back to the base.

"You know, the men on the field haven't a chance in the world," he continued. "The flying men are the only ones who are really safe. I couldn't tell you of the awful pitifulness of it all. Seen from the air, the men in the trenches and in the advance have a hundred to one against them. They look so weak and small, and the whole great game that is spread below is so cruel and so very, very futile. It's the only thing about flying that gives me the creeps — to see the poor chaps on the ground. You see them make an advance, and it looks like a long row of tiny sandbags moving across the open in a snaky form. Then come the white puffs of smoke from the enemy guns and you see arms and legs fly out from the sandbags and you know they are men, falling and agonizing."

The two men had flown over the German trenches and watched officers running up and down, rallying their men. Sutton had been kept busy reporting his observations despite repeated attempts by the Germans to jam their wireless. "On the second afternoon, one of the guns on our machine was knocked silly by a shell which nearly brought us down. I saw that there was a German machine a little below us, and in a good position for a shot, and I turned the other gun on it. But before I could fire the shot, the nose of the gun was shot away. It seemed to me we were drifting into unnecessarily dangerous ground above the enemy lines, and I looked back to signal my pilot."

Bea couldn't miss the bravado in the pilot's eyes. "Just as I took in this pretty situation —" he smiled at her, "a bullet caught me in the hip. I fell, and for a few moments, lost consciousness. I think it was another dose of shrapnel in the head that brought me to — I already had nearly a dozen pieces and was covered with blood. We were getting dangerously low, and the play of bullets on our planes was exactly like a hailstorm. I managed to crawl back from the front of the machine to the pilot's seat. Then I had to sit on the knee of the unconscious man and guide the machine to a safer landing."

"If I hadn't come to exactly when I did, they would have had us down sure. I just managed to land on the British side as it was. But our troubles were not over, for we came to rest on a rounded knoll in range of the German fire and found ourselves under a pelting rain of bullets."

Fortunately, according to Sutton, a reserve batch of British soldiers "ran out like one man" and pulled the plane into a hollow out of range of the guns. Ross had a badly crippled arm, but "nothing but luck" came Sutton's way. He expected to return to the front as soon as his wounds were healed.

Bea couldn't know that Sutton hadn't really climbed into the pilot's seat and flown the plane to safety. Instead, seeing that Ross was wounded and on the verge of losing consciousness, he reached over, patted him on the shoulder, and kept him awake until the pilot managed to land the plane. They didn't land on a knoll either, but crashed through two barbed wire fences and landed in a field. With Ross now unconscious, the wounded Sutton somehow managed to carry him to a nearby dressing station, where both men were treated and sent back through the lines.

While it was the embroidered story that Bea reported, there was little doubt about the courage of the two men. Fred Sutton would be promoted to flight commander and remain in the RFC until the end of the war — one of the Corps' lucky survivors.[21]

ROYAUMONT, France, July 1916. "We arrived at the nearest station and were met by a motor ambulance driven by a tall, fair daughter of Scotland who thinks nothing of making three trips in one cold dark night to bring her wounded along the roads from the evacuation hospital to Royaumont. She is one of the staff of three girl chauffeurs who run all the motors as well as the electric lighting for the Royaumont Hospital."[22]

The hospital that Elizabeth was visiting was a casualty clearing station only forty kilometres behind the front lines and forty-eight kilometres north of Paris. Staffed entirely by women, Royaumont was one of the units founded by the Scottish Women's Hospital (SWH) organization. When war broke out in 1914, SWH founder Dr. Elsie Maud Inglis approached

British military authorities with the idea of women's medical units serving on the Western Front. The British flatly refused their offer, but the resource-strapped French eagerly accepted their help. The hospital at Royaumont, established in 1915, was one of many that would run under the SWH banner throughout the war.

Situated in an ancient abbey, it was now inundated with wounded from the "big push." According to Dr. Agnes Saville, the hospital "had received warning that the offensive was to begin about the end of June and when we heard the guns thundering by day and by night from the 25th of June we realized that our share of the labour entailed by all military operations was about to commence. On July 2, the anticipated rush began and for ten days almost without intermission, it continued...."[23]

In the first twenty-four hours after the start of the battle, the hospital's four ambulances ferried 121 cases from the train station to the hospital. By ten o'clock that evening, there was a long line of stretchers lying in the corridors outside the X-ray rooms and operating theatre. For the next few weeks, surgeons, nurses, technicians, and drivers would be lucky if they could snatch a few hours of sleep each day. In one week alone, they operated on 160 patients, did 231 bacteriological tests, and took 406 X-rays.

"The wounds were terrible ... many of these men were wounded dangerously in two, three, four and five places," wrote X-ray technician Vera Collum. "That great enemy of the surgeon who would conserve life and limb, gas gangrene was already at work in 90 percent of cases. Hence the urgent need for immediate operation, often for immediate amputation. The surgeons did not stop to search for shrapnel and pieces of metal: their one aim was to open up and clean out the wounds, or to cut off the mortifying limb before the dread gangrene had tracked its way into the vital parts of the body. The stench was very bad. Most of the poor fellows were too far gone to say much...."[24]

The hospital had evacuated all but five of its patients in preparation for the expected influx. Three weeks after the Battle of the Somme began, it had four hundred patients. As more and more wounded arrived, staff worried about keeping up with the boiling of instruments and gloves, the laundering of acres of bloody sheets, and whether the gauze, wool, and swabs would last.

Fortunately for the men who ended up at Royaumont, they were being treated by nine of the most highly trained surgeons to serve during the war. They included Chief Medical Officer Dr. Frances Ivens, the most brilliant graduate of the London School of Medicine for Women and only the third woman in Britain to obtain the degree of Master of Surgery. (Elizabeth admired Ivens, and a photo of the doctor was found among her few possessions after her death in 1964.) Dr. Nicholson, her second-in-command, had served in the mission field in Palestine, and Dr. Saville, a distinguished graduate from Glasgow University, had extensive experience in radiology. They were reinforced by a constantly changing number of nurses, orderlies, cooks, maids, drivers, and additional doctors.

Writer Cicely Hamilton, Elizabeth Montizambert's friend from her London days, was now the Royaumont's administrator. In a column in the *Common Cause* suffragist newspaper in August 1916, she told readers that the "greater number of the cases have been exceedingly grave — some of the men have arrived actually dying. We are serving the Army of the Somme District where fighting is incessant and shows no sign of abatement. Every struggle and advance on the Somme means added work for the hospitals in the rear of the Somme line — of which Royaumont is the largest."[25] Wearing muddy boots, French workman's blouse, and shirt and tie, Cicely was a startling figure as she "travelled all over the war zone delivering food and clothes to refugees, collecting truck-loads of supplies from the Channel ports," according to her biographer.[26] That work was exhausting, and whenever she could, Cicely would travel to Elizabeth's "Paris flat now and then to get away from the milieu of doctors and nurses interested in little besides their gruesome work," wrote Elizabeth.[27]

Cicely was a superb organizer, always on the lookout for ways to boost the morale of staff and patients. They may have been in the midst of one of the war's worst battles, but with the encouragement of Dr. Ivens, she managed to organize an event to open the much-needed "Canada Ward," a wing equipped through donations from Canadians. She recruited her friend Elizabeth, one of the hospital's boosters, to perform the opening ceremony, along with representatives of the Canadian and French Red Cross.

As they drove in, Elizabeth could see patients wrapped in red blankets lying on beds in the open-air cloisters. She and the other guests ate lunch outside and then toured the X-ray department. Then it was on to the Canada Ward, in what had formerly been the monastery dining room. Now its giant stained-glass windows sent beams of coloured light onto one hundred beds arranged in four rows. Nearly every cot was filled with a soldier wounded at the Somme. Most wore red dressing gowns, the gifts of Canadian donors. Smoke hung in the air from the four wood stoves, around which were huddled the few patients who were able to stand or sit.

Elizabeth and the Red Cross officers were introduced, and the men listened politely as each officer gave a brief speech. Then it was Elizabeth's turn. She stepped up to the pulpit (now used to store bed pans), and with a smile, unfurled a giant Canadian flag and hung it from the front of the lectern. She spoke of the friendship between Canada and France and the need to keep the bond strong. The men in the beds gave a feeble cheer. But as Elizabeth stepped down, she could not help but remember the march of the Allied troops through the streets of Paris during the fourteenth of July Bastille Day celebrations a few weeks before. Now many of them were lying in hospital beds just like these.

LONDON, England, August 1916. The officer's footsteps echoed down the stairs. Bea sat in silence, the news still registering in her unwilling mind. Charles Adams was dead. The tall, kilted soldier who had danced her around the Chaloners' drawing room would never return. The reality was difficult to accept, "so tremendously alive had he been on that occasion."

The officer who had given her the news was full of comforting words. "His life was laid down as bravely as it had been lived. The fatal blow brought instant release." Platitudes. She wanted to know what had really happened to Charles. Within a few weeks she located one of the men who had fought with him, now home on leave. She learned that since his return to the front lines after Christmas, Charles had been attached to the intelligence department and had been brave, even a little reckless. In January he had been struck in the neck by a piece of shrapnel. When he woke in hospital, he was suffering from shell shock. Perhaps ashamed of his "weakness," he became impatient to return to the front and left the hospital sooner than he should have done.

The 16th Battalion was getting ready to go into battle. The Canadians were holding a hill called Mount Sorrel and a crest of land called Observatory Ridge. The Germans bombarded them day and night. The shelling was so intense that entire trenches were destroyed, and trees, weapons, and bodies were thrown up into the air. Then the enemy poured down on the Canadians like waves crashing on a beach. Observatory Ridge was lost, and the German army had the upper hand.

Now the Canadians were to charge the enemy and retake all the ground that had been lost. In preparation, Charles and his men were moved closer to the German lines. They took shelter under some low hedges in no man's land while rain and shells poured down on them continuously. The attack began at dawn. As their artillery roared, the sodden, depressed band emerged from the mud and began to move forward through the mud and the noise. They fought hard and finally regained Observatory Ridge, but Charles didn't live long enough to celebrate it.

"Lieutenant Adams fell in the thick of it as the objective position was won, killed instantly by flying shrapnel," Bea would later write. "Some time later he was buried with special military honors. Today he lies in a little cemetery behind the Canadian lines."

Beatrice's obituary for Charles would be a typical follow-up piece about a heroic soldier who had met his end, but it lacked the vivacity and sparkle that usually characterized Beatrice's writing. Up until 1916 the war had been an adventure to her, a cause that would be won quickly and gloriously by gallant soldiers. But this year, with the deaths of Harold Riddell and Charles Adams, the sacrifices of the nurses of Serbia, and the courage of pilots such as Fred Sutton, the conflict had become for her what it had always been for others — a grim, costly nightmare.

EDMONTON, Alberta, October 1916. Beatrice was back in Canada, at least temporarily. She was on the new train to Alberta's Peace River country, on a publicity junket sponsored by the provincial government.

Beatrice would serve two masters with one story — providing the *Province* with a full-page, first-hand account of the opportunities for settlers, while also acting in her capacity as publicity secretary, promoting immigration to the province. It was a welcome break after an emotionally wearing nine months.

The train was filled with journalists, government officials, and engineers, along with men and women returning to the north after visits to Edmonton. "It was a truly western trainload. Conductor, waiter and porter discussed with passengers the prospects for crops, oil and land in the various districts in which their particular interests lay, and from time to time the chef, with a postponed cigar tucked under the band of his cook's cap, poked his head in from the curtained-off kitchenette for a characteristic remark or to reply to an enquiry that 'the apple pie was fresh — certainly! — but he wouldn't go so far as to say it was made with fresh apples!'"[28]

Bea's journey began at six o'clock on the evening on October 1, travelling through endless poplar groves and along the shore of Slave Lake. The train reached McLennan, 422 kilometres from Edmonton, at eight o'clock in the morning, but stopped only briefly. Then the train snaked onward, twisting west. The countryside opened up, and here and there Beatrice could see signs of land being cleared and the soil being turned. Next, the train began a sharp descent, a dangerous journey (there had been several derailments in the previous months), and each minute had "its own special thrill," according to Bea.

The train stopped briefly at the Town of Spirit River, a collection of shacks scattered along a main street that was more of a roughly cut track than a proper road. The plump owner of the town's Palace Café lashed a pumpkin pie to a piece of cardboard and delivered it to Beatrice for the princely sum of thirty-five cents. To a woman who had been living on limited rations since the beginning of the war, it left an "outstanding impression."

When they reached Grande Prairie at seven in the morning, Beatrice was met by a car and driver. They drove along the rough road back towards Spirit River, past black cultivated farmland glittering with frost. Then it was on to Peace River, where "new stores and houses are being built in all parts of the town," a community ripe for settlement.

Bea returning home to Canada for a well-earned break.

As she gauged the area's potential for successful farming, Beatrice couldn't forget the struggle taking place on the western front. "We had seen not a few vacant homesteaders' shacks and on some of them the simple legend tacked to the door was 'Gone to the War.' It told its own tale of the sacrifice of these pioneers. I was reminded of the great stacks of soldiers' wills I had seen in the Estates Department of the Canadian War Office in London, many of which had bequeathed homesteads in the North Country to relatives, 'in the event of my death.' How far apart were these two scenes, yet how closely and pathetically associated."

One of the towns that Bea passed on the train.

FRANCE, October 1916. William MacLeod Moore, newly transferred into the 46th Battalion, was about to get his first taste of life under fire. The unit had arrived at the Somme on October 8. It was nicknamed the "Suicide Battalion," having fought in almost every major victory of the Canadian Corps since the war had begun and sustaining a casualty rate of over 90 percent in the process. Now the 46th was to participate in one of the last battles of the Somme.

In late September, the First, Second, and Third Canadian divisions had fought in the Battle of Thiepval Ridge. The battle was fought along a front that extended from the Village of Courcelette in the east to the German front line near the Village of Thiepval. In the centre of that front was Thiepval Ridge, a crest of land that was well fortified with trenches, craters, and dugouts. Despite the rough terrain, terrible weather, and constant barrage of German gunfire, Canadian troops managed to capture Courcelette on September 15. They continued their attack, only to face the almost impossible challenge posed by the German barbed wire and machine guns defending what became known as "Regina Trench."

By October 17, the divisions withdrew to a quiet sector near Vimy Ridge and the 4th Division took their place. Many of these men were inexperienced and faced conditions that even the most seasoned soldier would have found daunting. Eight platoons of the 46th Battalion had been called in to reinforce Winnipeg's 44th Battalion for an attack on Regina Trench. Four of the 46th's platoons would provide cover fire, and the other four would act as a digging party. The attack began on October 17 and would cost two hundred men, with the 46th suffering fifty-two casualties (including two missing in action).

On the night of November 11, the 46th joined the 44th in another attempt on Regina Trench. William MacLeod Moore was part of the attack. He was damp from the constant rainfall, his uniform coated in mud. Like the other men waiting at the fire-step, he was carrying four grenades, five sandbags, a shovel, and 220 rounds of ammunition. Then, just eight minutes after the Allied barrage ended, the 46th went "over the top." They managed to cover a lot of ground before the Germans realized what was happening. Then all hell broke loose — within minutes, two hundred Canadians were dead or wounded. The survivors slogged on, finally taking the trench, capturing four guns and taking eighty-seven prisoners. Those who survived were startled to discover that what they had risked their lives for was "a mere depression in the chalk, in many places blown twenty feet wide, and for long stretches almost filled with debris and dead bodies."[29]

By the time the Canadians withdrew from the Battle of the Somme, they had lost 24,029 men.[30] One of the casualties was Lieutenant William MacLeod Moore. Wounded in the chest and arm, he was treated at the Red Cross hospital at Rouen. His mother and sister would welcome him back to England just after Christmas. For them it would be only a temporary respite from worry. Within a year, Mac would return to his battalion and find himself in the thick of the fighting once again.

ROYAUMONT, France, December 25, 1917. The Canada Ward was decorated with ivy and lit with strings of Chinese lanterns, and the men looked especially festive in their scarlet dressing gowns. In one corner of the grey stone hall, a tall Christmas tree decorated with flickering candles had been installed and was being carefully watched by two young VADs, each holding a long broom handle with a wet sponge at one end.

Elizabeth was pleased to be back at Royaumont to share Christmas with its hard-working staff and their soldier-patients. When she had arrived at the ancient abbey, Cicely Hamilton had ushered her into the "Canada Ward," where the "fête" would soon begin. But first, even in the midst of the season of peace, there was to be a sharp reminder of the "glory" of war.

There was a loud bang as the heavy door at the end of the ward swung open. A French colonel strode in, followed by four buglers and a detachment of soldiers in trench helmets and blue army coats. The men stopped in the centre of the ward and the bugles were sounded. Whispers echoed through the hall that three men were to be "decorated by the colonel with the Croix de Guerre" they had won on the field of battle. The first to receive his medal was a young man who had lost a leg. The second was a "sad-faced" Algerian who had to be brought forward on a stretcher from another ward. The third was a young lieutenant who "looked far too boyish to have gone through the scenes which had earned him his country's thanks," thought Elizabeth.

With the ceremony barely over, Cicely stepped forward.

"Silence," she said majestically, "for the entry of Père Nöel." In the distance, Elizabeth could hear bells and the faint sounds of old English Christmas carols coming nearer and nearer. Then the oak door swung open once again and through it "advanced surely the most wonderful procession that had passed its portals since the days of the solemn monks of the time of St. Louis," Elizabeth observed.

"First walked a page dressed in green and red, followed by twelve merry VADs in short crimson tunics with coquettish little caps. With two ropes dragged over their shoulders they drew an old time sled laden with huge sacks and adorned with mistletoe and very realistic snowflakes. There were chuckles of delight from the luckier soldiers who had secured places in the pulpit when Father Christmas made his appearance. Some of her [Ivens's] very own patients didn't recognize her, though, when they found out they were immensely uplifted about it and had to be sat on by the men in the other wards for their repeated boasts that it was 'our doctor' who was the Pere Noel."[31]

The colonel who had earlier meted out the Croix de Guerre, now found himself taken forward to receive a gift from Santa Claus, and only betrayed his embarrassment by murmuring to Father Christmas, "*Merci, Madame.*" He was followed by the stout old *curé* of the abbey, who trotted down the hall hand-in-hand with his page, to the thunderous applause of the soldiers. After receiving his gift, he gave an enthusiastic speech, praising the women who had toiled so devotedly for the welfare of the soldiers of France. The wounded applauded and "there was no doubt they echoed his sentiments." Then the pages split open the sacks and tossed out gifts to each soldier — pipes, tobacco, chocolate, socks, and handkerchiefs.

While the men were receiving their gifts, Elizabeth glanced around the room and noticed that five of the beds in the ward were occupied by women. One had been the victim of an accident in a munitions factory and had lost one of her hands. "When we are not over-crowded, we like to do what we can for the people of the village," explained one of the doctors.

The gift-giving was followed by music, beginning with the singing of the well-known French drinking song "Auprès de ma Blonde." Then it was on to more traditional Christmas songs. As the men's voices echoed throughout the hall, "the war and its horrors were forgotten for the moment as the organizers of the fete wished them to be, for all these men had played a glorious part in the liberation of their country and had earned a right to all the merriment and spoiling that their British hostesses could give them," wrote Elizabeth. "The names of the Canadian donors over each bed and the warm Canadian dressing gowns worn by some of the men as well as the flag swaying in the air, all testified to the practical sympathy that had come to them from far away."[32]

Chapter 7

Women's Work

> Where do they think the world would have been without women's work all these ages?
>
> — Dr. Elsie Inglis, responding to the suggestion that women's war work had inspired the introduction of a bill granting women the vote in England

PARIS, France, January 1917. "[I]t is not an uncommon sight to see a woman dressed in handsome furs taking her turn in the long queue outside the coal shops where sometimes a two hours' wait in a temperature below zero ends in the devastating announcement that there is no more coal," observed Elizabeth.[1] As the fourth year of the war began, both the rich and poor of Paris were feeling the pinch. The German army was in control of the coal-producing areas of northern France, and heating fuel was in short supply in the rest of the country. Food was also more expensive. Although the price of bread and potatoes was controlled by the government, the price of meat, milk, and butter were not. As these became harder to get, prices soared.

Stores now had their electricity cut off at 5:00 p.m. and were forced to shut by 5:30. In an effort to save power, bread was not allowed to be sold until at least twelve hours after baking, and cakes, tarts, and buns could not be sold on Tuesdays and Wednesdays. This was just as well — sugar was scarce, and the government would introduce sugar ration cards in March. The pastries for which France was famous were now the stuff of dreams.[2] Elizabeth, who mourned the loss of cream-filled mille-feuilles, consoled herself with the knowledge that "the French culinary set is capable of making bricks without straw, or in this case, cakes without flour … we are promised a new sort of flourless brioche in a few days and already the choux a la crème and the éclairs made from revised recipes are filling the shop windows."[3]

The war weariness of those in the capital reflected the much graver situation on the Western Front. A sense of futility and stalemate greeted the dawn of 1917. The Somme offensives and the actions around Verdun had produced few gains in exchange for huge numbers of casualties. In the coming year, French troops would finally rebel against throwing themselves against barbed wire and machine-gun fire in meaningless actions that gained little ground.[4] Their families back home, caught up in the daily struggle to put food on the table, could do little to help them.

LONDON, England, January 1917. Mary and her mother had just finished eating dinner when a great roar shook their apartment, the windows almost rattling out of their frames. The women scrambled up from their chairs and ran to the window. They scanned the sky for Zeppelins, but found none — only a strange orange glow in the distance.

The blast had come from Silvertown, a smoky industrial corridor bordering the eastern edge of the capital. Since it was technically located outside London's boundaries, it wasn't subject to the capital's planning bylaws. That meant that Silvertown attracted businesses that wanted to produce dangerous products, such as caustic soda and sulfuric acid, without having to deal with pesky environmental or residential bylaws.

In 1915 the government approached Brunner Mond, a Silvertown chemical plant, to purify TNT for the war effort. The company resisted the idea because many workers and their families lived close to the factory in tiny houses sandwiched among factories, docks, and railway lines. The plant owners also knew that handling TNT was extremely hazardous, not only because of its explosive properties, but also because it turned the skin of munitions workers yellow and caused chest pain and nausea. Their objections were overruled by a War Office desperate for munitions, and the plant was forced to process the explosive.

Just before 7:00 on the night of January 19, a fire started at the factory in the "melt pot room." Tongues of flame spread out, igniting fifty tons of TNT, much of it stored in nearby railway wagons. The factory blew apart. So did nearby buildings and homes, many with sleeping workers and their families inside. The blast showered molten metal over several kilometres, starting wild fires that could be seen as far away as Kent and Surrey.[5]

"Within a few minutes families were swept out of existence, streets were in ruins, and the living were seeking the dead in wrecks of houses, in hospitals and mortuaries," wrote Mary. "All about that part of East London, close to the river, which one is forbidden to mention by name, there are scenes of tragedy. Men and women coming home from work found their homes gone up in dust and their relatives dead or dying. Small children were brought to one hall and kept there till a distracted parent arrived to seek for her own. One woman who had news that day of her husband's death at the front lost her two children; another her son, the only one at home."[6]

More than nine hundred homes near the plant were destroyed or badly damaged in the disaster. Thousands were left homeless. Millions of London windows were shattered, and about seventy thousand buildings were damaged, including factories, docks, and warehouses. More terrible was the human cost. Seventy-three people died, and more than four hundred were injured, ninety-four of them seriously. The dead included firemen from the local station, dock and munitions workers, and children asleep in their beds. The only thing that prevented an even worse disaster was the time — most people had left the factory by 7:00, and few people were in bed at that time (the blast mostly killed people in upstairs rooms).

London responded quickly to the disaster. "Nurses, VADs, clergymen, helpful men and women who hurried to the spot with the sole desire of being of use toiled for hours among the injured and dead and at once an enquiry office was opened and an emergency committee formed to deal with the questions of food and shelter, as well as to help to trace the missing," wrote Mary. "Over a thousand people are homeless and the difficulty is great of finding accommodation for them in crowded East London. To add to the misery involved, the weather is cold and raw."[7]

PARIS, France, March 1917. As she rushed to her morning interview, Elizabeth stopped briefly in the shadow of the white columned Pantheon, the burial place of the heroes of France, from Voltaire to Victor Hugo. Only one woman was buried there — Sophie Berthelot, chemist Marcellin Berthelot's wife. It seemed to Elizabeth that France now had many heroines worthy of the Pantheon, women who had produced "a mass of fine, solid, often unnoticed achievement as any country might be proud to recall." They included the woman whom she was en route to meet, the formidable Aline Boutroux, a wealthy intellectual whose contributions were often overshadowed by those of her husband and famous brother.

The beloved younger sister of the renowned mathematician Henri Poincaré, Boutroux was married to the French philosopher Émile Boutroux. Before the war, she and her husband had lived in and presided over the scientific research institution Fondation Thiers. When the war began, she transformed the Fondation into a hospital for French officers. Now Boutroux was undertaking a new plan — to mobilize women for national service in a scheme similar to the one already in place in Britain. The organization she was to direct was known as the Association de l'Enrôlement Volontaire des Françaises.

"Four thousand applications have been received since the first of January," Boutroux told Elizabeth. "As in England, the two most pressing needs are for munition and agricultural workers, but the French passion for multiplying office work of every description entails a vast amount of secretarial labour which can easily be accomplished by women. While visiting many French military hospitals I have noticed that in the last two months a great change has taken place in the secretarial staffs, which are now nearly all composed of women. The railways are also employing numbers of women secretaries as well as women to fill the more humble roles."[8]

Many working-class women, struggling hard to make ends meet, were glad to accept paid war work. Yet such jobs came at a high price. "[The Union Française pour le Suffrage des Femmes has] just held a meeting to organize a system of lady superintendents on the English pattern to look after the health and hygiene of the women factory workers.... A good deal of attention is being drawn to the fact that the high wages given to munitions workers has [sic] caused many women to risk their own health and their children's. The new movement proposed by the Assemblée Feminine will include the establishment of crèches for the tiny children where they will be kept while the mothers work, cantines [sic] where good food will be provided and rest rooms for all the women."[9]

Boutroux's efforts would pay off, as Elizabeth would write a few months later. Women across France were rolling up their sleeves and coming to the aid of the war effort. "So much ink has flowed over the creation of the volunteer women's movement in England that one is apt to overlook the silent revolution that has taken place in France in this respect," she wrote. "At the moment there is an army of no less than 150,000 women, not counting the munition workers who have been appointed to take the place of all the able bodied men formerly employed behind the trenches. Most of these women are employed in doing office work. Others are cooks, tailors, orderlies or washerwomen taking their place in the vast war organization with as much devotion to duty as their brothers and husbands in the trenches."[10]

LONDON, England, March 1917. Beatrice's interview with a British officer was going nowhere. She was hoping he would share some of his frontline experiences, but the man declared that it was impossible to "picture for others the horror of a big engagement." Then Beatrice noticed that he kept putting his hand to his ear in an absent-minded way and asked him if something was wrong.

"Oh, no, nothing at all. I just can't get used to the ringing in my ears," he replied quietly. "It has never stopped since the last night I was in the big battle." Then, as though her sympathy had opened a locked door, he went on to describe what a battle was like. "For twenty hours a day the earth shakes. It is quiet only when the guns are cooling. That usually happens for two hours shortly after darkness falls and again before dawn breaks. The first period of cessation is necessary because of the increased intensity of the guns to make the most of the declining day; the second to prepare for a vigorous resumption when light comes again. And often at night the star shells make a continual illumination." The story didn't end there. In a halting voice, the man confessed to what would one day be seen as a war crime, but which in 1917 was simply "one of the little tragedies of the trenches which few people are allowed to hear."[11] One afternoon on his rounds of the trenches, he had come upon a man in the act of committing a "flagrant crime." The soldier had likely fallen asleep on sentry duty — a serious crime that could put his comrades in danger — or was perhaps stealing from one of the other men. It was the officer's duty to report him and he knew that the penalty for the crime was "certain death."[12]

"I simply couldn't let him die like that," said the officer. "So I covered him with my revolver and forced him out of the trench and into the open. I held him there until the Germans shot him. If they had not done so I should have had to shoot him myself. Now his name is on the honor roll

Eat Less Bread: With food in short supply, consumers were urged to eat less.

and his people believe he died gloriously in action. But the experience was as unnerving to me as if I had bayoneted a dozen Germans."

Beatrice's story of an officer effectively murdering one of his own men was allowed to be published in *The Daily Province*, untouched by the Canadian censor. Perhaps the powers that be saw it as a tribute to the "compassion" of British officers or as a warning to troops to follow the rules or face the consequences. Bea let the story stand on its own without comment, buried in an article that contained a series of vignettes on life in London in 1917. Whatever way it was viewed by the writer, or by those who allowed its publication, the story revealed one of the ways in which the war had created parallel worlds, with one law applied to combatants and another to those living in a seemingly safe world, far distant from the fighting.

LONDON, England, April 1917. Soldiers on leave couldn't understand it. Why were Londoners acting as though they were on the front lines rather than living in relative safety and comfort? How could any of them compare their experience with the mud and blood of Flanders? Few of them knew that England was on the brink of starvation. Germany was waging unrestricted U-boat warfare against all merchant ships travelling to and from Allied ports. In April 1917 five hundred and forty-two thousand tons of British shipping would be sunk, and rank-and-file Britons would feel the loss at their own kitchen tables.[13]

On April 8, the *Observer* reported, "The usual weekend potato and coal scenes took place in London yesterday. At Edmonton [in the London borough of Enfield], 131 vehicles were lined up at the gates of a coal depot at nine o'clock in the morning, while the crowd numbered several hundreds. There were also bread and potato queues of such length that the police had to regulate them. In south London trolley men with coals were besieged by people who had requisitioned all types of receptacles, including perambulators, wheelbarrows, go-carts and trucks, while others brought sacks, baskets and boxes."[14]

While Londoners were occupied with keeping food on the table, the Canadian Corps was making history at Vimy Ridge. The heavily fortified seven-kilometre-long ridge in Northern France had been in the possession of German troops since October 1914; since then, over one hundred thousand French soldiers had lost their lives trying to reverse the situation. Now it was the Canadians' turn. At 5:30 a.m. on April 9, four of their divisions stormed the slippery ridge. The battle continued until April 12, with the Canadians in decisive control of the escarpment. The victory was a huge morale booster for the Allies, but came at a high price — 3,598 Canadian dead and seven thousand wounded. These losses would be a dress rehearsal for an even more costly battle later in 1917 — Passchendaele.

———

PARIS, France, May 1917. As Elizabeth walked along the Rue de la Paix, she thought how different it looked compared to the pre-war days. All of the big dressmaking establishments were closed and guarded by groups of blue-coated policemen. Instead of sitting behind their sewing machines in airless back rooms, Paris's *midinettes* (garment workers) were on strike. They had gathered in the Place Vendôme, laughing and chatting — but their purpose was serious. They wanted an extra franc a day in wages, and the adoption of "what they call the English week, meaning a half holiday once a week."[15]

It had begun quite modestly, but had "grown to alarming proportions and now includes not only the dress makers but the modistes, the corsetieres, the workers in fur, embroiderers, lingerie and waterproof makers," reported Elizabeth.[16] Although Paris's fashion trade had declined sharply at the beginning of the war, it had begun to recover in 1916. Well-to-do women in America were now buying up the latest fur-trimmed, cloud-blue "military coats" from designers such as Paul Poiret. Trade was brisk, and prices were higher than in pre-war days. And back at home, the need for fashionable mourning clothes was as relentless as the war. However, the workers who produced these garments were not profiting from the renewed boom in French fashion.

"[H]ats for instance now cost more than before the war and the trade is brisk while the modiste salaries are still so remarkably low as $30 a month for the skilled hat trimmers and sums ranging from $4 to $20 a month for the unskilled work. If these are the before-the-war wages it is difficult to see how these workers can have existed on anything less," Elizabeth wryly commented. To add insult to injury, government laws that mandated safety measures and regular days off were also being constantly ignored.[17]

Initially, the government didn't pay much attention to the strike. It seemed more like a party than a serious labour disruption. The *midinettes* were dressed fashionably, and laughed and sang as they marched along. "Now and then a staid old workman stops and advises them to go back to work but they pay no attention," Elizabeth wrote. But the garment workers' strike quickly spread, with shell-fitters and gunpowder makers joining in. By June, one hundred thousand women were on strike in seventy-one industries in the Paris region.[18] Like the garment workers, they demanded that conditions in the factories be improved and their wages increased to keep up with rampant inflation. Failing this, they simply wanted their men back from the front. "Give us back our *poilus*!" they demanded.

A few media commentators criticized the women, saying that they just wanted the extra money for "luxuries." Elizabeth and most others disagreed. "As to the rise in wages, everyone is thoroughly in sympathy with the work girls. A few statistics of the rise in the price of food were published not long ago by the French newspaper *La Battaille* providing that the cost of living is now just three times as much as it was before the war. The price of meat is two and a half times greater. Eggs, cheese, and butter cost twice as much, while the price of dried vegetables, oil, soap and wine has been trebled. As for clothes and boots, they are fifty percent dearer. *La Bataille* also quotes the price of coal, but as it is now practically impossible to get any the price has no meaning for the moment."[19]

The women's strike mirrored the growing anger of French soldiers. Over one million had died since the beginning of the war. The losses at Verdun and the Somme were creating despair, and most soldiers would have been more than happy to respond to the pleas of the *midinettes* and return home. Their rage would be expressed in what became known as the "soldiers' mutiny." After ninety thousand were wounded in useless, ill-conceived actions on the Western Front in mid-April, a depleted battalion refused to go back on the attack. Then, a whole division refused to follow orders on May 3. Between mid-April and the end of June, the number of desertions increased, along with confrontations between soldiers and officers. On

May 27, thirty thousand French soldiers defiantly left the front lines and retreated to the rear. The men were tired, exhausted by often-futile battles and life in the trenches. Many had not had leave for years, and when they did, they were still expected to do work behind the lines.

Afraid that opposition to the war would spread on the home front and in the trenches, the French government chose to take a conciliatory approach to the strikers and mutineers. Garment workers were lured back to work with the promise of an extra franc a day and half a day off on Saturdays.[20] As for the soldiers, fifty-five mutineers would eventually be executed, but the military brass would start to deal with the men's concerns. Regular leave became mandatory, and putting men on leave to work behind the lines was forbidden. Grievances about food were addressed.[21] Yet it was clear to all that both behind the lines and on them, the idealistic, patriotic fervour that had gripped France in the first years of the war was now dead and gone.

ROYAUMONT, France, May 1917. Strings of lanterns hung from the trees bordering the stream that meandered near the abbey at Royaumont. A boat decorated with coloured lights played the role of a gondola, and underneath an ancient chestnut tree sat a flower-strewn table which "groaned as much as was consistent with wartime economy under the best efforts of the French chef."[22]

Instead of directing the festivities, Elizabeth's friend Cicely Hamilton was the guest of honour. She was leaving her position at Royaumont to join "Concerts at the Front," the acting company managed by Canadian-raised Lena Ashwell. Ashwell, a renowned actress who had once appeared with Ellen Terry and Henry Irving (and attended Bishop Strachan with Elizabeth), had established the company early in the war. Military authorities had initially opposed the idea of an acting troupe at the front (citing the "immorality" of actors), but eventually allowed it to tour the front under the auspices of the YMCA.

Cicely had become bored with her administrative duties at the abbey and wanted to return to the grease paint and footlights once more. Her job would entail directing plays in the shadow of the front lines, where she would witness terrible destruction, death, and mutilation. While she was touring, a bomb would destroy her office in Abbeville and her staff would survive only by sheltering in a deep stone cellar. The fear and anger she experienced would stay with her all her life. "On one of those nights, the worst that I remember, the invaders scored a direct hit on an ammunition dump in the Somme valley; and it was while I lay and watched the glare in the sky that the world was changed for me,"[23] she would write. Later in 1917, Cicely would write a book called *Senlis*, about German war crimes inflicted on the occupants of the French town of the same name.

On this May evening, Cicely, the centre of the party rather than the organizer, basked in the warmth of her friendship with Elizabeth and with the staff of the hospital. "As Miss Hamilton has always been the Master of Ceremonies, everyone was determined to do her best in her honour, and certainly no fault could be found with the party of six strolling players dressed in Italian peasant costumes who took possession of the bridge arching the stream and gave an excellent programme of old English and French songs." Elizabeth stayed the night, listening to the music under the stars and hoping and praying that her old friend would remain safe as she ventured out into the war zone.

LONDON, England, July 1917. Beatrice sat at her desk, tapping her pencil on her typewriter. She was fed up. Not a single Alberta nurse was running for a seat in the upcoming provincial election. It was the first time in Alberta history that women were being allowed to vote and stand for office. Bea's second cousin, Liberal premier Arthur Sifton, had extended the franchise in the hope that women would repay him with their support. Knowing that soldiers tended to vote Conservative, he also passed legislation hiving off Alberta's thirty-eight thousand soldiers and military nurses into their own constituency, with two members-at-large to represent them. The province-wide poll would be held in June, and the soldiers' and nurses' poll in August.

In London, twenty soldiers had put their names forward as overseas candidates. At the eleventh hour, Beatrice decided to take matters into her own hands to ensure that a woman would enter the contest.

On Friday the thirteenth (nominations were to be in by noon on July 16) I thought that to be really worthy of the name suffragette I ought to have a woman candidate in the field for our overseas elections. Consequently, acting on a good hunch, I set out at five in the evening to find one, taking Mrs. D. [Nell Dennis, her cousin] along for ballast. We went to the office of the Director of Medical Services first and interviewed numerous colonels and majors and even a captain or two to try to get a line on someone who would be suitable and eligible and would consent to stand for election. We wasted a lot of time this way and got nothing. Then we went to dinner somewhere and about this time I had a brain wave and remembered a girl who had come into the offices about a year ago and who was on the staff of the Ontario Military Hospital at Orpington. We came back to the office and called her on the long distance (trunk call, it is called over here!). Of course the poor girl nearly passed away when I asked her if she would let her name go up. However, I was lucky enough not to scare her absolutely to death and she said she'd think about it and would see us if we went to Orpington the next day. Well, we got there at five in the afternoon after missing two trains and it was not till ten that evening that we finally got her consent.[24]

The "girl" was an Alberta domestic science teacher by the name of Roberta MacAdams. Now a nursing sister and dietitian for a thousand-bed military hospital, the intelligent, reserved, and beautiful Roberta would prove to be the perfect candidate. "[W]e began our campaign with the press by demanding an interview with Lord Beaverbrook and asking his assistance. He was formerly Max Aitken you know. We were nearly a day getting on his trail but finally he asked us to come to his office at some bank or other in the city (which he also owns I believe) and agreed to come to the rescue. He took us down to the Express and introduced us to the editor. Luckily I was ready with all biographical details of the candidate and our campaign was soon launched. We rushed Miss M. up to town and she sat for her picture."[25]

Beatrice didn't take Roberta to just any photographer; she took her to see Emil Hoppe. The Karsh of his day, Hoppe took photographs of some of Europe's most famous figures, including Virginia Woolf, George Bernard Shaw, Rudyard Kipling, Richard Strauss, Einstein, and many others. The photograph he took of Roberta made her look like a military Madonna, her gaze direct, her white muslin veil framing her face. Beatrice placed the photo at the centre of a flyer that read (among other things): "Give One Vote to the Man of Your Choice and the Other to the Sister." It was an inspired campaign slogan that appealed to the loyalty of soldiers to the nurses who cared for their wounded comrades. Seven thousand copies of the flyer would be circulated to Alberta men in camps and hospitals in England, France, and the Mediterranean.

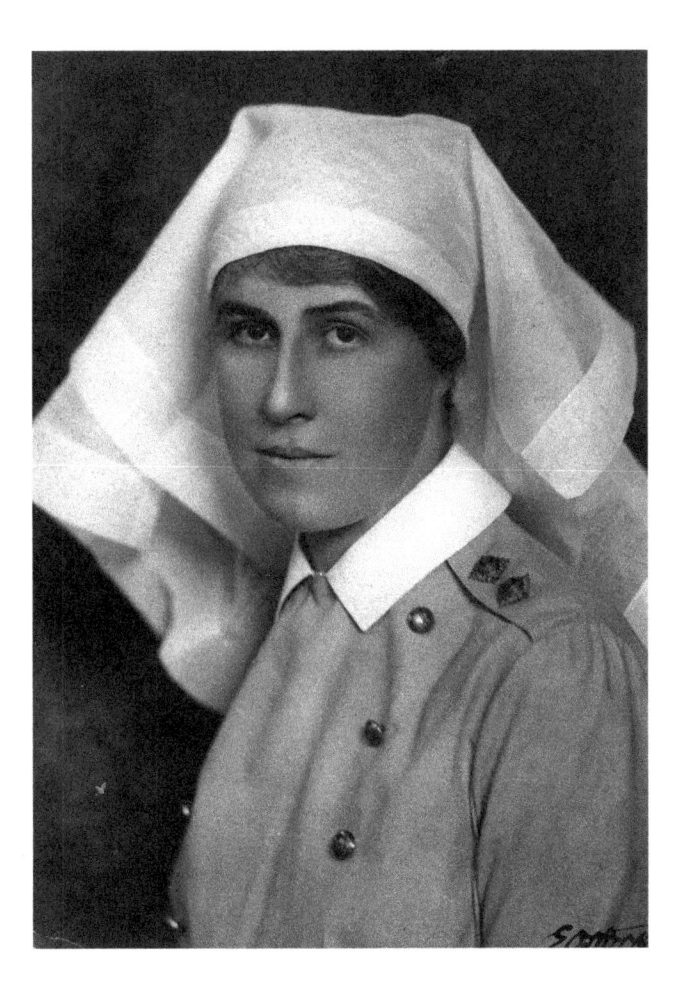

Lieutenant Roberta MacAdams.

Many of the soldiers and officers against whom Roberta was running were famous for their bravery on the battlefield, but Beatrice was not daunted. She organized speeches, press luncheons, visits to hospitals and military camps, and a letter-writing blitz. Realizing that she was clearly in a position of conflict of interest — working as both an employee of the Alberta government and publicity secretary for a candidate running for election, not to mention her family relationship with the Siftons — Beatrice kept a low profile, and Roberta would refer to her new friend as her "silent partner." Not everyone was fooled. Officer Harold McGill, writing home to his wife, argued that Roberta was "palpably the candidate of the Alberta government and I am strongly of the opinion that the interests nearer her heart will not be those of the soldiers but those of A.J. Sifton."[26]

McGill was wrong about one thing. Roberta, whose brother and nephew were both on the front lines, did care deeply about the soldiers. Her election platform focused on military pensions, land and employment for those returning home after the war, and the establishment of good hospitals and schools. The heroes of Ypres and the Somme deserved to return home to a nation that was ready to receive them.

Roberta took two weeks' leave, and she and Beatrice made their headquarters in a quiet corner of the Agent General's Office. It was there, at the height of the campaign, that Guy Furniss re-entered Beatrice's life. The pair had corresponded since the war's outbreak. Guy's military career in the Argyll and Sutherland Highlanders had taken him to the fighting front and back again to England to train recruits. Now he became a familiar figure at her office, dropping by to offer moral support or to take Beatrice out for a meal.

It finally dawned on Bea that Guy wanted to be more than a friend. "He has an immense sense of humour — which I am only beginning to understand a little bit, a love of books and art, and the good taste to find my companionship absorbing — not having had much of it," Beatrice would later tell her parents.[27] She had many male admirers, including a well-to-do upper-class Brit and a Canadian soldier. He may have had competition in the race to win Bea's heart, but the persistent Guy Furniss wasn't about to give up. On a brief visit to London, he hopped a cab to visit Bea in her new suburban digs. When the cab driver said that he wouldn't go that far out (gas was rationed), Guy pulled out his Webley revolver and said "Drive!"

Whatever Guy's feelings were, Beatrice had little time to worry about them. In late August, the election campaign ended and voting began. Roberta returned to her work in Orpington, and Beatrice attempted to catch up on the backlog of work at the Agent General's Office. Election results would be announced on September 18.

Guy Furniss.

LONDON, England, September 1917. It had been a bad week — air raids every night, six people killed, twenty injured, and great caverns carved into London streets by German bombs. Bea had been in the thick of it, a passenger on a bus during one of the raids. "[E]veryone on the street was running pell-mell — a weird effect, all these shadows flying through the darkness. Another block further on the guns started and then a bomb dropped with a resounding crash — probably a mile away but as usual seemingly on our very heads. The driver seemed to lose all control of himself and then began the wildest joy ride I have ever known." Despite anti-aircraft guns popping and shrapnel flying, she managed to reach her destination unscathed.

Beatrice would soon have an even closer call with death. She was just getting ready to go to bed — she was now sharing a house with a friend in an area of Westminster supposedly "immune from bombs" — when another air raid began. "I do not like to think even yet of how near to my house the bomb fell, and certainly I can never forget my sensations immediately following the explosion when the door blew in, the windows shattered, and the pictures fell rattling from the walls. I soon decided to remove myself from this 'immune' neighbourhood before the next moonlight period enticed the baby killers from Hunland."[28] The anti-German rhetoric was unusual for Beatrice, but she had been badly frightened. She would soon move to a "safer" suburb on the outskirts of London.

A few days later, all thoughts of narrow escapes were replaced by jubilation with the news that Roberta MacAdams had become one of the first two women elected to a legislature anywhere in the British Empire. Bea's slogan "Give Your Other Vote to the Sister" had been prophetic. Captain Robert Pearson, an officer with the 49th Battalion, was the first-place winner, with 4,286 votes, while Roberta MacAdams won her seat with four thousand votes, defeating her nearest rival by seven hundred votes. The news flashed around the world. "When the results were first made known, she was inundated by a wave of congratulation and good wishes — a wave which swept her into half of the illustrated papers and proclaimed her a wonderful boost to the women's cause in England," wrote Beatrice.

One British editorialist declared: "In Alberta, manifestly, women have established their claim to share the burdens and responsibilities of citizenship, and men do not regard this claim as unreasonable or as the assertion of a novel right which has to be limited and safeguarded by all sorts of checks and balances. To those who have watched the slow progress of the women's cause in this country, this straightforward and very matter-of-fact recognition of woman's citizenship is refreshing. By contrast, our timid and half-hearted concession of a truncated franchise for women looks ridiculous and the bitter struggle that the women of this country have had to wage to get even this small measure of justice can be seen in its true light as a tragic waste of energy."[29]

PASSCHENDAELE, France, October 1917. The Canadians were back in the Ypres salient. British field marshal Douglas Haig had ordered them to take Passchendaele ridge (its name taken from the devastated village of the same name) located east of Ypres and eight kilometres from the Roulers railway junction that was an important part of the German army's supply network. Haig wanted that supply line cut, and believed that the Canadian troops, who had performed so well at Vimy, were the men to do the job. On October 18, the four Canadian divisions relieved Australian troops in the area between Gravenstafel Ridge and the heights at Passchendaele. It was the same area that the Canadians had held in April 1915 at the time of the first gas attacks. Now, two years later, the battlefield was a sea of mud. One of the Canadian officers sent to report back on the conditions recalled that "all you could see was shell holes with a group of men in them, and you could look perhaps two hundred yards over and see the Germans in the same position."[30]

Canadian commander General Arthur Currie warned Haig that there would be sixteen thousand casualties in the action. In an effort to reduce those losses, the Canadian general made extensive preparations, ordering roads rebuilt, drainage ditches dug, and supplies collected. The attack began on October 26. The Canadians fought through mud- and rain-filled craters against a well-entrenched enemy, some of whom were protected by concrete pillboxes. By October 30, aided by two British divisions, the Canadians reached the outskirts of the village.

One Canadian soldier, Sergeant Major George Horne of the Royal Canadian Regiment, would receive the military medal for his actions during those terrible days. Horne had already served with gallantry on the Somme, hauling Lewis gun equipment so heavy that his legs developed severe varicose veins. At Passchendaele, he faced a new challenge. German fifty-pound bombs whined through the air and exploded into the ground, churning up the mud and entombing men alive. Horne — a strapping six-foot-tall hockey player — wasn't going to let them die. In the face of enemy fire, he "worked tirelessly in digging out buried men."[31] A store clerk from Winnipeg, he wasn't a commissioned officer, so the more prestigious Military Cross wasn't available to him — but he would go on to receive the bar to his medal in later actions.

The offensive ended on November 11, 1917, but despite the heroism of men like Horne, it was a hollow victory. The Germans had simply fallen back to equally well-defended positions, and the Allies had failed to make a significant breakthrough.

The news of the battle seeped slowly back to London. Mary MacLeod Moore received a letter from a Canadian officer. "The Canadian Corps is very delighted about Passchendaele," he wrote. "Who would have thought when a little more than three years ago the First Contingent arrived here that the Canadians would prove equal to the best British regiments in the field? Our Corps is proud of this year's work. Vimy, the Battle of Lens, and now Passchendaele. The last, the most important operation the Corps has undertaken, has been a complete success."[32]

As Mary reminded her readers, the success had come at a high price. Currie had been right — 15,654 Canadians had been wounded or lost their lives in the battle. "With pride, but in anguish, the names have been read in Canada of those who died for others, who have not counted the cost, who have forgotten self, and happiness and love and future joys that they might offer themselves for the greater good."[33] Safe from the absolute horror of a stinking battlefield covered in the bodies of men and horses, Mary MacLeod Moore had little idea of how those who survived really felt. In the wasteland of Passchendaele, many had lost all thoughts of the "greater good" and simply prayed for an end to the horror.

AMBOISE, France, October 1917. Elizabeth had her precious new red identity card in the pocket of her canteen uniform. The French government had recently made it law that all foreign nationals had to carry one. However, the wheels of the bureaucracy turned slowly, and it had taken weeks for it to arrive, and another few weeks for the corresponding *ordre de transport* required before she could embark on any further journeys into the *zone des armées*.

"Most people's existence has become more or less kaleidoscopic since the war and the need of workers shifts constantly from place to place, producing a corresponding shuffling of human beings out of their wonted routine," wrote Elizabeth. "The temporary need of someone to fill a gap between the departure of one worker and the arrival of another was the reason for my coming to this quaint little red-tiled French town, where a few British women have been working for many months among the French soldiers."[34] This time, Elizabeth was filling in for a worker in L'Oeuvre de la Goutte de Café, a voluntary group that provided coffee, vegetable soup, meat, and bread to hungry *poilus* from 4:00 a.m. until nearly midnight. Most of the men visiting the café were convalescents from nearby hospitals, now back on their feet and waiting for orders. As the gramophone blasted from one end of the room, many settled into comfortable chairs and wrote letters home. Some leaned over the counter and challenged Elizabeth to dominoes. Others told her stories of their war service: "how Pierre enlisted when he was only seventeen, being the youngest of four brothers, two of whom have been killed and two wounded; his mother and sister are in the [invaded areas] and he would like to know how to get word of them."[35] Sometimes she met Frenchmen who had immigrated to Canada. At the outset of the war, they returned to their homeland and joined the French army. Later, when Elizabeth returned to Paris, she received a letter from one of those men.

"Dear Madame. Your kind letter was a great comfort to me, and I was very glad to read you; many thanks for the congratulations the so good wishes you make to me. I am very pleased to see so many Canadian ladies holding canteens. It shows there is as much heart in Canada as in any other country. I wish you would express my best admiration to the Canadian ladies who are with you, wishing you my best luck for the success of your kind work."[36]

Soon, three Canadian ladies — Elizabeth, Beatrice, and Mary — would be touring France and witnessing the impact of women's war work first-hand.

Chapter 8

Lines of Communication

"Have you news of my boy Jack?"
Not this tide.
"When d'you think that he'll come back?"
Not with this wind blowing, and this tide.

"Has any one else had word of him?"
Not this tide.
For what is sunk will hardly swim,
Not with this wind blowing, and this tide.

— "My Boy Jack," Rudyard Kipling

SOMEWHERE IN FRANCE, December 1917. "It is easier, I am convinced, for a camel to go through the eye of a needle than for any unauthorized person to go to France during war-time," wrote Mary MacLeod Moore.[1] Mary, Beatrice Nasmyth, and Toronto writer Florence McPhedran had arrived in Boulogne to participate in the first tour of the lines of communication by female journalists from Canada. Also along on the tour was Elizabeth Montizambert, who had travelled up from Paris, and Roberta MacAdams, who was visiting her soldier-constituents in France. All of the journalists were familiar with one another, having crossed paths in women's press clubs and, if nothing else, having read one another's copy.

It's difficult to know just how the tour came about. From the beginning of the conflict, the British military had made it clear that female journalists were unwelcome in France (Elizabeth was an exception since she already lived in Paris). Male correspondents were only marginally more fortunate. Truly "embedded" with the military — seconded to British forces and given officer status — a chosen few were assigned to headquarters at St. Omer and occasionally allowed to make carefully guided forays to the front lines. Some important strings had been pulled in order for a similar door to be opened temporarily to a group of female journalists. The person who pulled those strings may have been Lord Beaverbrook, head of the Canadian War Records Office.

Beaverbrook had already helped Beatrice Nasmyth in her campaign to have Roberta MacAdams elected. He may have hoped that a tour of France by a group of high-profile female journalists and a popular female politician would drum up further support for the war effort. This was especially important following the unpopular introduction of conscription in August and the death or wounding of nearly sixteen thousand Canadians at Passchendaele during October and November.[2] French Canadians and farmers in the West heartily opposed conscription. After being urged to "grow more" for the Allied cause, few farmers could afford to lose the labour to harvest it, and most people from Quebec opposed conscription because they had no loyalty to Britain or to France. The long lists of war dead and the sight of maimed men returning home were also dampening the war-passion of those who had once shamed men into joining up. It couldn't have been worse timing, from a military point of view. The war was losing favour in the eyes of Canadians at a time when fresh troops were desperately needed on the Western Front.

The journalists' tour would also coincide with the first federal election in which some Canadian women were allowed to vote. Under the Wartime Elections Act of 1917, the franchise was extended to women in uniform and female relatives of soldiers (and denied to conscientious objectors and recent immigrants from "enemy countries"). The government hoped that women whose husbands and sons were facing the horrors of war would be happy to vote for a government that had taken measures to force "slackers" to join up.³ Mary, Beatrice, and Elizabeth celebrated this extension of the vote, truncated though it was. They planned to show how women had earned that right in a series of articles profiling the lives and work of Canadian women behind the lines.⁴ In particular, they wanted to describe the contribution of women in Canadian hospitals and to the Canadian Red Cross. The International Red Cross had just won the Nobel Peace Prize for its work during the war. It seemed particularly appropriate that a group of female journalists should write about an organization that was largely staffed and supplied by women.⁵

There were other motivations for the tour. "For [Canadian women] the war is a dark impenetrable curtain which envelops her soldier, letting through no glimpse of his later life on which she can rely," wrote Beatrice. "So, if I can bring to those at home just a few of the human pictures in which I saw their men in France, if I can make the war curtain just a little less impenetrable, I shall be glad."⁶ She didn't mention, of course, that it would also draw the curtain back on the experience of the man with whom she was now in love. Guy Furniss was back in France, fighting with the Argyll and Sutherland Highlanders.

The journalists weren't the only women crossing into France that cold December. On board their ship were members of the Women's Army Auxiliary Corps (WAAC), "looking like the women soldiers they are, in their khaki and their greatcoats and their army hats," wrote Mary MacLeod Moore. The unthinkable had happened: British women were taking on pseudo-military roles in the theatre of war.

The establishment of the WAAC was not a victory of feminism but of warfare. At this point in the war, half of all soldiers who had enlisted had been killed or wounded, a figure that rose to 60 percent for those who served on the Western Front. By 1917, Allied governments were desperate for men to fill the gaps left by those who had been lost in over two years of fighting. The British government established women's paramilitary organizations such as the WAAC so that men who were doing military tasks behind the lines could be relieved of those duties and be sent to join their comrades on the killing fields. Women would do the men's former jobs, working as drivers, clerks, cooks, typists, telephone operators, mechanics, and waitresses. Recruiting for the women's corps began in the spring.⁷

The first stops on the women's tour were the Canadian Red Cross depots in Boulogne. Located in six different locations "so that one bomb cannot wipe us out entirely,"[8] these warehouses were filled with towers of wooden crates. "Jam, gramophones, crutches, chewing gum, nuts, work materials, coloured tissue paper, pipes, tobacco and cigarettes, tinned peaches, maple sugar, books, playing cards, chairs, tables, beds, even bird cages and sewing machines, stationery, pianos and cinemas were among the comforts which the Red Cross stood ready to give," according to Mary.[9] Tons of socks, pajamas, and shirts, along with jars of peaches, beans, jams, and jellies had been sent by women's groups across Canada, from IODE chapters in rural Ontario to the Women's Institutes scattered across the prairies. Everyone was canning all they could and "knitting their bit" for the soldiers. By the end of the war, 248,673 cases of home canning and fresh fruit would be sent to England and France, valued at £1,971,118.[10]

As Beatrice wandered among the crates, she could smell cinnamon and a vague scent of molasses that reminded her of fruit cake. Then she saw the reason why — three wooden boxes stood open along the wall, filled with bulging Christmas stockings. "Every Canadian in hospital in France received a stocking and a special gift on Christmas," she would later write. Even the holly used to decorate the wards was provided by the Red Cross. The organization arranged for cozy "extras" like these to make soldiers' lives more comfortable, but as the women learned, most of the organization's contributions were of a more serious nature. Out of their stores in Boulogne and Paris came ambulances and X-ray machines, stretchers and bandages. Hospitals were often fully equipped by the Red Cross, the cost covered by over seven million (Canadian) dollars in donations. The money and materials weren't earmarked solely for Canadian hospitals; by the end of the war, seventy-five thousand cases of supplies would be given free of charge to over four thousand French hospitals.

It is almost certain that one of the women's guides was none other than Mary's brother, William. Still recovering from his wounds, Mac had been temporarily attached to the Red Cross in Boulogne, this time to the Advanced Stores Department. Under his watch, urgently needed medical materials were sent forward to the advanced dressing stations near the front lines. Shortly after the women's tour ended, Mac would be transferred into the CAMC for a stint of hospital administration before returning once again to active duty with the 46th Battalion.

The women's second stop in Boulogne was Number 3 Canadian General Hospital on the heights overlooking the ancient city. Built among the ruins of an old Jesuit college, its staff was made up of doctors, nurses, and medical students from McGill University's medical school. Established in 1915, the hospital was an important hub in the network of British, American, and Canadian hospitals strung throughout the lines of communication. The head of the hospital was Colonel John McCrae, by now famous for his poem "In Flanders Fields." McCrae wasn't in evidence on the day of the women's tour; instead, Chief of Surgery Colonel John Elder led the tour.

A blue light shone down from the skylights in the ancient Jesuit college onto rows and rows of wounded men lying in cots on the great stone floor. "[W]hen we stepped into the old theatre we became the centre of a hundred pairs of eyes," wrote Beatrice.[11] According to Elder, Number 3 had a capacity of roughly 2,400 beds, and it needed every one of them. In 1917 alone, 48,465 patients had come through its doors — ninety-three thousand since the establishment of the hospital itself. Such demands entailed a major conversion of the broken-down college. "Things are not what they were," Elder told the women. "This admitting room, now, was a hay barn, the operating room was a cow stable and our largest ward was the theatre of the original Jesuit institution."[12] When big convoys came in, explained Elder, patients passed through the admitting room at the rate of two a minute, often for several hours at a time.

The hospital's three hundred nurses ministered to these men, preparing and changing their dressings, stocking ward kitchens, making beds, checking pulses and temperatures, and assisting in surgery. One of the more demanding tasks facing them was the irrigation of wounds. The shrapnel and bullets that maimed men's bodies carried with them the mud of Flanders, a bacteriological soup made up of soil mixed with dead bodies, rats, and manure. The result was deadly. Without immediate care (and sometimes in spite of it), a bacterial infection would grow in the wound that would produce gas in the tissues and eventually kill the patient. "This war has produced more so-called antiseptics than have been evolved in all the previous history of surgery," according to Elder. Nurses were the front-line troops in this war against bacteria. Each day, they would regularly fill open wounds with these pungent saline solutions, treating men who were often without the benefit of painkillers (which were in short supply).

After their whirlwind visit to Boulogne ended, the women were bundled into a large staff car to begin their tour of the "lines of communication." The "lines" were the vast network of ambulance convoys, hospitals, supply depots, convalescent homes, repair shops, laundries, training grounds, prisoner-of-war camps, postal services, and cemeteries that were arranged along the northwest coast of France. These vital services were linked together by railways, roads, canals, and rivers. Twenty thousand trucks and 250 trains per day serviced this network. A quarter of a million men sorted, transported, and stored food, uniforms, and whatever was needed by the soldiers at the front.[13]

Their car drove quickly through the snow-covered French countryside, the roads dipping and rising before them. "By day you note how few men out of uniform are to be seen, the number of British women in uniform and the number of residents in mourning. You pass shawled working women, who make a cheerful click as they walk the cobbled streets in their sabots; here is a Sister of Mercy with her wide coif, and there a priest in his cassock. Here an old man, wearing a blue blouse, stumps beside a cartload of dull red carrots, with the tall gray houses for a characteristic background, and there a dog pulls a little cart filled with milk cans," wrote Mary.[14]

Soldiers were everywhere — English, Irish, Scottish, Canadian, Australian, New Zealand, South African, Indian — all marching in long lines or gathered in clumps at the side of the road, eating their rations or smoking. A truck carrying Chinese labourers passed their car, the men waving at the women from the back of the truck. The air was crisp and cold — a "real Canadian winter" according to Mary — with snow on the ground, frost in the air and a "dazzle of ice-encrusted trees." As their car rushed onward, a flight of dark birds formed a black, billowy line against the cold blue sky. They passed a rest home for nurses and then pulled up to a hospital for sick and wounded horses.

"The hospital has four wards, reception, medical, surgical, and lame, and the horses and mules, for twenty percent of the patients are mules, which come down from the front for treatment, are placed in one or another as the case requires," observed Mary. She petted the nose of a large black stallion whose coat was scarred and bandaged, its pride all but gone. It had arrived from a Divisional Ammunition Column, where it had pulled guns, supplies, ammunition, and heavily laden wagons and ambulances through the mud and along bombed-out roads. A treatment card hung next to its stall, listing the date the horse had come in, the nature of his wounds, and the treatment prescribed. The stallion was condemned to death, too badly wounded to return to "active duty."

It seemed an unfair fate, thought Mary. The brawny Scot who oversaw the care of the horses hastened to reassure her that many more did recover from their wounds and illnesses. "Some are able to continue on active service after been sent from hospital or from convalescent horse depots to a remount depot," she noted. "Even blind horses may be of use, as they are valuable for transport work."[15]

The establishment of veterinary hospitals had begun to grow quickly not long after the war began. After suffering huge equine losses from cavalry charges into machine-gun fire early in the war, the British and French military had decided to use horses mainly for logistical support — to pull artillery and supply wagons and ambulances through the terrible mud of Flanders. The horses suffered as the men did, wounded and killed by artillery fire, poisoned in gas attacks, expected to pull loads beyond their prewar capacity, malnourished and overworked.

By 1917, the mortality rate of horses and mules had skyrocketed. Between the Somme in 1916 and the end of the war in November 1918, 58,090 British horses would be killed and over seventy-seven thousand wounded by gunfire.[16] As the war progressed, the health of the animals became almost as important to the military as that of the soldiers they served. There were no "Blighty wounds" for horses, however; many were treated and sent back to the front, but those whose wounds did not permit them to work were shot — the fate of the black stallion. Back home, stories of heroic "war horses" soon became popular, but few people had any idea of the hell that these animals endured in the muddy morass of Ypres and the "bloody Somme."

With only a few days for their tour, the women couldn't stay long at the veterinary hospital. Although their articles are vague about the exact sequence of events, they went on to visit a number of casualty clearing stations and stationary hospitals during their tour. One of these was Number 7 Canadian Stationary, established by Dalhousie University in the Village of Arques. "Being but a few kilometres back of the lines, it is sometimes bombed and the nurses are ordered to their dugouts," wrote Beatrice.

The hospital was located in a cluster of tents and huts within the shadow of a ruined mill. Stationary hospitals like this one were the third or fourth stop for a wounded man. His journey usually began when he was removed from the field of battle on a stretcher carried precariously over slippery duckboards by two weary bearers. After initial treatment at a first-aid post, he would be placed in a motorized or horse-drawn ambulance and driven over bumpy roads to a casualty clearing station, a war-front surgical clinic where a skeleton crew of doctors and a few nurses would clean his wounds, do necessary surgery, or, if he was too far gone, try to make him comfortable and allow him to die peacefully. Those who were well enough would be sent farther back from the lines to stationary hospitals such as Number 7 for final preparations before being sent on to the large general hospitals on the coast, or home to "Blighty."

"At the casualty clearing stations — the nearest to the front line that nurses were permitted to go — the ambulances rolled up in a steady stream, and for hours the tramp of the stretcher bearers might be heard as they moved the wounded to the wards to which they were assigned," wrote Mary, who would visit a number of these before the end of the war. "Many of the men were gassed and choking for breath; others fearfully wounded, their faces ghastly and their clothes dirty and blood-stained. All must be cared for at once, fed, and clothed in clean garments."[17]

Several hundred patients could be cared for at a time at Number 7 Canadian Stationary. Such an operation was small compared to the vast hospital complex and military base at Étaples, the next stop in the women's itinerary. That complex included a motor ambulance convoy situated near the railway lines that bordered the base. "None of us, I feel sure, had more than the haziest notion of what an ambulance convoy was like when seen on its home ground," wrote Beatrice. "We thought of the long lines of ambulances we had seen leaving the London stations with their loads of wounded men and of the very smartly tailored girl drivers we had envied at the steering wheels of handsome staff cars in town; but to each of us the real picture came as a surprise, one revelation further of the work of women behind the lines in the war zone."[18]

As the Canadians stepped from their car, they saw two long rows of ambulances and several young women dressed in leather skirts, heavy gauntlets, khaki great coats, heavy boots, and puttees. They were oiling machinery, filling radiators, painting wheels, and cleaning the insides of their ambulances. "Their faces glowed ruddily in the frosty air," wrote Beatrice. "Their whole appearance suggested sturdiness and pluck.... Eleven months ago this convoy was taken over from men and placed in charge of women. Today finds a happy and efficient company of a hundred girl drivers 'carrying on.'"[19]

The sixty-five vehicles that were being cleaned and polished were labelled with the names of the Canadian groups that had funded them — "Women and Girls of Peel County," "WCTU of Toronto," "Women of Montreal," and so on. In one year alone, these ambulances would carry 180,745 patients to the hospitals at Étaples. They would also transport the dead for burial.[20]

The women interviewed a few of the drivers, including Grace MacPherson, a Canadian who had lost her brother in the Dardanelles campaign and was now trying to "do her bit." In a photograph of the twenty-three-year-old Vancouver woman taken around the time of the Canadian visit, her dirty jacket sleeve is drawn up to her elbow and she is pouring water into the car's radiator from a large white metal jug. There is a broad smile on her face that doesn't hint at the fact that MacPherson's brother was already a casualty of war.[21]

Elizabeth, always conscious of fashion even in the midst of war, couldn't help but comment on the drivers' appearance. "Vanity, indeed, is hardly compatible with the work they do. No one can keep her hands neatly manicured if she has to clean an ambulance car once every 24 hours, but these girls are out to win the war, and they have let such frivolities as rosy fingernails go overboard with many other things in their life. They came over to France to replace the men last March. At first there was much skepticism and doubt as to whether they could manage the work of the eighty men they had come to set free to do important war duty. There are ninety-six of these girls in this convoy and they have certainly made good. With the assistance of seven men mechanics to do the roughest work that is physically impossible for them, they manage all the running repairs for themselves."[22] Elizabeth didn't mention that the reason these women knew how to drive and repair cars was that they were all middle- and upper-class women whose families had owned cars (an expensive luxury) before the war, and they had been allowed to operate and care for these expensive toys.

After chatting with the drivers and promising to return for tea later, the women continued on to the base camp itself. In 1915 the British established four military hospitals, an infantry base depot, and new railway siding near the small coastal village of Étaples. By 1917 this camp had become the largest complex of military hospitals any country has ever built abroad. There were nearly twenty hospitals, able to accommodate more than twenty thousand patients at one time. Most were general hospitals, but some specialized in certain illnesses — such as venereal disease — or other special needs. There were separate hospitals for officers, women, and German prisoners. Laundries, kitchens, bakeries, and living quarters for the medical staff provided for the needs of the living, while a mortuary and growing cemetery ministered to the dead.[23]

Étaples wasn't only a medical compound. It was also a training ground for new recruits, many of them recent conscripts. These men were trained by foul-mouthed tyrants in the infamous "bull ring" training ground. The poet Wilfred Owen, who passed through Étaples, described it as a "vast, dreadful encampment. It seemed neither France nor England, but a kind of paddock where the beasts are kept a few days before the shambles.... Chiefly I thought of the very strange look on all the faces in that camp; an incomprehensible look, which a man will never see in England; nor can it be seen in any battle, but only in Étaples. It was not despair, or terror, it was more terrible than terror, for it was a blindfold look, and without expression, like a dead rabbit's." Just a few months before the women's visit to the base, soldiers rebelled against the inhuman conditions to which they were being subjected each day. There were riots and mob scenes, and the WAACs stationed at the base had to lock themselves into their quarters after threats from the rioting men. Like the soldiers who mutinied in France that same year, British soldiers were no longer coping well with the terror and monotony of this seemingly endless war.

If the journalists knew about these events, they chose not to report on them, preferring to portray Étaples as the "great white city of healing." They visited the two Canadian hospitals at the base — Numbers 7 and 1. Like the other hospitals in the complex, these were long corrugated iron huts lined with asbestos and rough wood panelling. The men lay in metal cots arranged in orderly rows along both walls. When there was a big "push," cots also filled the aisles, and the nurses struggled to find their way among the beds. The blankets covering the beds were bright red — gifts from the Red Cross warehouses in Boulogne. Miniature canvas hammocks were suspended above some of the beds to immobilize fractured legs. The air was hazy with cigarette smoke, and the scent of wound-cleansing solution hung in the air. It was mixed with the even more pungent smell of gas gangrene, the gas caused by bacterial infection in wounds.

Stepping outside, the women watched as a group of planes flew in the sky above them, locked in combat. It was a reminder that Étaples, with its training ground and supply depots, was also a military target. Within five months, the journalists would find themselves reporting that the very hospitals they had visited had been bombed. On a warm May evening, German fighters would drop 116 bombs on the camp. While the camp was still under fire, Grace MacPherson (one of the ambulance drivers whom the Canadian journalists interviewed) would treat the wounded and get them to safety. By the next morning, sixty people were dead, including three Canadian nurses.

But for now, that was still in the future. The Canadian journalists returned to the ambulance convoy, where they stepped out of their car "into the very midst of an exciting hockey match, and ducked in and out among the healthy, cheerful girls who were enjoying a little recreation in their off time."[24] After a welcome cup of café au lait in the women's recreation hut, they left Étaples behind, driving on past prisoner-of-war camps and ammunition dumps, camouflaged guns that looked like cubist sculptures, and air fields "with a succession of speedy war planes floating from them into space and rising with singing engines to the blue heavens."[25] The women did not record where they slept most evenings, but it was likely that they were given refuge in nurses' quarters and military rest homes along the way. Their final destination was Paris. There they planned to enjoy an evening of dancing with soldiers in the "Christmas leave clubs" and visit Number 8 Canadian General, located at a nearby racecourse. But there was one more stop they had to make before they could let down their hair.

"It was a proud moment for the first Canadian women writers who visited France when they were presented to the Canadian Corps Commander General Sir Arthur Currie, and thought of Vimy Ridge and Passchendaele."[26] For Mary, even this would not be the highlight of the tour. Instead,

> the outstanding memory is of soldiers. Soldiers playing football behind the lines, soldiers smiling at the strange sight of civilian women driving on the roads dedicated to war uses, soldiers in packed lorries going up to the line, soldiers walking with French children and talking in a mixture of French and English, soldiers marching in the gloaming, soldiers in beds in long hospital wards decorated for Christmas, soldiers with the Maple Leaf in their caps, who smile at you and are ready to tell what part of Canada they come from — "Ontario and perhaps you know my home town?" — soldiers sound and well, wounded and ill, but always friendly and cheerful. Lastly, soldiers lying very still with a little cross above them, for they have fought their last fight and have died for the honor and the preservation of a land across the sea — a land which will cherish their memory and make their record an example for the safe and happy children of the future, whose safety and happiness were purchased in part by these men "who from their labors rest."[27]

The women would visit Paris, dancing at the Canadian leave clubs before they returned home to celebrate Christmas. The experience of touring France had established a professional camaraderie and respect among them. While they did not develop close friendships — there were too many differences of class and background among them — from this point forward they kept abreast of each other's work and promoted it wholeheartedly in their columns. Mary, Beatrice, and Elizabeth knew that they shared an unusual bond as women writers in a time of war.

Christmas 1917 would be relatively peaceful for those stationed on the Western Front. Germany now controlled one-quarter of France. Soldiers on both sides of the trenches had dug in for the winter, fearful that the glistening snow would act as a spotlight on any troop movements. As Mary, Beatrice, and Elizabeth returned to their typewriters, they could not know that the respite being enjoyed by the troops after the brutality of Passchendaele would soon be swept away. The hardest months of the war still lay ahead.

Chapter 9

When Your Boy Comes Back to You

> When your boy comes back to you
> And the bands are playing too,
> Won't your heart be beating fast,
> Just to welcome him at last?
> When your boy comes back to you.
> — "When Your Boy Comes Back to You," Gordon Thompson

LONDON, England, February 1918. "May I have some sugar for my tea, please?" Beatrice asked the harried waitress. The woman disappeared into the café kitchen and returned with a small bowl gripped in her left hand. "'Ow many?" she asked. "Three," replied Beatrice, throwing caution to the winds. "Kin only 'ave two," the waitress replied, tossing two meagre lumps into Bea's saucer and bearing the bowl away. Rationing was now law in Britain.

The sinking of merchant ships by German U-boats was making food supplies run dangerously low. In January 1918, sugar was rationed, and by the beginning of May, meat, cheese, butter, and margarine had been added to the list. Ration cards were issued, and everyone was asked to register with a butcher and a grocer. Customers had to present their ration cards when going to stores and restaurants, and there were many rules and regulations about what one could substitute for commonly available items such as bread. For the average consumer, a shopping expedition was now a complicated process.

"'Cake is bread and sausage is meat!' That is today's pronouncement by the powers that control the national rations," wrote Bea. "So you know that if four pounds of bread weekly do not afford you sufficient nourishment you may not supplement them with cake (deductively, you have been eating cake all along), and similarly if your weekly allowance of two and a half pounds of meat leaves you with an underfed feeling, you may not bring it to repletion with sausage! Probably by next week we shall be told that syrup is sugar and those who have been learning to use it as a substitute for sugar in tea and coffee will be obliged to discontinue such an unpatriotic practice."[1]

Although she was making light of rationing, the government's new food rules were having a direct effect on Bea's health. One evening, during one of Guy's visits to the Alberta office, she fainted in his arms. At the hospital they learned that Bea was suffering from malnutrition. Guy insisted that she "put more fat on" and Bea responded by moving to a home in the leafy suburb of Golder's Green with her friend Sibyl and Sibyl's mother. "[I]t is impossible to work and feed yourself at the same time," she wrote to her parents. "One has to spend hours in queues to get the necessities and [Sibyl's mother] would be the queue lady and would look after us."[2]

Even after her move, Bea still managed to run into trouble. Once, on the way to work, her train caught fire while stalled between stations. As smoke began to seep into the darkened railcar, she wrapped the strap of her purse around her wrist so that if the worst came to pass, it would be found with her body and identify her. "What a pity to pass out on the very day the meat and margarine cards become effective," she would later claim to have thought regretfully. Luckily, at that moment, the conductress broke into the cabin and managed to lead them along the rails to safety.

It wasn't Bea's first mishap, nor would it be her last. She finished work late one evening and emerged from the Golder's Green railway station into a pitchy blackness so dark she could barely see the curb of the street. There were no street or house lights, since these were forbidden due to the risk of air raids. It was five blocks to her home, and she set out in the thick London fog, fumbling along the sidewalk.

"The unaccustomed silence about me told me that practically all traffic in that district had stopped. The footsteps of others in the murky street sounded groping and timid. But there was nothing to do but trust to my sense of direction to lead me safely home.... After numerous plungings off curbs and brushing into hedges I considered I had gone three blocks. All I really knew was that my feet were still on the pavement and as I was returning thanks for this somewhat limited blessing I walked into somebody's front gate."

The gate inspired an idea, and Bea fumbled for the latch, lurched down the walkway, and banged on the front door. A maid appeared in the light, and Bea asked to borrow any kind of light they might have. A carriage lamp was found, and with its dim light in hand, she started out again. To her surprise, she soon found herself with a following of "at least a dozen people, all crowding more or less closely upon my heels and remarking how fortunate they were to have found someone with a light and that we were all going in one direction." By the next block another dozen had been added to the parade until "I could not see through the fog the tail of my own queue." Eventually Bea managed to guide a few people home and was forced to abandon the rest when she reached her own gate. The story didn't end there, though. The next day she discovered that she had unknowingly borrowed the lamp from one of London's most famous women — Marie Lloyd — the music-hall actress famous for her sexy wartime song "Now You've Got Your Khaki On."

Bea included these stories in her columns, always emphasizing the funny side of wartime life. In the coming months, however, her sense of humour would be severely tested. The war was about to take a dramatic turn.

LONDON, England, March 1918. "This is written during the early days of the great battle. We are passing through perhaps the most momentous days of our history as a nation. We read, only half realizing what it means, of the tremendous number of German divisions massed against our men and we dimly understand what the conditions must be like when war is waged on so gigantic a scale," wrote a subdued Mary MacLeod Moore.

"No one who has not passed through such days as a combatant, or at least as a spectator and non-combatant, can realize other than dimly what is going on. We only know that the tragedy of the war would seem to have reached some climax. Thousands and thousands are dying and thousands and thousands injured and suffering for the sake of a Cause, for the sake of a country and an Empire, for the sake of the people at home in these countries. It is hard for the people at home to live up to the heroism and the awful sacrifice. Few can be worthy of it, but to know unworthiness is a step towards better things. A cleaner, humbler nation this must be, because of being bought with such a price."[3] It was the worst news possible: German troops had broken through the Allied lines, and British troops were in retreat.

The United States entered the war in 1917, and by early spring 1918, American soldiers were arriving in the war zone at the rate of ten thousand a day. German military leaders knew it was only a matter of time before fresh American troops would begin to swing the war in favour of the war-weary Allies. Germany had to act fast. The withdrawal of Russia from the war effort allowed them to redeploy fifty thousand troops in an all-out effort to break through the Allied lines. They would begin with an intense barrage aimed at taking out Allied artillery, machine-gun positions, and communications. The next step would be to cut through the line of trenches, and then, if all went well, head northwest to cut British lines of communication. Once they were cut off from their supply lines, the British would be forced to surrender. Elite storm troopers, the best that Germany had left, would lead the charge.

The attack — called Operation Michael by the Germans — began on the twenty-first of March with a terrific bombardment of British positions over 240 square kilometres in the Somme sector between the River Oise and the River Sensée. The British had already anticipated the large-scale German offensive and had begun to shore up their defences — upgrading fortifications and strengthening their communications. It was not enough to stem the German tide. The British War Cabinet's decision not to provide the additional reinforcements requested by General Haig, together with French requests for British troops to cover a longer front, meant that they were stretched to the limit and vulnerable. As the Germans swept forward, the order came for British troops to retreat.

"About 10:30 came the order and off we went leaving the camp we had improved so much for the Germans. It was a lovely moonlit night for which we were thankful and what a tramp it was," wrote Private J.L. Bramley of the Worcestershire Regiment. "Everywhere the roads were full of troops and transport and guns of all descriptions moving back in one continuous stream. Scores of times we were held up and had to stand there with packs on and blankets too. Out on our left great fires were burning — an aerodrome being destroyed before the Huns could get there. His aeroplanes were over us bombing and if they could only have hit the road would have done us some damage."[4]

Despite being tired and depleted, British troops managed to hold on to Arras, but lost many other Allied strongholds. Within three days, the Germans reclaimed all the positions they had lost during the Battle of the Somme. By the end of the month, Albert, Noyon, Montidier, and Peronne would fall into their hands.[5]

Back in London, the usual bombastic tone of Mary's articles was replaced by sober reflections on the changing situation in France. Her "London Letter" no longer portrayed Britain as a triumphant Crusader, but as a courageous and wounded George facing a terrible dragon. "Everywhere there are wounded men with the blue band on arms which have struck good blows for you and for me," she wrote. "Overhead drone the aeroplanes, and the kite balloons wobble about in the air in seemingly unwieldy masses. At night the searchlights sweep the sky with clutching fingers, and below them walk people like shadows, through the dimly lit streets. But despite all that war has brought, cheerfulness abounds and beauty and music and laughter and high courage and a great unselfishness."[6] Allied soldiers would need that courage, with the German army nipping at their heels.

PARIS, France, March 1918. Elizabeth was just finishing her after-lunch coffee at the Canadian government offices in Paris when three explosions rattled the windows. "The noise was at once explained by the thick cloud of dense creamy smoke slowly climbing into the absolutely clear sky," she wrote. Although she would have preferred to visit the scene on behalf of the *Gazette*, she had already committed herself to an interview at Number 8 Canadian Hospital in St. Cloud, on the outskirts of Paris. When she arrived at the hospital, she found that several members of the staff (including those she had come to visit) were already organizing an ambulance convoy to go to the scene of the bombing. Elizabeth joined the group, travelling in the chief medical officer's car while an ambulance sped ahead of them, driven skillfully by "Miss McLaughlin of Ottawa, whose performance would have threatened a British policeman with an attack of apoplexy." They rushed through the Bois de Boulogne at sixty kilometres an hour, slowing only at the Boulevards Extérieurs, "where the traffic was thickest." Soon the boulevards gave way to streets filled with chaos: buildings crumbled, streets strewn with broken red roof tiles, a dead horse lying on the ground. People in bloodied clothing wandered about as though they couldn't quite take in what had happened to them.

"As we came nearer to the scene of the disaster the number of people lessened," wrote Elizabeth. "Here and there the owners of a café that had had its front wall blown to bits were serving drinks to agitated customers in the midst of the debris.... Nothing in the immediate neighborhood was left standing and melancholy shells of what had once been cottages and business premises showed up against the blue sky." A pillar of brown smoke hovered over the scene, and now and again there was a minor explosion. The convoy came to a halt and McLaughlin and the other medicos began to treat some of the more seriously wounded while ambulances from other medical services began to arrive. One of the American drivers casually picked up a grenade for a souvenir. When told it was live, he tossed it into an adjacent field, where it exploded on contact. Many were already speculating that a German airplane had dropped a box of grenades on the area.

The horrors of the unorthodox daylight bombing would pale into insignificance within days. During the last week of March, the Germans began to shell the city with a gigantic long-range siege gun. Between March 23 and 25, the "Paris gun" lobbed seventy-three 280-pound shells into the heart of the capital. Not accurate except with large targets such as cities, the giant weapon was designed more to undermine the morale of Parisians than to destroy the city.[7] According to Elizabeth, that desire was unlikely to be fulfilled.

"Once more the Germans have shown their utter inability to understand the psychology of their adversaries, for they could not have chosen a time to bombard Paris more likely to find the spirit of her people tempered to a fine endurance than at a moment when she can feel she too has a part, however small, of the appalling risks her soldiers are facing a few miles away," she wrote. "It is extraordinary how soon one becomes accustomed to the sound of the shells dropping in the city. On the first day business was more-or-less disorganized, because no one quite knew what was happening, but there seemed little difference in the number of people in the streets and most of them had their noses in the air looking for enemy planes. Having an innate distrust for anything that smacks of an 'abri' [undercover shelter], I avoided the metro and did my errands on foot in the sunshine, but many unwary people were caught for hours in the underground railways that stopped running in the belief there was a raid."[8]

Although many people were leaving Paris for refuge on the coast or in Britain, Elizabeth was not among them. Even the fact that one of the long-range shells landed just outside her home and "spat up a little mud but failed to even break a window" did not destroy her equanimity. She continued to attend the theatre, do the rounds of the few art galleries still open in Paris, and, more importantly, write columns for the *Gazette* about life in Paris under bombardment. On Palm Sunday, she attended worship despite the fact that shells were falling on the city at intervals of ten, twenty, and thirty minutes.

"A raid at nine o'clock, when one is surrounded by after-dinner guests, is a thing to be supported with equanimity, but when the German planes arrive at three a.m., one is really annoyed," joked Elizabeth, sounding more like an upper-class hostess than a war reporter.[9] Despite the bravado, the constant German bomb attacks, together with repeated shelling from the Paris gun, were taking a terrible human toll. Nowhere was this more in evidence than on Good Friday, when a shell hit the roof of St-Gervais-et-St-Protais Church, showering worshippers with concrete. Eighty-eight people died and another sixty-eight were wounded.

That same day, while the shells were still falling, Elizabeth was across town at a canteen for refugees at the Gare du Nord (north train station). As the German army marched farther into France, the displaced were pouring into Paris, and the journalist wanted to see for herself how they were being treated. The smell of sweat and fatigue hung in the air of the large dining hall. Worn-looking women, children, and the elderly crowded around long trestle tables. Women in starched blue uniforms and white pinafores were pouring coffee into white china cups and handing out bowls of soup and bread.

"[The refugees] come in by the hundreds and are taken at once to the canteen where they get a good meal served by American and French women," observed Elizabeth. "All the sick are made comfortable and kept for the night in the canteen, which is provided with about a hundred beds."[10] Doctors, housing workers, and transportation coordinators were also there to deal with the needs of the exiles.

Several Canadian ambulances were assigned to drive displaced people to reception centres and shelters. From there they were ferried to safe locations scattered throughout unoccupied France. Once again the intrepid driver, Miss McLaughlin of Ottawa, was called into action. "The state of these unfortunates is lamentable," McLaughlin told Elizabeth. "They are so dazed with fatigue and grief that they can hardly speak. One old woman was asked if she had any choice as to what region she would like to be sent to, but she replied listlessly that she didn't care; all places were alike to her since she had lost everything."[11]

LONDON, England, March 1918. The bad news at the front inspired one happy decision in the life of Beatrice Nasmyth. "The truth is that 'a marriage has been arranged and will shortly take place (English joke) between Beatrice Sifton, only daughter of Mr. and Mrs. J. Hay Nasmyth, Woodstock, Ontario … and Captain Guy Mackenzie Furniss, 1/8 Argyll and Sutherland Highlanders, third son of Harry Furniss, Esq and Mrs. Furniss, "The Mount," High Wickham, Hastings, Sussex.'"

Beatrice knew that her marriage plans would come as a shock to her parents; indeed, it had come as a surprise to the bride herself. In fact, in February she received several proposals. "At the very last I found myself called on to decide between [sic] three — two with much more of this world's goods than Mac and one a Canadian who meant home and native land to me. I never want to go through such an agonizing month again," she wrote to her Canadian friend Blanche. "I know now I made the right choice — at the same time I realize that I descended to the rankest sentimentalism by marrying the man I wanted to marry regardless of all other considerations."[12]

She didn't mention the other men to her parents, but did reveal her earlier uncertainty. "One thing I may mention is that a few months ago I had no intention of marrying Guy.... But his bombardment has been terrific and my defenses too weak and my reserves too few so I have cried 'Kamerad!' Even in the past few months, however, things have been too uncertain for me to put anything on paper for you. One doesn't feel nowadays that it is possible to make plans — let alone speak of them — more than a fortnight ahead."

Bea and Guy's courtship had been carried on "in spasms of from two to five days' leave during the past three and a half years and that time includes a solid year and a half in which we never met once. This month we spent the longest time together in our joint history — ten days! He arrived from France January 31st; we left for the Mount, Hastings, February 1, spent a week there and then three days in London (out of office hours!). He has since returned to his regimental depot where he improves the shining hours by lecturing, being an expert in musketry and Lewis guns. However, he is under orders to proceed again to France in March and as there is some slight probability of my returning to Canada for a little while before long we have decided on the fatal step."[13]

Guy's parents, who had met and fallen in love with Bea, celebrated the match. His father, Harry Furniss, a famous *Punch* cartoonist and well-known lady's man, wrote "Dear Guy, you are indeed a very lucky fellow. As a matter of fact, I was about to invest in some very subtle poison, a wig and hair dye, order new suits with small waists and patent shoes too small for me and had already selected a secluded spot in Fairlight [a village near Hastings] and a tablet for your mother. Alas! All this dream is over.... Miss Nasmyth is most charming and delightful and extremely clever. The one thing that puzzled us was that you may not have discovered this for yourself. You ought to feel very happy and fortunate.... Your mother and Buzz [Guy's sister Dorothy] have, I believe, written to Miss Nasmyth. I shall offer her my sympathy verbally."[14]

Guy and Bea took "the fatal step" on March 28 at St. Martin-in-the-Fields Anglican Church in Trafalgar Square. The groom had just been given leave; realizing the dire straits that the war was in, the couple knew that this might be the last opportunity they would have to make their vows. Bea rushed in with a babe in arms. It wasn't hers — she had been watching a friend's baby and couldn't find anyone to take her place. Despite the rush, she still managed to dress as though she had just stepped out of the pages of *Woman's Life*. She wore grey gloves and hat, matching shoes, and a burgundy suit with a few violets tucked into the belt. Grey fox furs were draped over her shoulders. At Bea's request, Guy wore a uniform that had seen long service rather than buying a new one, since "the war will end soon and once it does I never want to see him in khaki again." Fifty people attended, including Guy's mother, father, and sister, and Bea's friend Muriel. After the minister pronounced them "man and wife," they walked out of the church, bells ringing, under an arch of swords presented by some of Guy's fellow officers. There was no time for the customary wedding lunch. Time was precious. Instead, the couple took the train to a seaside hotel on the Isle of Wight, where they spent their honeymoon. They would have ten days before Guy would rejoin his unit and depart for France.[15]

PARIS, France, May 1918. "While the Boche is joyfully depicting Paris as the prey to abject fear of their long distance cannon, Paris is jauntily opening her first Spring Salon since the war," wrote Elizabeth. Although the Grand Palais had been transformed into a hospital early in the war, the nearby Petit Palais was now hosting an exhibition by artists whose names would undoubtedly have been included in prominent pre-war catalogues. The weather may have been grey, but there was a riot of colour inside the gallery with the paintings of Jean Beraud (whose paintings depicted the gaiety of Paris before the war), Abel Faivre (designer of many French propaganda posters), and poet Henry Bataille, along with sculptures by Jean-Paul Laurens.

Paris shopkeepers were also creating their own kind of wartime art. A letter to a local paper had suggested that Parisians should protect their windows from the violent vibrations caused by the shelling of the Paris gun by gluing strips of paper to the glass. In true Paris fashion, the shopkeepers responded with an "orgy of paper decoration." "Coty, the beautiful perfume shop on the Place Vendôme, has its windows protected with black paper bars that harmonize with the ironwork. Some of them are merely ingenious, like the window in the Faubourg Saint-Honoré that is adorned so as to give the passer-by the optical delusion that the centre of the window is projecting ... all sense of protection for the glass has been lost in the decorative idea, for the window is merely covered with a patchwork of inefficient and detached designs."[16]

Paris had changed in another way as well. According to Elizabeth, fewer upper-class children were "taking the air" in the Avenue du Bois de Boulogne, Paris's most expensive street. Those who could afford to do so were sending the younger members of their families to relatives in the country, away from the fighting. Sanatoriums had been established for those children suffering from shell shock, while youngsters who had lost both parents in the war and had no other family to take them in were being housed in orphanages.

In Elizabeth's columns of May 1918, Paris was still a proud capital in which citizens of all ages were keeping cool heads and passionate hearts. Yet Elizabeth — like most Parisians — was well aware of just how serious a turn the war had taken. By the end of the month, German troops would be just ninety kilometres from Paris.

LONDON, England, May 1918. "The eyes of the world are turned with wonder and admiration on the British Army holding its own so splendidly against the swarming hordes of Germans thrown against them," wrote Mary. "London has been very brave and quiet through these tense days since the Great Fight began. There is no panic, and rumor is quieter than usual. People are brave and cheerful. If there are mourners, they mourn quietly and privately. The stricken do not call for public sympathy. Most of them have taken for their motto and watchword, 'Who dies if England live?'"[17] Tension lined the faces of most Londoners; everyone knew that Germany now had the upper hand in the war. As if to emphasize the point, the last (although no one knew it at the time) air raid on London occurred in May, with 49 people killed and 177 wounded. That same month, the Étaples hospital camp that Mary, Beatrice Nasmyth, and Elizabeth Montizambert had visited in December was bombed. It was one of the lowest points of the war — but worse was yet to come.

LONDON, England, June 1918. The fourteen nurses aboard the *Llandovery Castle* were enjoying a well-earned respite. They had been posted to hospital-ship duty as a reward for their hard work in casualty clearing stations and in military hospitals in England and France. It was relatively light work — accompanying nearly two hundred convalescing Canadian soldiers to Halifax and then returning to Liverpool and regular duty. Before the war, the *Castle* had been a comfortable second-class ship well fitted out with all the latest conveniences. There were private bathroom facilities and running water, comfortable beds, lounges with wide-seated wicker chairs and upholstered couches, and a grand staircase and spacious entry hall. It was heaven to women who had been bunking in tents and dormitories, enduring bombing raids and twelve-hour shifts.

It was quiet on the evening of June 27, as the *Llandovery Castle* neared Fastnet Rock on Ireland's coast. They would soon be back in Liverpool. All the lights on board the *Castle* were burning, and a huge electric cross was lit over the bridge to alert enemy submarines that it was a hospital ship. Unfortunately, this did not deter Lieutenant Helmut Patzig, the commander of German *U-boat 86,* from torpedoing the unarmed vessel. As the ship listed to one side, the 258 passengers and crew clambered on board lifeboats. The nurses were wearing a combination of nightgowns, uniforms, and heavy coats. Few could swim. When their boat entered the water, they struggled in vain to keep it from drifting back toward the sinking ship. Sergeant Arthur Knight was on board the lifeboat with them and later reported that the Matron Marjory Fraser asked, "Sergeant, do you think there is any hope for us?" He replied "No," and a few moments later, the craft was sucked under the water. Only Knight would survive.

Patzig didn't want any evidence left behind of the war crime he had committed. He ordered that the surviving lifeboats be rammed; only one managed to escape. As the next day dawned, floating chunks of debris and a lone lifeboat carrying twenty-four people were all that was left of the *Llandovery Castle.*

The sinking of the *Llandovery Castle* was not a sign that the Germans were still holding the upper hand. In fact, they were losing momentum. Out on the Western Front, with fewer horses than the Allies, the Germans were having difficulty moving much-needed artillery and supplies to their new front lines. Their troops, deprived of decent food and clothes, stopped all too often to plunder the booty left behind by the retreating Allies. These delays would prove their undoing.

HASTINGS, England, October 1918. It was a quiet fall evening in late October, and Harry Furniss could hear the swallows singing in the garden beyond the open window in his study. He was dashing off a quick letter to his daughter Dorothy. Usually he was in an ebullient mood, ready to share the latest society gossip. But not tonight. His daughter-in-law Beatrice was visiting and had shared some worrying news she had culled from her sources at the war office. "B was very upset as she had just heard officially that the Canadians have been wiped out at Cambrai," he wrote. "They don't exist — there is no Canadian army now and c. 45,000 casualties. It appears they were promised support and went on to find themselves left and absolutely lost. So we have paid a heavy price for Cambrai. B was and is — naturally — very dejected."[18]

Bea may have been dejected, but as she would later learn, the sacrifices being made would form the final chapter of the war. The Battle of Cambrai was one of a string of battles that would turn the tide back in the Allies' favour. The first took place in Amiens, an ancient city located just 120 kilometres north of Paris. On August 8, an Allied force spearheaded by Canadian and Australian troops led a surprise assault on German defences, advancing thirteen kilometres through enemy lines. At that point, the Germans rushed reinforcements to stop the offensive. While the cost to Canadian forces was high (with nearly twelve thousand casualties), damage had been done. Allied morale had been raised, and German faith that they would be able to complete their sweep to Paris was shaken. Now Allied commanders would coordinate an offensive that would become known as the "Hundred Days" and would end in the defeat of Germany. Cambrai would be one part of that offensive.

On August 26, Canadian forces spearheaded the British First Army's attack on the Arras front, through the German defensive lines stretching between the French towns of Drocourt and Quéant. By the time they crashed through the heavily fortified "D-Q" line, there would be eleven thousand Canadian casualties. But the carnage wasn't over. After nearly a month of planning and preparation, on September 27, the Canadian Corps attacked across the nearby Canal du Nord. With the help of military engineers, the Corps crossed the canal and pushed through the enemy defences, eventually capturing the strategic positions of Bourlon Wood and Cambrai on October 9. Beatrice was fairly accurate in her assessment of the impact on Canadian forces. Amiens had cost Canada almost twelve thousand casualties; the Arras and Canal du Nord battles, over thirty thousand.[19]

Allied troops were now pushing the exhausted Germans back by leaps and bounds. That hopeful news and its personal implications were also included in Harry Furniss's letter to his daughter. "[Beatrice] had a letter from Guy this morning — he is in great form," wrote Harry. "Was thirty-six hours without any food so quickly are things going there."

LONDON, England, November 1918. The sound of maroon bombs echoed through the streets of London, the signal that the war was over. Within minutes, Union Jacks were waving from almost every house. Mary stood on the sidewalk in front of her flat, wondering what to do, who to see, how to celebrate. A messenger girl biked past her, British flags flying from her fender. People were everywhere, waving flags, laughing; there were munitions girls still in their uniforms, British and Canadian soldiers, all marching arm-in-arm, singing patriotic songs. Mary felt herself drawn into the crush, pushed along to Trafalgar Square and then on to the gates of Buckingham Palace. At Victoria Station, soldiers were storming the buses, climbing into and onto taxicabs. Bands were playing, and the king came out onto the balcony of Buckingham Palace and waved to the crowds below.

"Today, November 11, 1918, the men who have died during four years and four months of war share with the glowing living the greatest victory in history," Mary wrote that evening, worn out from the mixed feelings that had warred within her all day — the vacillation between adrenaline-fuelled excitement and relief from a terrible burden that had been carried too long. "The victory not only over the most dishonorable, the most cruel and the most brutal and gross of enemies, but over the doctrines by which they swore; of Might and Force and the Sword, and the subjugation of the weak and small."

PARIS, France, November 1918. It was Armistice Day at last! Crowded around her dining room table in Elizabeth's Paris flat were an American journalist, an English officer, and a French friend who had shared canteen duties with her during the war. Despite the noisy rejoicing taking place on the street outside, those inside seemed solemn, perhaps remembering lost friends and comrades.

After a light lunch — still on rations — the group boarded the officer's military car and swept across the river to the Place de la Concorde. It was black with people. Trucks were passing, filled to overflowing with soldiers waving flags and singing La Marseillaise. One man rained champagne on the crowd as his vehicle passed by, despite the fact that on this day the beverage was worth more than its weight in gold. Passing the other way was a YMCA truck filled with Canadian soldiers waving their national flag (the Canadian Red Ensign). Troops of seamstresses marched along the road, their hair decorated with tricoloured ribbons, some stopping to dance with a grizzled *poilu* and an embarrassed English officer. A news vendor selling the *Paris-Midi* was mobbed, while at another corner a busy street merchant was selling paper flags of all nations at five cents apiece.

Every window was decorated, every restaurant overflowing. That night at the Folies Bergère, the dancers draped themselves in the flags of the

Allies. English soldiers politely applauded whenever the flags of other nations appeared, while Australians and Canadians went wild with enthusiasm every time one of the many members of their own military climbed onto the stage to persuade a scantily clad artist to remove their flag and wave it to the audience. Then dancers holding swaths of red, blue, and white bunting sped across the stage to form the French flag, then equally quickly rearranged themselves to form a Union Jack.

A few days later, a crowd of tens of thousands gathered in front of the Paris opera house where Canadian singer Decima Moore (an old school friend of Elizabeth), draped in the Union Jack, called for cheers for every celebrity connected to the war. The British Horse Guards band played; a French airplane circled above. For Elizabeth, "it was an unforgettable time, and those who have lived through those long-ago days of mobilization in 1914 will have two memories of Paris, valiant and gay, that will never be effaced."[20]

LONDON, England, December 1918. As the war came to a close, questions of reconstruction began to arise, and women's issues were among them. "The question of how the women will vote is debated anxiously, regardless of the fact that a very great body of the less-educated women have not been instructed in the matter, and in some cases, do not even know what it means to vote."

It was the first national election in which British women were to be allowed to vote. The Representation of the People Act of 1918 had extended the franchise to all men over twenty-one without any property requirements, and enfranchised women over thirty who owned property or were university graduates. It was the first step in what would ultimately lead to full enfranchisement for women. The long-sought-after vote was finally in women's hands, and already critics were complaining that women were apathetic about it. Others wondered if women would vote for women.

Mary believed that the criticisms were unjust. "The granting of the suffrage came at a time when the war was absorbing all one's attention and all one's thoughts and there has not been time to teach the women simply and plainly why they should use their vote," she replied. "It's a pity, as this is the great reconstruction election, but there it is. The women who have been working with men in factories and elsewhere understand the question pretty well, but there is a vast army quite uneducated in the matter of how politics affect them and their home, and why they should use their influence in one direction or another."

Christabel Pankhurst, eldest daughter of Emmeline Pankhurst, who had for many years led the suffragette movement in Britain, was running for election, along with fifteen other women candidates. Christabel was representing the Women's Party, a political party that she and her mother had established during the war. She would lose the race by 775 votes. Constance Markiewicz, representing Sinn Féin, would be the only woman elected. Hers was more of a symbolic victory, since, as was usual policy for Sinn Féin members, she refused to take her seat in the House of Commons. It would take Nancy Astor, a non-suffragette running in 1919, to become the first woman to take her seat in the House.

Mary was elated that women were finally able to run for office. But it was just as important to her that whomever was elected — male or female — would be ready to roll up their sleeves and address the pressing issues facing both men and women in the post-war era.

> Reconstruction takes the place in the public mind and public press that propaganda, camouflage and other words associated with the war did a short time ago. The papers devote much space to all the serious questions that arise through the demobilization of millions of men, and the consequent shifting of millions of women who have been working hard during the war, many of them filling the places of men. This is a very difficult matter to deal with. Many of the married women will go home when their husbands are again earning good wages. Many who worked from patriotic motives and not because they needed the money will retire from paid jobs. There are still left the thousands and thousands of women in this country who, through war losses, both of men and

money, must earn their living and assist their relatives, as well as those who have always worked. These are the sufferers, or will be unless very great care is taken.[21]

On the home front, the war's end brought challenges that were harder to solve than some of the struggles and sacrifices of the war itself. "This period of reconstruction and of the settling down of millions of people who have been thrown out of their accustomed ways for years, teems with difficulties. There is not the great stimulus which has kept us straining every nerve to support the men and to be worthy of the men. It is uphill, steady, dull work, at a time when the natural reaction after tremendous effort has set in. For some reasons this time is the real test for us."[22]

The Great War would continue to affect and shape the lives of Mary MacLeod Moore, Elizabeth Montizambert, and Beatrice Nasmyth for the final decades of their lives. In the interwar period, they would reconstruct their lives in its shadow, observe as Britain and Canada struggled with the social, economic, and political changes wrought by the war, and hear again the echoes of 1914 in the rise of Germany and the march to yet another world war.

Part III
Last Words

Work is and always has been my salvation and I thank the Lord for it.
— Louisa May Alcott

Chapter 10

Beatrice Nasmyth

> Time and trouble will tame an advanced young woman, but an advanced old woman is untamable by any earthly force.
> — Dorothy L. Sayers

VERSAILLES, France, June 1919. The afternoon sunlight poured into the Hall of Mirrors as reporters jostled one another, each vying for the best seat from which to witness one of the most historic moments of the young century. Beatrice, her hair damp with sweat, finally found a chair close to the front and watched the action unfold. The Versailles Peace Treaty was about to be signed.

Beatrice's journey to Versailles had begun in October 1917, when Arthur Sifton resigned as premier of Alberta and joined the Union Government of Sir Robert Borden. In 1919 he became one of four Canadian delegates to the Paris Peace Conference, and asked Beatrice to be his publicity secretary.

The Canadian delegation was officially made up of fifteen people. In addition to Sifton, it included Prime Minister Borden, two cabinet ministers, five businessmen, two legal experts, and two military representatives (including Lieutenant-General Sir Arthur Currie). Two journalists, John Wesley Dafoe (representing English-language newspapers) and Léon

Trépanier (representing French-language newspapers), acted as representatives of the Department of Public Information.[1] Bea, the invisible "sixteenth" member of the team, likely wrote copy for Dafoe. Her press pass also entitled her to attend daily press conferences and gave her access to a cable service for wiring stories back to Canada.

The peace conference began in Paris on January 18, 1919. Allied leaders, including those of the dominions, met to discuss and set the terms of peace with Germany. Canada had little influence on the shape of the final treaty. Nonetheless, Borden and Sifton worked hard to ensure that Canada's equality of status among the nations would be recognized in any agreements made. Sifton would later write, "Canada has no desire in return for or in regard to her sacrifices save that in matters in which she is vitally interested she should be treated as an equal."

Such recognition was difficult to obtain; the British and the Americans kept trying to include Canada as part of the British Empire instead of as a nation with interests of its own. In the end, it was agreed that Canada would sign the final peace agreement along with the other dominions

Arthur Sifton and Guy and Beatrice Furniss in Versailles.

(albeit indented under the signature of the British prime minister). This was an important victory; ultimately it would ensure Canada would have its own seat when the League of Nations was established in 1920.

It was widely reported that Bea wrote many articles about the peace conference and the signing of the peace treaty. "Crowning an extremely eventful and interesting career, Mrs. Furniss was sent to the peace conference at Versailles, where, in addition to her official work, she turned out much characteristically clever newspaper and magazine copy."[2] However, no articles about Versailles appeared under Beatrice's own name. The old prejudice about female journalists not writing "serious news" may have meant that her byline was omitted. An anonymous article that may well have been penned by Beatrice appeared in the *Vancouver Province* on June 28, 1919:

> The signatories of the "second peace of Versailles" in the long Hall of Mirrors in the château of France's great monarch Louis XIV today restore to Versailles its old place as the stage of "all the glories of France" dimmed in more recent days by the memories of mob excesses during the French Revolution, the military downfall of France in 1870, and the proclamation of the German emperor in the same hall. Representatives of the nations of the world gathered there to sign and seal the instrument undoing the work of the conquest of Bismarck and von Moltke and inaugurating the sway of the League of Nations in place of the ill-adjusted European balance of power.

No authorship was provided — but it has the ring of an article by Beatrice. She was among the scrum of reporters who earlier that day had crowded into the far end of the Hall of Mirrors. In front of them were tables filled with secretaries from various delegations. Then there was a long horseshoe-shaped table for the representatives of various countries. At the centre of the horseshoe was a chair and ornate desk on which the peace agreement had been placed, ready for signatures. Beyond this were rows and rows of chairs for invited guests. By the time the delegates took their seats, nearly one thousand people would be packed into the long chamber that had once been home to Marie Antoinette. Sir Harold Nicholson, a member of the British delegation, recorded what happened next:

> [T]he delegates arrive in little bunches and push up the central aisle slowly. Wilson and Lloyd George are among the last. They take their seats at the central table. The table is at last full. Clemenceau glances to right and left. People sit down upon their *escabeaux* but continue chattering. Clemenceau makes a sign to the ushers. They say "Ssh! Ssh! Ssh!" People cease chattering and there is only the sound of occasional coughing and the dry rustle of programs. The officials of the Protocol of the Foreign Office move up the aisle and say, "Ssh! Ssh!" again. There is then an absolute hush, followed by a sharp military order. The Gardes républicains at the doorway flash their swords into their scabbards with a loud click. *"Faites entrer les Allemands,"* says Clemenceau in the ensuing silence.[3]

The German delegates, Doctors Müller and Bell, entered the hall and took their seats next to the table holding the treaty. After more words by Clemenceau, the German delegates rose and signed the document, followed by the Americans, British, and other delegates. Sir Robert Borden had returned to Canada, so Sifton and fellow cabinet minister Charles Doherty signed for Canada. The war was now officially over. As news of the signing spread, the crowds outside the palace cheered, fountains sputtered to life, airplanes soared over the palace, and cannons were fired from the forts in the hills surrounding Paris. After shaking hands with delegates and friends, President Wilson, Prime Minister Lloyd George, and Prime Minister Clemenceau emerged onto the terrace and waved to the crowds.

Beatrice eventually found herself outside the palace. She noticed that some of the staff at the palace were piling together some broken cane chairs, perhaps damaged in the melee of observers and delegates inside. The cane on one of the chairs was shaped into the letter "b." Somehow

Beatrice managed to remove it and slip it into her handbag, a souvenir of an unforgettable day. Then it was on to the telegraph office to cable home the final "wartime" stories of her career.

———

MONTREAL, Quebec, September 1920. Guy had a job. He was now a half-tone etcher for the printing division of the *Montreal Gazette*, a relief after a rocky start in Canada. He had been demobbed in April 1919 and travelled to France to be with Bea while she covered the peace talks. Bea met him at Le Havre, where they stayed for two romantic nights at the Hôtel Moderne before Bea had to return to Paris. After the treaty was signed, they returned to London, where Bea discovered she was pregnant. Guy didn't have a job, and economic prospects in post-war Britain were grim. The pair decided to take their chances in Canada, where Bea would have the support of her parents.[4]

Unfortunately, Canada was suffering an economic depression all its own. British immigrants weren't especially welcome in a country that was enduring high unemployment, labour unrest, and anger from returning soldiers over low military pensions and benefits. The country was also still recovering from the shock of the bloodshed and upheaval of the Winnipeg General Strike. In May and June of 1919, thirty thousand Winnipeg workers — including police officers, fire fighters, and factory workers — had walked off the job and effectively shut down the city. At one point, the mayor also called in the Royal Northwest Mounted Police to attack the strikers violently. The federal government intervened at the urging of influential bankers, business leaders, and politicians, forcing workers to return to work.[5]

The crushing of strikes such as the one in Winnipeg was part of an overall strategy designed by businesses to quell the rise of labour organizing in Canada. During the war, companies had made immense profits from military contracts and depressed wages; they did not want to see that trend reversed, and the government gladly supported them. As unsettling as the situation was, it would ultimately benefit Guy and Beatrice.

A former assistant manager for an English photo-engraving company, Guy applied at every newspaper and print shop he could find.

Finally an opportunity presented itself. The etchers and engravers at the printing company of the *Montreal Gazette* went on strike in 1920. Companies were now using replacement workers as part of a larger strategy to break the union movement,[6] and the *Gazette* was no different. Guy was offered, and he accepted, a non-union job as a half-tone etcher for the newspaper. When the strike was over, he was transferred to the sales department. Management probably realized he wouldn't be given an easy road in the print department, where he would have been seen as a "scab engraver."[7]

The couple moved into a small, furnished apartment. In February, Bea had given birth to their first child — a boy they named Harry, after his grandfather. Guy's salary gave them much-needed security, but there was little left over from the monthly bills to pay for any extras they might need. Bea happily filled the gap by freelancing once again, writing regularly even after the couple's second child — a daughter they named Monica — was born in 1924. Like so many women who combined writing and motherhood, Bea snatched time to do her work when her children were asleep or at school. "I remember hearing her lamp come on — it had a chain that would clink," Monica would later remember. "She'd scribble on a pad beside her bed."

Bea now wrote fiction for *Modern Woman*, a British magazine catering to educated middle-class women. In the late twenties she would also begin to write for *Chatelaine*, a brand-new Canadian women's magazine. At that time, its content teeter-tottered between in-depth commentary on issues such as divorce and maternal mortality and traditional advice on child-rearing and cooking. There was a short story or serial installment in every issue, and over the next few decades Bea's stories featured frequently.

In the interwar period, Bea's fiction varied among fluffy romances, humour pieces, and psychological dramas in which relationships were complex, dark, and often unresolved. "A Bed of Her Own," in *Modern Woman*, describes a widow who longs all her married life to get rid of the ornate bed chosen by her husband. After his death, her daughter tries to persuade her to keep it, while her son sets it on fire. "Nancy Grows Up," a 1934 story in *Chatelaine*, tells the tale of a relationship that is ended because the woman involved has tuberculosis. Not the typical fare served up to female readers in the 1920s and '30s.

Some stories were clearly based on Bea's own experience. "Without References" tells the tale of a romance between a Canadian journalist and an Englishman during a cross-Canada train ride. "He was good to look at, big and rather brown, with happy blue eyes and well-shaped hands. But he was English. Margot had lived most of her life in a town where 'remittance men' were still a recognized type and the Englishman's lack of subtlety in the uptake was a frequent subject of stage jest."[8] The romance mirrored Bea's first meeting with Guy on that train journey back in 1914.

Another story reflected more recent times. "The game started in the lean years following the War when Bart walked the streets trying to forget that he was an ex-officer with those years of active service immediately behind him; and Anita, in a ferment of suppressed energy and ambition after years of canteen and ambulance work in France, stayed at home and looked after baby," Bea wrote in "Lawyer's Letter," a story about a game of make-believe between a young couple. "It began as a happy bit of make-believe at the close of a nerve-fraying day when a jobless peace seemed a poor substitute for the thrills of an uncertain wartime life."[9]

Bea could easily have been describing her own life as a young mother. While pregnant with Monica, she took a job writing catalogue copy for Simpson's. Sitting behind a desk in a dusty office, trying to write inspiring sentences about women's underwear, was a long distance from the knife-edge that she and Guy had lived on when he was fighting in France and she was a jobbing journalist in wartime London.

VICTORIA, British Columbia, March 1928. Beatrice was visiting her parents in Victoria, to which they had retired some years before. She was just tucking Monica and Harry into bed when the doorbell rang, announcing the arrival of a telegram from Guy. "A wettish day, a late parson, a tokio topper, a crying baby, a weepy soul, a crowded carriage, a tight shoe, a choppy sea, an inquisitive officer, a late tea, a new husband, a shiny ring, an adventure started, then ten years of wonderful memories love in every petal, Guy."[10] Her husband may have been at home in Montreal, but he hadn't forgotten that day ten years earlier when they had made their vows.

Bea was able to afford the cross-country trip to visit her parents as a result of some freelance work she was doing for the Canadian National Railroad (CNR). In those days, children travelling on the train were given special menus filled with illustrations of the great outdoors and rhymes about the sights they would see from the train. In exchange for free travel, Bea wrote many of the poems that filled these menus. "Here's the station! Watch your step! Now hurry through the gates! Down the platform with the crowd, where the long train waits."[11]

Poetry had always been part of Bea's life, from her childhood in Stratford to her friendship with writer Pauline Johnson. She wrote rhymes for her children and, eventually, her grandchildren. While her poems would never match the calibre of Pauline Johnson's, they would fill her scrapbooks, buy her many train trips, and become a treasured part of her family archive.

MONTREAL, Quebec, December 1929. Bea's favourite correspondent was dead. James Nasmyth was visiting his son William in his home in Sumner, Washington, when he passed away in his sleep at the age of eighty-two. The bond between father and daughter had always been strong. "From her first glimpse of day, Beatrice has been 'Dad's' girl, an affectionate — a darling daughter," James had written to Guy when he and Bea had announced their engagement. "That affection I know has been mutual and has grown steady as the years pass and I don't recollect anything that gave me more pleasure than canoeing or boating or strolling through the woods with her."[12] James had preserved all of Bea's wartime letters, and these were now forwarded back to her for safekeeping.

Bea was now forty-four, with grey streaking her wavy brown hair. The love and affection she had experienced as a child was now lavished on her own children. "Unlike her own mother, she was thrilled to have a daughter and always made me feel wonderful," Monica later remembered. "But how she adored Harry! My dad was my defender when I needed him, when I did things that displeased my mother. 'Oh now, Bea, it's all right … she's just a little girl!' Then there was always 'Oh, Guy, he's just a young boy!' Harry was a very bright personality, and I was supposedly bright but quieter and shy."[13]

Bea was as full of humour as ever — well known for accidentally twisting words in sentences, "as in her famous haughty order to a Pullman porter, 'Would you please put my cabbage in the lug!'" remembered her daughter Monica. She was also a stickler for good manners, telling Monica to keep her back straight and always be polite.

MUSKOKA, Ontario, June 1932. Dust flew in the air as the horse clopped along the dirt road. Bea sat in the front next to the farmer who had picked them up at the railway station. Twelve-year-old Harry and eight-year-old Monica sat in the back, crammed between boxes of empty quart sealers and trunks filled with their summer clothes. They were making their annual summer trek from Montreal to Glenwilde, the two-storey house on the banks of the Muskoka River where Bea had spent so many happy summers as a child. James Nasmyth had given the house to Beatrice and Guy as a wedding present, and now their children were enjoying the same golden summers. There was canoeing and tree climbing and visits from Dignam relatives. For Bea, the holiday also involved a lot of work, hauling water from a spring down by the river, weeding the garden, chopping firewood, and preparing meals on a wood stove. The children pitched in, too, picking "strawberries, raspberries, blueberries, pears, peaches, vegetables, and anything else we could get free," Harry Furniss remembered later. "For these were the years of the Great Depression."

Bea would pay Harry one cent for every "ten pails of water I carried up a steep path to the house from the spring down by the river." With cash in hand, he and his sister would take turns manoeuvring the family rowboat down the Muskoka River and then hiking one mile up the gravel road at Mary Lake to Hoth's General Store in Port Sydney, where they would buy candy and any groceries their mother wanted.

In the evenings Harry and Monica would pump the old melodium in the parlour and Bea would play some of the classical music that she had learned as a child. Then, as the darkness deepened, they would light oil lamps and play card games. Guy would join them for the last ten days of their vacation, taking Harry fishing and going on long tramps with Monica. When the long, hot summer drew to a close, Bea and Guy would close up the house and the whole family would return once again to city life.

MONTREAL, Quebec, September 1937. Guy was in his element at the *Gazette*. He was now sales manager in the printing department; the huge contracts he had been able to secure from government and big business were helping to create large profits for the company. A witty speaker and sportsman, Guy was popular with prominent clients like the Molsons. He nurtured those relationships the way men of his time often did — by joining the Kanawaki Golf Club, the Royal Montreal Curling Club, and the Canadian Club. He played billiards, golfed, curled, and painted and sketched just like his father.

At home, however, there were problems. Harry had always been mischievous and wild. Now his school marks were slipping and his relationship with his parents was deteriorating. One day, after he was rude to his mother, Guy handed him a pair of boxing gloves and challenged him to a round. Harry was no match for Guy. At the end of the match, his father told him never to speak to his mother in that way again. Harry never did.

Guy confided their worries to his boss, publisher John Bassett. Bassett persuaded him that Harry should be sent to Rothesay, a private school in New Brunswick designed to prepare students for Royal Military College. When Guy discovered that the fees were beyond their means, Bassett insisted on paying the costs himself.

Harry's marks gradually improved as a result of the rigid discipline and rigorous teaching. "We all wore uniforms, joined the cadet corps, and marched," Harry later remembered. The teachers were strict, too. "We'd get hidings with canes. I realized I'd better learn or I'd never get out of there." Despite the strict regime, Harry's love of adventure continued to flourish. Unbeknownst to his parents, he began using his allowance to take flying lessons during his free time.

When Bea and Guy realized what Harry was doing, they were horrified. Based on her experience interviewing Great War pilots, Bea saw flying as a dangerous pursuit. She also knew that Harry was likely to enlist as a fighter pilot. "Of course, as mature adults they were much more aware than us teenagers of the terrifying dangers lurking ahead in the belligerent politics in Europe," Harry would later write. "I had my head in the clouds and could think of nothing else but a glorious career in aviation. The perils of mortal combat in a catastrophic World War never entered my mind."[14]

MONTREAL, Quebec, July 1939. Harry had been accepted as a pilot in the RCAF. The only fly in the ointment was that he needed a parent's signature on the enlistment papers. "For some time [the enlistment papers] laid [sic] there on the desk, silently urging us to sign away the paltry history of a childhood that is gone," Bea would later write. "Give this youth the title to his own life, they urged. Don't try to withhold what is already his. That life you have so painstakingly nourished has now outgrown your mould and impress; it now begins to expand into that freedom which is its own inherent radiance. You can only hold it in your heart by letting it go free."

Bea was deeply conflicted. On the one hand, she was proud of her son's achievement. On the other, she had lost loved ones to war and didn't want to lose Harry, too. That evening she and Guy sat in silence and listened to the nightly forecast of ominous events in Europe. Bea couldn't cope with it any longer.

"I'll get the drinks," she volunteered, pushing herself out of her comfortable Morris chair.

"Bea," said Guy, catching hold of her hand. "Would you like me to dissuade him from flying? He hasn't the faintest idea of what he's getting into."

"You couldn't dissuade him. Nor could I," answered Bea.

Guy signed the papers. In August, Harry reported to the Montreal Light Aeroplane Club hangar at Cartierville, north of Montreal. He could live at home while learning to fly in old Gypsy Moth biplanes, another echo of the Great War.

The Second World War began in September, and after passing his final flying test and ground school exams, he was transferred to Camp Borden, near Toronto, to complete his training.

Just as she had in that earlier war, Bea volunteered with local women's groups. No record exists of just whom she worked for or what jobs she took. She must have been busy, however; a poem sent to friends in 1943 informed them of the Furnisses' move to an apartment on Sherbrooke Street where "Bee, she finds it grand to have the shops and shows at hand; her wartime tasks are half the care and she gets home with time to spare."

Guy was back in khaki, too. During the week he worked at the *Gazette*. On weekends he volunteered as a weapons instructor with the Canadian Officers' Training Corps (COTC) at McGill University. All of the male students at the university were now required to take military training. Before the war ended, more than twelve thousand would participate in the COTC.[15] The seven-day-a-week schedule didn't seem to affect the quality of Guy's work at the *Gazette*. In 1940 he was promoted to director of the company.

Monica was still at home and attending McGill University. She would eventually become a journalist, and then later a schoolteacher. Out in Ontario, Harry earned his wings, only to learn that he was being held back to train other fighter pilots. In 1941 he also began a passionate romance with a dark-haired French-Canadian singer named Terry Dusseau. With the possibility of an overseas posting at any time, the two married quickly. Their son Guy was born in 1943, just two days before Harry was shipped out.

ENGLAND, March 1945. Harry Furniss woke with a crushing hangover on the first day of March 1945. He didn't even have time for a cup of coffee before he got the command that he was to lift off with the 126 Wing for a bombing mission over Northwestern Germany. As they flew near Dorsten, more than forty German ME 109s and FW 190s came in to attack. The Allied flyers managed to destroy four German aircraft. Just as Harry was evading a German fighter, several sharp explosions flashed on the engine in front of him. In his rear-view mirror he could see a plume of black smoke pouring from his wounded Spitfire. He flew into a layer of clouds at two thousand feet and turned his plane toward the Netherlands. However, as the oil pressure dropped and his engine began to overheat, Harry knew his minutes airborne were limited. As his plane slowly descended, it became the object of enemy ground fire. With fifty-five gallons of high-test gas underneath him, a forced landing was inadvisable. Instead, he slid open the canopy over his head, opened the door on the port side of the cockpit, released his safety harness, and disconnected the oxygen and radio lines. A sheet of flame shot out of the engine as he stepped over the side of the plane and pulled his ripcord.

MONTREAL, Quebec, March 1945. "Regret to advise that Flight Lieutenant Harry Peter Mackenzie Furniss C1081 is reported missing after air operations overseas March 1. RCAF Casualties Officer." The telegram, in its black-and-white starkness, summed up their worst fears. Guy was stoic and Monica was in tears, but Bea refused to believe Harry was dead. The telegram said "missing," after all. Until provided with evidence to the contrary, she would not accept the idea that her son was not going to return from war.

While his family was struggling with the terrible news, a hungry and aching Harry Furniss was being marched south to a military jail in Frankfurt, Germany. He had managed to land safely, his plane a ball of flame as it hit the ground. After a short and relatively benign interrogation in Frankfurt, he would be taken to a prisoner-of-war camp known as Dulag-Luft.

"This might have been an ominous move had we known then about the German death camps," Harry was to reflect later. As it turned out, Dulag-Luft was a transit camp and was comparatively comfortable — prisoners were given Red Cross supplies, soap, and two meals a day. Unfortunately, their stay was temporary. Within days they would be transferred to work camps. Harry, whose ankle had been injured as a result of his parachute jump, was allowed to remain a little longer than normal at Dulag-Luft. He was lucky; those who left the camp were sent to local coal mines where they were starved, beaten, and worked nearly to death.

In May, Germany surrendered. The guards at Dulag-Luft fled the day before American troops arrived and cut open the wire gates of the prison camp. Harry had survived. It was time to go home.

MONTREAL, Quebec, May 1945. The train slowly drew to a stop and soldiers tumbled out onto the platform, each scanning the crowd for familiar faces. Harry soon spotted his grey-haired parents and his sister Monica. Absent, however, were his wife and two-year-old son. "As soon as the hugging and kissing was over, I asked where my wife and baby were. Mother and Dad waited in embarrassment as my sister gave me the bad news," Harry wrote later. "My wife, she said, had left Canada and our family circle two years ago with my child to sing in a dance band in the States. She had sent word that she was not coming back."

Harry realized that his pre-war romance and marriage were truly over and that there was nothing he could do about it. "The following weeks were hard to cope with," he would write. "I didn't want to admit it publicly, but I was still physically and mentally impaired by the trauma I had experienced as a prisoner of war. And now the family breakup."

Beatrice and Guy were just glad to have their son home and did everything they could to get him back on his feet again after his discharge from the RCAF. After a few months of casting around for something to do, Harry became a journalist, eventually working for the *Toronto Telegram* and later the *Vancouver Province*, just like his mother.

With Harry's return and the end of the war in Europe, life settled back to normal for Beatrice. She even had time to visit her old friend Roberta. The two had kept in touch since their Great War days. Roberta had married and now she, her son Robert, Bea, and Monica spent three days together in Banff. Robert, unlike Harry, had not enlisted during the war. According to Monica, Roberta had ensured that her son enrolled in university — a common way to keep young men out of military service.

Bea also returned once more to her writing. A tongue-in-cheek 1945 clipping described the process she went through whenever she got a new idea for a story:

> Mrs. Beatrice Furniss tells us that the urge to write a short story comes on like an attack. Preceding symptoms: exhilaration, depression, uplift, confidence, general nostalgia. These obviously take outward expression, because

members of her family comment dryly: "Oh leave her alone. She's got that look on her face again!" Mrs. Furniss then proceeds to get the short story out of her system.

"First, I cannot even think without a pencil in my hand," Mrs. Furniss says. "Once I have the pencil, the ideas begin to form. The pencil may be used only for the most random jottings, but it has a stimulating effect." Next she vanishes behind a closed door in her Montreal apartment.

"Propped up with a couple of pillows, a good scratch pad in hand, I begin to feel the attack approaching a favourable crisis, and I can relax and let it take its course. The more severe attacks may take several days to finish off, and then I know the glorious feeling of being back to normal. But it never lasts! A few light-hearted days and I go through the dread of recurring symptoms."[16]

In 1947, Monica graduated from McGill and married a young fighter pilot named Eric Newton. They would soon start a family and Bea would gain three grandchildren — Debby, Sally, and Rod. The children would call her "Goo-Goo," and she would write them poetry and stories, just as she had for her own children back in the 1920s and '30s.

MONTREAL, Quebec, 1952. The heart attack almost killed Guy. The once-robust soldier and sportsman was now barely able to walk. It had been a close call, and the specialist told Bea that Guy would have to stop working. After a brief convalescence, the two decided that perhaps Vancouver — Bea's old stomping grounds — would be a good place to retire and enjoy life at a slower pace. Their life together had come full circle from that first meeting on the train thirty-eight years earlier.

Life in Vancouver would be busy for Bea. In 1958 she would become president of the Vancouver and Mainland Branch of the Canadian Authors' Society, organizing a symposium on writing and publishing. She would continue to write short stories (with middle-aged characters now). She would also spend many hours with her children and grandchildren, since Harry and Monica had both relocated to Vancouver.

At the start of his retirement, Guy embraced life once again, taking watercolour courses in Banff with Canadian artist W.J. Phillips. But as the decade progressed, his health deteriorated. He became diabetic, and sometime in the late 1950s lost a leg to complications from the disease. It was heartbreaking for a man who had prided himself on his robust health. He died in December 1963.

"My father had been retired from the *Gazette* some years before his death," remembered his son Harry. "There was no formal pension plan then for officers of the company; the directors voted funds each year as they saw fit. After father died, this arrangement was continued with my mother, who lived on for another sixteen years."

VANCOUVER, British Columbia, January 1977. Beatrice was curled up in her favourite chair, her granddaughter sitting on a footstool in front of her. Sally's grade eleven English teacher had assigned her to interview a family member about her life, and she had chosen her grandmother as her subject. The room was warm from the crackling fire in the grate as the animated elderly woman told story after story and the young girl recorded everything she could in a little spiral notebook. Sally would describe her grandmother as "friend, comforter, teacher, someone to giggle with, all the priceless, wonderful things a grandmother can be."

Now ninety-two, Bea had been living with Sally's parents, Monica and her husband Eric, for five years.

The central role that she played in the family was evident in Sally's essay. "Although the years separating us are many — a separation of three-quarters of a century is a big generation gap — Goo Goo and I have an easy rapport. We share so many things: our love of classical music, our joy of writing and reading, our unpredictable and slightly wacky sense of humour, our delight in the world as a whole. Perhaps these are qualities Goo Goo has taught me, or perhaps they have been passed on to me through heredity, but whatever the method, they are a strong and invaluable tie 'twixt my grandmother and me.... She is the shining beacon that attracts my older siblings back to the nest; she is the reason for many rainy Vancouver evenings around a fireplace together."

Decades earlier, Beatrice had penned a few pages of memoir. "Parental affection between generations may stretch like an iridescent rainbow but it is not something tangible one can travel," she wrote. "It is like a mountain from which one has travelled far and thought never to see again; yet when afternoon lingers towards evening you look back and there it is, just behind you, all rosy and revealed and very real. Before the glow fades I must paint a picture of it for my children, one of strong brush strokes and sensitive outlines. And perhaps if it is hung in that long blind corridor between this generation and the next they may place a little candle of understanding before it and if it does not lighten the picture it may perhaps serve to make the corridor less black."[17]

The glow finally faded for Beatrice Sifton Nasmyth Furniss on October 23, 1977. She died peacefully in her sleep, her daughter Monica sitting next to her, holding her hand. In her entry in *Canadian Women of Note*, she was described as a "pioneer in women's rights and a writer who didn't let being a woman stop her. She was a correspondent for the *Vancouver Province* on a special assignment for the Alberta government when she was allowed behind Canadian lines in France during the First World War."[18] The war would forever be the story for which she was best remembered.

After Bea's death, Monica found several cardboard boxes in her closet. They contained a stack of calling cards, on the back of which were listed the names of all of her wartime features for the *Province* and how much she was paid for each. There was a letter "b" made out of shiny brown cane and a press pass to the Paris Peace Conference. Photo albums and scrapbooks held many of her post-war stories, and a bulging file folder contained the precious letters she had sent home during the First World War. It was Beatrice's archive of the best stories of her life. They would one day illuminate the corridor down which her biographer would travel through war and peace and into the heart of a young, ambitious journalist.

Chapter II

Mary MacLeod Moore

The hours slip by. I am alone still, but the anguish is subsiding. The evening sunlight pours through the golden leaves of the delicate birches. I feel overwhelmed by its beauty. In this tragic world there must be purpose. Perhaps for me it is that I must live to see that the names of the men who gave their lives for this beautiful country should not be forgotten.
— Grace Morris Craig, at the death of her soldier fiancé in 1919.
He died of endocarditis, an after-effect of trench fever.

LA HULPE, Belgium, April 1919. Mac stood on the table and looked through the open casement window at the stars and then down at the cobblestones below. The edge of the table began to teeter, back and forth, back and forth. He swayed faster and faster until he felt himself pitch forward, through the window and into the open air while the ground rushed up to meet him and the moonlight was gone forever.[1]

LONDON, England, April 1919. The officer who gave the news to Mary and her mother said it was an accident. Seconded to 4th Canadian

Divisional Headquarters in Brussels, Mac had been trying to shut a window in his billet when he fell to the street below. It was salt in their wounds — he had endured and survived terrible injuries. To die like this after the war was over made their grief even more unbearable.

A medical board was called. There was some sort of controversy over Mac's death — a question of suicide. It was soon brushed aside. "A court of inquiry convened to investigate the circumstances of his death, after hearing all the evidence and visiting the scene of the accident, is of the opinion that he came to his death by falling from the window of his billet while walking in his sleep and that his death was entirely accidental and that no blame is attached to anyone."[2] No military court would allow a decorated officer's memory to be stained with controversy. Yet the two different explanations of his death suggest that no one was really quite sure what caused him to fall from the window that night.

The obituary in the *Sunday Times* revealed just how similar he and his sister Mary had been. "Mac, as he was known to his friends in and around Fleet Street, was a man of outstanding ability, unusual resource, and most generous disposition. A staunch Canadian and an ardent Imperialist, he used to say that in Canadian messes he spent time explaining the Englishman, and in the English messes explaining the Canadian. He had the gift of friendship developed to an extraordinary degree, and for his friends he spent the best that was in him at all times and in all seasons. He was essentially of the type which binds and cements the union between the Colonies and the Motherland."[3]

Although a funeral was promised, none was held. Instead, Mary travelled to Belgium to say a final farewell to her brother.

LA HULPE, Belgium, April 1919. "The difference between invaded France and Belgium, and the British Isles stands out very clearly when one drives through miles and miles of places which were once part of a happy provincial country, rather aloof from international politics, but very busy with their affairs and their domestic life, and are now places of the dead. No description can do justice to the sight," mused Mary. "Towns and villages, their shops, villas, cottages and churches, silent, heaps of dust and mortar and bricks; sandbags, rusty wire, torn railways and broken bridges make the country a great refuse heap. Occasionally the desolation is emphasized by a few figures as women search for some reminder of their old homes."[4]

The tiny cemetery in La Hulpe, with its orderly gravestones and carefully tended flowers, had somehow emerged unscathed amid the destruction that otherwise blanketed the countryside. Mary stood silently in front of the raised hump of earth where her brother was buried, the only First World War casualty interred there. Soon a stone would mark his grave, the same size and shape as those erected above all Commonwealth war graves. Her brother's marker would read: "Captain William MacLeod Moore MC, The Only Son of His Mother and She Was a Widow, St. Luke 7.12." The quote, from the story of Jesus bringing an only son back to life, described what Emily MacLeod Moore must have longed for when she received the news of her son's death.

Mary would not write publicly about the loss of her brother or her visit to his grave — her family life would continue to be intensely private. However, her trip would form the basis for several articles about war cemeteries and what life was like in the former war zone. Despite the many journeys she had made to France during the last year of the war, the utter devastation overwhelmed her. "The destruction seems almost incredible. Yet on the famous road between Cambrai and Arras (try to think of it as part of the road from London to Brighton), which is linked with much of the war's story — a road that has been shelled and shelled and lately repaired — you pass for miles through war ruins. Great black signs tell the name of the town that was and has ceased to be; a higher ruin here and there indicates a church; another pile must have been a row of shops; trees in the distance are Bourlon Wood from which troops watched the great fire in Cambrai; the dark criss-cross lines are trenches; over there is the Hindenburg Line; empty dug-outs, some still strong and firm, with their steps clearly outlined, speak of the men who lived and fought a little while ago — now all is silence."[5]

Now and then that silence was punctuated by tragedy. As in all wars, the debris left behind was still lethal. Time and again, children would be killed while playing with shells found in the battered earth. A man who had witnessed one such event told Mary that "the pathetic part was that the war zone children were not frightened in most cases, for these younger ones could not remember any other existence. War and all its accompaniments were as natural as thunderstorms."[6]

The peace talks were now in progress and Mary believed that those who opposed heavy reparations from Germany should visit "the old war-zone, where they will see at firsthand what the invaded countries have suffered, and can guess how long — and how much — it will take to rebuild what has been devastated."[7]

The landscape was thronged with the ghosts of the dead, but now and again she could see signs of life — a small hut with clean lace curtains blowing in the window, Chinese workers clearing away "war-rubbish," and gangs of German soldiers mending the roads. But the most hopeful sight was that of a man in uniform and a woman in black looking at the ruins of what had once been their home. "In the dust knelt a small child intent upon building a house with the best pieces of brick within reach. It seemed like an allegory, for a new and better world must be built by those children on the wreck of the shadowed lives of this generation, else men have died in vain."[8]

LONDON, England, May 1919. The fighting may have been over, but the struggle for justice on the home front continued. "These are grave days, [for] besides all the trials and pitfalls of the Peace Conference — too big a subject to be touched on here — there is the general industrial unrest," wrote Mary. "At the moment, war or peace hang in the balance, for the railway men, the miners and the transport workers are considering their position and negotiating with employers and with the Government. There has been no more critical time than this in years, but to the eye and ear there is little sign of a great revolution. There is no Roll of Honor to be read in the newspapers, no long account of battles and of suffering, no stirring news to thrill us, yet affairs which will affect the life of this country and of others for many years are being discussed and settled as these bright spring days dawn and die."[9]

Low wages, rising food and housing costs, and fewer jobs made many returning soldiers wonder if this truly was an "England fit for heroes."

In 1919, 2.4 million British workers went on strike, including tube and underground train workers, who had hit the pavement in March. "It was a week of intense cold and of great discomfort — one long to be remembered," reported Mary. "The only means of transit were the tramways which run but in certain parts of London, and the buses. All were crammed and jammed and a clamoring, struggling crowd of hundreds tried for standing room only."[10]

A month later, the miners went on strike. Estimates vary, but somewhere between twenty-five thousand and forty thousand coal workers walked the picket lines. They were no longer content to put up with the dangerous conditions, low pay, and long hours. Despite the shortages of coal during one of the coldest winters in memory, Mary sided with the striking miners. "Nothing of all that is going on in the industrial world of this country has struck the general public so much as the account of the conditions under which the miner lives and works. The miners' demands are being talked of with more sympathy since the readers of the daily press have heard of the appalling housing conditions, the indecent crowding and the fact that a miner's life is a more dangerous one than that of a soldier in wartime."[11]

LONDON, England, June 1919. The Great War was officially over. A slim column on page five of the *Times* declared that Germany had signed the formal peace treaty at Versailles. Mary sighed as she set the newspaper down on her typewriter. A little clipping was pinned on the wall above her desk. It read "Lest We Forget," and listed British casualties during the war — 670,986 killed, 2,041,040 wounded, 350,243 missing.[12] The conflict might be over, but the suffering it had caused would last for years to come.

Mary would use her weekly "London Letter" to explore her feelings about the anticlimactic end to more than four years of pain and loss:

> There are all the millions in the other countries of the Allies as well who have suffered and died, not just to beat the Germans, but to root out the things for which German tyranny and militarism and deceit and lack of

honour and treachery stood — to give the world new standards, or rather to revive the old, and to make the world cleaner and better. If Peace means all this, either now or as the nations slowly grow, then we may well rejoice. But we have suffered too much and too long to greet Peace with wild gaiety. These men and boys who have passed into another life while this was still so sweet have gained us the victory. We owe it to them to use well the freedom they won.[13]

The Canadian "men and boys" who did survive the conflict wanted to return home. It was nearly a year after the war's end. Many were still in England, and some were getting into trouble. "The most painful subject of the moment is the outbreak at Epsom of Canadian soldiers and the consequent death of Station-Sergt. Green, and the injury of a number of policemen," wrote Mary. On June 17, Canadian soldiers stationed at Woodcote Camp on Epsom Downs had rioted when two of their comrades were arrested after a fight in a pub. Some attacked the police station to secure the release of the two men. Eleven policemen were injured, and fifty-one-year-old Green was hit with an iron bar. He died the next day without regaining consciousness. There was one positive outcome of the Epsom riots: British ships were pressed into service to help get Canadian troops home faster.

Back in London, one form of demobilization was putting smiles on people's faces. Military planes were now being used to take holidaymakers into the sky for half-hour trips. "These 'flips' cost two guineas each," wrote Mary, "but according to the enthusiastic, they were well worth it, for cares and strikes and cold weather and high prices charged for everything necessary to civilization were all-forgotten as the earth slipped away and one was alone with the clean air and the empty clouds."

LONDON, England, July 1919. Mary slit open the cardboard box and drew out a small green hardcover book with a white maple leaf stamped on the cover. It was her first book, *The Maple Leaf's Red Cross: The War*

Story of the Canadian Red Cross Overseas. Commissioned by the Canadian War Records Office, it was an in-depth look at the work of the organization, from the cases of food and clothing sent by women from homes on the Prairies to the overseas work of doctors, nurses, and ambulance drivers. Mary had begun researching the book during her tour of the lines of communication and in a series of brief follow-up visits. Its pages were filled with front-line stories and appendices listing the people who served with the Red Cross (including her late brother), the money spent, and amounts of food collected and distributed to hospitals in England, France, Serbia, and Russia.

The Maple Leaf's Red Cross is the clearest indication of just how strongly Mary felt about Canadian women's contributions to the war effort. She meticulously catalogued everything from the number of cases of jams and preserves sent overseas during the war years (248,673 cases, worth two million pounds) to the number of socks knitted for the men in the trenches (868,629 pairs). "The gifts from Canada of clothing, dressings, blankets and socks were invaluable. In many instances it is difficult to realize how the hospitals would have managed without them."[14]

There were long descriptions of overseas organizations almost totally staffed by women. These included the Information Bureau of the Canadian Red Cross Society, which answered inquiries from relatives about the sick, wounded, and missing; the Prisoner of War Department, which ensured that food and clothing were regularly distributed to Canadian POWs; and the Supply Stores, which provided necessities for both soldiers and refugees throughout the war. The terrible demands placed on ambulance drivers, VADs, and nurses are explored in two chapters. Nearly one hundred years after its publication, *The Maple Leaf's Red Cross* remains one of the few in-depth contemporary sources of information about Canadian women's home front/war front activities during the Great War.

The book marked the beginning of a busy period in Mary's life. Having spent half her life in journalism, she was now at the top of her game. A regular columnist with the *Sunday Times* and *Saturday Night Magazine*, she was now also a contributor to popular publications such as *United Empire*, the *Illustrated London News*, *Land and Water*, *Baby's World*, *The British Dominions Yearbook*, and many others. In an article for *Cassell's Weekly*, she looked back at her career:

> I have had intimate and beautiful confidences from strangers; I have been sent photographs of babies, brides, soldier sons, and houses which the owners trustfully hope I shall be able to let for them. I have been asked to find furnished flats, lucrative posts, secluded country villages for the nervously exhausted, lost relations, elusive quotations, and homes for the aged. I have come to the conclusion that Fate never intended me for a great writer or even a mildly distinguished one, but for a useful Information and Advice Bureau.[15]

An uncharitable historian of the *Sunday Times* writing in the 1970s would say that Mary wrote a "Wilhelmina Stitch kind of column."[16] The comment was intended as a sexist put-down, but was really a compliment of sorts. Stitch — the pseudonym for Canadian journalist Ruth Jacobs — was a brilliant book reviewer, literary editor, translator, and poet whose poems and advice columns were syndicated throughout Britain. Her poems were sentimental, upbeat, and uncritical and the frequent target of jabs by "serious" journalists.

Mary wasn't a poet or translator like Jacobs, but she was a regular reviewer, promoting books such as Elizabeth Montizambert's *Unnoticed London* and Vera Brittain's *Women's Work in Modern England*. In her magazine articles, she aired her opinions on everything from the changing length of women's skirts to the joys of travel. Yet, unlike Jacobs, Mary subversively layered serious concerns, such as women's rights, between trivial ones such as the latest dog show or the recent holiday of the king and queen. One issue that she would return to again and again was the necessity of jobs and housing for women. After the armistice, women who had worked in war industries were pushed out of their jobs to make way for returning soldiers. Yet with the loss of so many men on the battlefield, few could return home and expect a man to provide for them. Instead, they found other jobs, usually at lower pay. In the early 1920s, eight hundred thousand women would be working for a living in London.

"One might have supposed even the most prejudiced and old-fashioned would realize that girls have to work if they would live," wrote Mary. "Yet there are still people of both sexes who complain that girls are going to work daily, filling the trains and omnibuses and taking the places of young men. But if they did not work, who would support them? Few girls nowadays, except those with really wealthy parents, can afford to be quite idle. The days of staying at home to arrange the flowers and help mother with the tea parties have gone."[17]

Another issue that would emerge in Mary's columns for the next two decades was the new internationalism. During the war, she had opposed all attempts at diplomacy, writing in 1918 that "the wonderful patriotism of the majority makes one even more indignant with the miserable disloyal pacifist minority, always ready to admire what is inimical to their own country and to slur over the crimes of the enemy with a loud cry of internationalism and a general kiss and make friends policy."

That attitude, so consistent during the war, altered soon after the loss of her brother. Perhaps the change of heart was the result of her tour of Belgium, where she witnessed the terrible destruction wrought by the war. The establishment of the League of Nations in 1920, the first international organization dedicated to maintaining world peace, may have also been a catalyst. Whatever the case, like so many of her post-war contemporaries, Mary began to promote that very internationalism she had once adamantly rejected. At a 1922 meeting of the Society of Women Journalists, she "made an eloquent and valuable plea on the importance of establishing international press relationship. There never was a time when the friendship among nations was more important than now," reported the *Evening Post*.[18] Time would prove her right.

YPRES, Belgium, March 1923. A thousand people gathered in Ypres's town square in the shadow of the ruins of the ancient Cloth Hall. There were British soldiers, a London military band, and hundreds of relatives of the dead. They came from "places as far apart as Llangollen and Glasgow, Exeter and Montrose, Llanfairfechan and Chester, Aberdeen and London and Liverpool." Mary MacLeod Moore was among them, reporting on the pilgrimage to Ypres for the *Sunday Times*. The St. Barnabas Hostel had organized and funded the tour; twenty-five hundred people had applied to come, but subsidies were only available for one thousand. Daughters and sons, mothers, fathers, and wives were there to see the graves of those they'd lost. Their first stop was Lijssenthoek Memorial Cemetery, a military burial ground that would eventually be the second-largest First World War cemetery in Belgium.

"A long, pathetic procession trudged down the sunny, dusty road, carrying the flowers they wished to place on the graves.... As the vanguard of pilgrims entered, there fell upon the soft air the first notes of 'For all the saints who from their labours rest.' Hardly a face but was wet with tears as the people streamed in," observed Mary. "Sometimes a sob broke the quiet, and I saw an elderly father and mother holding toil-worn hands as the tears streamed down their poor faces."[19]

It would not be the last time that Mary would visit the military cemeteries in Belgium and France. She would be in France on July 1923, when the Canadian war memorial at St. Julien was unveiled. It was a single shaft of granite from which emerged the bent arms and bowed head of a Canadian soldier. Mary listened intently as Marshal Ferdinand Foch — the head of the Allied forces — spoke movingly about the bravery exhibited by the Canadians in the face of the first gas attacks of the war: "The Canadians paid heavily for their sacrifice and the corner of earth on which this Memorial of gratitude and piety rises has been bathed in their blood." But what impressed Mary most were the "Big men in khaki, dazzling with ribbons," who had survived those attacks and were now talking intently in the cafés of Ypres, greeting "others with whom they had fought side by side. They said, 'Do you remember?'"[20]

Mary would never forget the sacrifices of war. Until her abrupt retirement from writing in 1940, her columns in the *Sunday Times* would mark every Armistice Day and regularly remind readers of the cost of the Great War and of those who paid it.

LONDON, England, June 1923. It was the perfect day for a wedding. The sun poured in through the stained-glass windows at St. Mary Abbots Church in Kensington. The bride was slender, her round face remarkably unlined for a fifty-two-year-old woman, her hair dark and cut in a fashionable bob. She wore a soft grey dress and a wide-brimmed hat.

The groom, a widower fourteen years her senior, was short and balding, with a monocle and a small moustache. The church was decorated with white lilies, and the pews were filled with some of London's most influential political and literary figures. There were T.P. O'Connor, Lord Riddell, Mr. and Mrs. Gomer Berry, and John Steele, London editor of the *Chicago Tribune*. They were gathered to witness the marriage of their friends Mary MacLeod Moore and *Sunday Times* editor Leonard Rees.[21]

Mary and Leonard had worked closely together for more than ten years. It is not known whether the two had carried on an extramarital affair while Rees's wife was alive or their relationship had simply deepened following her protracted illness and death. Whatever the case, her marriage brought Mary (whose mother would die a few months after the wedding) a loving new family.[22] Leonard had three adult children — Lawrence, Herbert, and Phyllis. Herbert would emigrate to the United States, but Lawrence and Phyllis would be close to Mary throughout their lives.

Leonard was an outgoing, friendly man who loved golf and chess and had the kind of personality that drew people to him. He was also a brilliant editor who persuaded some of the best writers to work for the *Sunday Times*, including Sir Edmund Gosse, Desmond McCarthy, Ernest Newman, and James Agate. Leonard counted these men among his friends, along with politicians, peers, statesmen, and a host of other well-known literary and society figures. Mary and Leonard moved into a large flat at 31 Bullingham Mansions, and over the next decade became a literary power couple, hosting and being hosted by the prominent and the influential, from Thomas Hardy to Neville Chamberlain.

LONDON, England, June 1924. It was the kind of party that Leonard and Mary liked to attend, a gathering of literary lions and exciting new writers. Novelist Vere Hutchinson and her partner, illustrator Dorothy Burroughs, had invited Michael Arlen, the toast of London, to attend. Newman Flowers of Cassells Publishing was there, too, promoting a promising young novelist whose book *The Unlit Lamp* had been signed by his company. The writer was Radclyffe Hall, and she and partner Una Troubridge were among the guests of honour that evening. Hall, striking in her finely tailored man's suit, short hair, and high collars, was reticent in social situations. As the glasses clinked and guests peppered her with questions about her new book, she responded in a shy, almost inaudible voice.

Watching Hall fumble with social niceties, Leonard Rees — with his unerring instinct for quality — decided he would help Hall navigate the stormy waters of London's literary society. In the months and years following the party, he and Mary would help her make important contacts and coach the awkward Hall on how to make a splash in London's social scene. Mary would review *The Unlit Lamp* in the *Sunday Times* and Leonard would regularly publish her poetry. The couple would also invite her to parties in their home, where she could meet authors, artists, and publishers, such as painter Augustus John, humorist E.V. Lucas, writers Edmund Gosse and Netta Syrett (whose novels featured strong female protagonists), and publisher John Murray. Writer Rebecca West, whom she would meet at the Reeses' home, would become Hall's lifelong friend.

One of Leonard's first suggestions was that Hall should frequently attend the opening nights of as many major London plays as she could. As her biographer Sally Cline points out, "Sometimes she [Hall] and Una attended as many as four matinees and evening performances in a week. Hall in her man's stock, high stiffened collar and romantic sweeping cloak made heads turn. She never carried a handbag but had special pockets sewn into her skirt. In her box she often cut a figure more dramatic than the plays she attended."[23]

Radclyffe and Una became close friends with Mary and Leonard, often visiting back and forth. In May 1925, Leonard's daughter Phyllis — who had married and moved to Accra, Gold Coast (now Ghana), with her husband — died suddenly of a tropical illness. Mary and Leonard had recently returned from a visit with Phyllis at her home in the Gold Coast and couldn't believe that the vibrant, healthy young woman they had left behind was now gone forever. Hall went immediately to the Reeses' apartment and spent the morning helping the couple cope with the shock.

Hall would be awarded the Prix Femina and the James Tait Black Memorial Prize for *Adam's Breed*. In July 1927 she threw one of the most memorable literary parties of the year, and Mary and Leonard were on the guest list. Composer J. Rosamond Johnson and singer Taylor Gordon sang spirituals in Hall's drawing room while London's literary elite, including writer John Galsworthy, actress Sybil Thorndike, Wilhelmina Stitch (Ruth Jacobs, the columnist to whom Mary would later be compared), biographer Margaret Irwin, poet John Adcock, novelist Sheila Kaye-Smith, and publisher Newman Flowers crowded onto pillows and improvised rows of stalls.

The test of the friendship between Hall and Mary and Leonard Rees would come in July 1928 with the publication of Hall's most famous book, *The Well of Loneliness*. The novel explored the life of Stephen Gordon, an Englishwoman who discovers that she is an "invert" (an early term for lesbian). The book was hugely controversial, with James Douglas, the editor of the *Sunday Express*, writing, "I would rather give a healthy boy or a healthy girl a phial of prussic acid than this novel."

Leonard Rees was not cowed by such criticisms and opposed censorship; he immediately passed the book to *Sunday Times* reviewer Ida Wylie, who wrote, "Radclyffe Hall writes with distinction, with a lively sense of characterization and with a feeling for the background of her subject which makes her work delightful reading. And, first and last, she has courage and honesty."[24] Mary was likewise undaunted by the controversy, and while she did not promote the book in her columns, Hall would continue to be a close friend.[25]

LONDON, England, November 1929. "No sane person wants war, admires war, glorifies war, or excuses war, but we deserve to perish as a nation if we forget the magnificent record of those four terrible years." Mary was preparing to observe Armistice Day at the cenotaph in Whitehall once again. This time, however, she was feeling angry and irritable. The way that people were thinking about the Great War was shifting, and she didn't like it one bit. "Lately there has been a fashion in strong war books. From the stories of actual events which thrilled us and filled us with pride in our men for years, the pendulum has swung to the purely sordid. Stark realism with a wealth of shocking detail, recorded by brilliant pens, seems to have wiped out the memory of nobility and self-sacrifice."[26]

Some were arguing that Armistice Day (later known as Remembrance Day) should be abandoned altogether, since unemployment, poor housing, and inadequate pensions for soldiers proved that "remembrance" itself was a hollow homage to those who had sacrificed their lives. Mary understood all this and was slowly beginning to re-evaluate the war. However, she did not believe the current challenges facing Britons could possibly outweigh the need to spend a few moments once a year to "commune with the vast unseen host" and remember those who had not returned from the war.

LONDON, England, May 1931. Flora Lion's dog was curled up on the coal heater in her spacious Fulham Road studio. He was watching his mistress painstakingly mix colours for a large portrait she was working on for a new client — Mrs. Leonard Rees. Lion, a popular society portrait artist, was well known for her portraits of suffragette Flora Drummond and wartime munitions workers. Now she was intent on capturing the likeness of long-time women's rights advocate and writer Mary Rees. Her subject sat patiently in an ornate armchair, wearing a sleeveless evening gown and filmy stole, her hair waved and parted on the side, drop earrings framing her round face, a heavily jewelled necklace at her throat. She was a bit stiff, though, and Lion wanted her to look more relaxed. "Raise your arm," commanded Lion. Mary complied, a slight smile hovering around her lips as she held her left arm up as though to snap her fingers. It was just the look that Lion wanted. The finished portrait would be displayed in a show at Burlington House before being received and displayed at Bullingham Mansions.[27]

The portrait suggests that Mary was not suffering financially at the start of the Great Depression. Leonard had a well-paid job, and Mary had not stopped working since their marriage. That didn't mean, however, that she had forgotten her own early struggles. Over the next ten years, Mary would use her columns to call for justice and compassion for those suffering from the Depression's greatest effects, especially the women and the men who had once fought for king and country.

Three million Britons were now unemployed, an all-time record, and those who had jobs were facing wage reductions. The Labour government, unable to cope with rising unemployment, resigned in August 1931. A new "National" government was formed, made up of members of all three parties — Liberal, Conservative, and Labour. An election on October 27 would result in the electorate giving the coalition its stamp of approval.

For many, the economic situation coupled with the political crisis raised questions about the kind of Britain for which men had died in the First World War. "Have we failed the dead?" Mary wrote in her 1931 Armistice Day column. "It is true that we did sincerely believe that there would be a new heaven and a new earth paid for by the blood and suffering of millions," she wrote. "The world which was to be made fit for heroes, and happy and safe for the children of the new generation, has been a disappointment."

Since the war had ended, she argued, Britons had been "weary, disillusioned, and listless" and suffered from "internal dissensions." The election of the National Government, however, signalled that the country was once again on the right track. Britain was "consolidated" for "peace and the rebuilding of the country." Mary described the response to the crisis as being similar to the way in which Britain approached the declaration of war. "Once again the nation has been stirred by danger and has proved its courage, its sanity, its sense of oneness. From the calamity which has threatened, the people have risen with the same unity of purpose, the same determination to see the country through its worst trials."

Unfortunately, the trials were only just beginning. The 1930s would be a terrible time for many Britons. Mary would not be exempt from suffering; her losses would not be economic, however, but deeply personal.

LONDON, England, January 1932. Leonard Rees was a confirmed workaholic who rarely missed a day at the office. That was why Mary was surprised when he decided to stay in bed on a crisp Tuesday morning in January. He was feeling under the weather, but it would turn out to be much more than that. By the end of the day, Leonard's condition had worsened, and he passed away in the early evening of congestive heart failure. He was seventy-five years old.

The funeral was held at the cathedral-like St. Mary Abbots Church in Kensington. Journalists, writers, lords and ladies, military officers, peers, and politicians crammed into the pews. The Earl of Dundonald, Lord and Lady Camrose (owners of the *Sunday Times*), a representative of the Canadian high commissioner, and the presidents of the Lyceum Club and the Society of Women Journalists were all present, along with many close family friends. Those who couldn't come, such as Neville Chamberlain, would send letters.

Mary's old friend Alfred Noyes was in the congregation, along with almost the entire editorial staff of the *Sunday Times*. Rees had given many famous writers their first chance, and although he wasn't always easy to work with, he fostered an intense loyalty. "I came to him a raw recruit," wrote Gerald Barry, "but I never met with anything at his hands but generosity." Writers badly wanted to live up to his expectations, remembered Herbert Sidebotham.[28]

A few months after Leonard's death, Mary moved to a flat at 22 Abingdon Gardens. Leonard had left her comfortably off, with nearly seven thousand pounds (worth over half-a-million pounds today). The woman who had once thought a fifty-dollar dress an unutterable luxury would live in comfort for the rest of her life. She would continue to write for the *Sunday Times* and *Saturday Night Magazine*, participate in the Society of Women Journalists and the Lyceum Club, and travel throughout Europe (a hobby developed while she was married to Leonard). Although she put on a brave face, however, Leonard's death was a terrible blow. Mary had found her soulmate in the perceptive, serious Leonard, and nothing could replace him. She would have his tombstone inscribed, "I thank my God upon Every Remembrance of You."

LONDON, England, May 1932. "A luncheon in honour of *Napoleon: The Hundred Days*, the play by Signor Mussolini and Signor Forzano at the New Theatre, was given at the Lyceum Club yesterday."[29] Mrs.

Leonard Rees (a.k.a. Mary MacLeod Moore), chairman of the Journalists' Board of the Club, was presiding over the event. The Italian ambassador was present, along with playwright John Drinkwater (who had adapted the play for the English stage) and lead actor Robert Atkins. The play's London debut had been marked with rave reviews, comparing it to Shakespearian dramas. The ambassador read out a personal telegram from Mussolini praising the British adaptation of the play; that Il Duce was at this time considered a friend of England was expressed by Robert Atkins, who shared the "honour" he felt at being associated "with so great a man as Signor Mussolini."

It was not an uncommon sentiment. In the early 1930s, many Britons were embarking on a romance with Italy and its leader. While Britain was suffering from slums and mass unemployment, Italy was ending strikes and pulling down "derelict areas" in Rome. Together with its glittering history of ancient empire and rich cultural heritage, it seemed to be a model of what a civilized society could and should be.

Such beliefs were actively nurtured by Italian diplomats stationed in Britain. Beginning in 1932, Italy initiated a policy of strengthening ties between Italy and prominent Britons, including writer Frances Yeats-Brown (author of *The Lives of a Bengal Lancer*), journalist Charles Petrie, and Vice Admiral Henry Usborne. Not only were they attracted by Italian culture, they were persuaded that Italy's brand of fascism was essentially benevolent, unlike German Nazism. They were what historian Claudia Baldoli calls "Italophiles" — people who believed that Italy "was a rising nation, as opposed to a declining Britain."[30] They also believed that building stronger links with Italy would prevent that country from allying itself with an increasingly aggressive Germany.

A careful reading of Mary's columns indicates that she shared those beliefs. In a December 1933 column in the *Sunday Times*, she would describe spending Christmas in Merano. "No one can stay in a place where different nationalities mingle without thinking of what is usually called internationalism, a word which frightens many kindly folk. And in thinking of it, one blesses all agencies by which people of various countries can know one another better." Merano was a "veritable oasis of tolerance," with German ("for Merano was Austrian in pre-war days"),

English, and Italian spoken. "So far as a stranger can judge in a short time, Italian rule is kindly and tolerant," Mary observed. Like so many Britons, she would soon change her opinion.

―

BERLIN, Germany, January 1933. Adolf Hitler stood in the window of the Reich Chancellery and waved to the adoring crowd below. He had just been sworn in as chancellor of Germany, and his mood was jubilant. In February, he would establish Nazi rule and give the government the power to censor publications and crack down on political agitation. In March, he would pass the "Enabling Act," giving him total dictatorial powers. He would soon put into action his "final solution," the killing of millions of Jews in Germany and the countries it occupied.

In October, Germany withdrew from the League of Nations. The horrors of the Great War were returning to haunt Britons once again. "The agitating news of the past week with regard to Germany seems to create a gulf between those who went through the war, whether as fighting men or as civilians suffering anxiety and grief at home, and those too young to remember the war," Mary wrote in the *Sunday Times*.

> The first feeling of many who heard the news on Saturday night over the wireless was a sort of sick foreboding and a curious revival of dread memories. The very young could have no background for such news. Their sensations must have been quite different. Most thinking people must realize that simple friendship between the people of different nations and the same aims and ideals, such as many of the women's organizations possess, is the best guarantee of peace and good understanding. But do they stand the strain when national feeling flames high, and the rights and the viewpoints of other countries are forgotten? I suppose there is no way of gauging the real power of these friendly international societies, but men by the

million have died in vain unless they have something more to show than holding meetings and making vague speeches.[31]

Mary had already observed the changes in Germany first-hand during a brief stop in the port of Hamburg in September, following a tour of Sweden. As she stood at the rail of her cruise ship, she observed German soldiers and cargo boats "flying the red flag with the black swastika" watched by "fair-haired German girls giving the Nazi salute." The obvious militarism and rampant nationalism horrified her. She wasn't alone; a man standing next to her whispered "cannon fodder" and Mary "prayed that it might not be so."[32]

LONDON, England, November 1934. Another Armistice Day had rolled around, but this time Mary linked the end of the Great War not with soldiers, but with women. In "Lest We Forget Women in Need," she described the "great need for improvement in the care and treatment of poor women, among whom the maternal death rate is so sadly high." A government report by the "Maternity Mortality Committee" had expressed the "need for better food, especially where unemployment was high." Mary noted that "mothers of families are often the last to be well fed as they sacrifice themselves for their children" and that there needed to be "wider provision of midwifery services." As the Depression continued, unemployment, poor housing, and maternal mortality rates were all rising. Mary could not help but contrast society's impotence with the "all hands on deck" attitude of the war years. "The difficulty is not want of heart (though sometimes want of imagination), but the feeling that there is nothing the individual can do. In the war every man and woman knew what to do and we worked for a common cause. Now sympathy may be offered, but comparatively few can be told definitely how to help in a great effort to invade and vanquish slumdom. Can anyone tell us?"[33] In another echo of her Great War writing, she catalogued the cost of living in London and called again for reasonably priced housing for single and elderly women — "no one is deeply interested in quiet elderly or middle aged women who have had to retire from active work on a tiny income or a small annuity."[34]

Now elderly herself, Mary likely understood what it was like to be slowly shoved to one side by society. For the previous two decades, she had written regular articles under her birth name, as well as her weekly "Pandora" column. In 1933 those articles disappeared, although Pandora continued on. Mary was slowly becoming yesterday's news.

LONDON, England, December 1938. It was a picture-postcard London Christmas, complete with deep drifts of snow and ice crystals on the holly berries. Despite the perfect holiday weather, Mary experienced a deep sense of apprehension. "Probably the wish that is strongest in all our hearts today is that 1939 may mean peace, not only for us but for the world, and that a better spirit may influence the nations," she wrote just before Christmas. "None can think of the weeks which led up to the crisis without pain and horror.... And at least in counting up last night the gains of the old year, which brought much trouble and anxiety, we counted as the greatest blessing the months brought the fact that we have been saved from a world war with consequences which cannot be estimated."[35]

Mary was referring to Prime Minister Chamberlain's flying visit to Munich in September 1938, in which Hitler agreed to sign a peace treaty between the United Kingdom and Germany in exchange for British acceptance of Nazi Germany's annexation of parts of Czechoslovakia. Chamberlain later made a speech saying that he had brought about "peace for our time." Yet few Britons believed him, and many opposed the agreement itself. Winston Churchill would famously remark, "England has been offered a choice between war and shame. She has chosen shame, and will get war."

In the days leading up to the Munich crisis, there were real fears that Germany would declare war on Britain and bomb British cities. Civilian defence measures were quickly put into action. Miles of trenches were dug in London parks to act as air-raid shelters, and over a few days, all

British residents were measured for respirators. Many who recalled the use of poison gas in the First World War believed that this weapon would be used against British civilians. Air Raid Precautions (ARP) wardens were called into action, distributing gas masks and providing people with information about how to protect themselves.

"The defense of civilians is the one [service] in which I am interested at the moment," wrote Mary, who was now one of those wardens.[36] She — like many who had lived through the Great War — believed that the Munich agreement had simply postponed an inevitable conflict with Germany. Despite the fact that "peace for our time" had been declared by Chamberlain, the ARP and other civilian defence measures continued after Hitler had signed the agreement. Mary and her fellow wardens went house-to-house in their neighbourhoods, providing people with special government-issued boxes in which to carry their gas masks, and taking a census of the number of people in each home for future use in the event of bombing raids.

LONDON, England, March 1939. "The visit, literally a flying visit of the famous woman who is head of all the women's organizations in Germany, has brought forward the question, 'Do we in England want one woman to represent us?'" Mary was describing the four-day visit of Frau Gertrud Scholtz-Klink, leader of the National Socialist Women's League in Nazi Germany. Scholtz-Klink was a leading Nazi appointed by Hitler to promote his views on women, including the need for German women to produce more children and care for their households. Scholtz-Klink visited the Women's League of Health and Beauty (WLHB), Lapswood Training School for Girls, the South London Hospital for Women, and the Mothercraft Training Society.

While in Britain, Scholtz-Klink spent time with Lady Douglas-Hamilton (also known as Prunella Stack), who was a leading proponent of women's physical fitness in the service of the nation. She was the head of the WLHB, an organization dedicated to "racial health." Stack had visited Germany in 1938 for a Physical Education Congress, where she and some of the League women watched German physical education demonstrations and where she reputedly gave the Nazi salute. Stack was also married to Lord David Douglas-Hamilton, a member of the Anglo-German Fellowship, an upper-class right-wing group. Many of its members were openly pro-Nazi and anti-Semitic. The organization had invited Scholtz-Klink to "study the work done by and for English women," but in reality planned to use her visit to promote the connections between the two nations. The Fellowship also sponsored a formal dinner at Claridge's for the Nazi women's leader during her visit.[37]

Mary MacLeod Moore was clearly unimpressed by Scholtz-Klink's visit. "In Germany, this lady is the acknowledged head of 40,000,000 women and girls. All the organisations with which women are connected are under her control, and nothing can be done as regards changes and courses of action that has not her consent.... Such a position, one would imagine, is possible only in a dictator country, as in a democracy differences of opinion as to the best woman for the post would be discussed aloud and in public and not only in whispers."

The fact that Scholtz-Klink only visited a few women's organizations — traditional, non-feminist organizations — disturbed Mary. "We have a great number of women's organisations, of which the woman leader from Germany was obviously able to visit only a few, or even to learn of the work of a comparatively small number," she wrote. "A longer stay might have given her a better idea of what is being done in this country by women, not under compulsion, and under no control but the constitution of their society and the rules by which anyone is governed." Scholtz-Klink was nothing but a kind of dictator, according to Mary. "But how would we respond to the idea of a woman chief over all women's organisations? With complete disapproval, I imagine. True, we have the National Council of Women, which includes many organisations of all kinds, but the officers are in no sense dictators, so that question does not arise."[38]

Mary did not like the news she was hearing about the atrocities going on in Nazi Germany. She had met many Jewish refugees who had fled to Britain in the wake of the Kristallnacht pogrom and was horrified. She was well aware of the struggle they faced — Britain was not very welcoming to Jewish refugees (authorities would famously turn away a ship filled with Jewish exiles in May, sending them back to Germany and certain death).

However, others managed to gain entry as domestics, students, and on work visas. By September 1939 there would be seventy thousand of these exiles from terror in Britain.

"One wonders, as one hears a man and a woman speaking in a foreign language, if they have left behind them loved relatives who may be cut off from them for years, and of whose lives these emigrants to England may know nothing, but fear the worst," wrote Mary. "One thinks too, though it is a point seldom stressed, of the grief it must be to those who have known no other nationality, and whose forbears belonged to one country for generations, to find themselves people without a country, disowned by their native land, exiled, and compelled to begin again. Whatever they have suffered in that land from which they have been driven out in pain and humiliation, many must be homesick for countries lost forever." One woman interviewed by Mary told her, "Now we have no country. Our Germany is gone."[39]

WARSAW, Poland, September 1939. German troops had swarmed into Poland. Hitler had been planning this attack since his forces had occupied the remainder of Czechoslovakia in March. In the days leading up to that country's dismemberment, Britain had pursued a policy of appeasement with Germany. Now that would change. Britain and France had sworn to defend Poland, and sent ultimatums to Hitler demanding his withdrawal from that country. Hitler declined to respond. On September 3, just as Mary was settling down to enjoy her Sunday dinner, Prime Minister Chamberlain announced that Britain was once again at war with Germany. Just as she had in 1914, Mary supported the government's decision. "And we, all around the world, who are British, are proud as never before of the leaders who have spoken with no uncertain voice about our duty to our friends and to the whole world, to destroy Hitlerism, which means tyranny and the crushing of all freedom of speech and action."[40]

"Those who listened the other night to a broadcast of a soldiers' concert must have felt a pang as they heard the old war songs and realized that the sons of the men who once sang those words are now giving themselves to the cause which we hope will win a better and a safer world," Mary wrote a few months later. It was now the time of the "phony war." British troops were not yet engaged in fighting, but everywhere there were signs that violent conflict was imminent. Training camps had been set up, Canadian soldiers were once again wandering the streets of London, and vans with loudspeakers were driving through residential neighbourhoods, telling people where they could go to get gas masks. Great War–style trenches continued to be dug in the parks, and schoolchildren were being evacuated to the countryside. Sixty-eight-year-old Mary, in her role as an ARP warden, was handing out gas masks to endless anxious queues of Londoners.

As she knocked on doors and measured children for gas masks, Mary was flooded with emotions and memories of the Great War. "Even the songs are Old War, for we hear 'Tipperary,' the 'Long Trail' and 'If You were the Only Girl' with a feeling of homesickness for another world. And sailors, soldiers and airmen still need socks, scarves, and caps; the hospitals still want supplies of all kinds towards the days when the wounded arrive." Women were once again applying to do war work — "learning to drive ambulances in the dark, wearing gas masks" and training to "do work which would release a man for more urgent duty." It was all too familiar.

This new war would be fought differently, with new technology. "What is different is the invention of the radio — so that people know what is going on overseas much more quickly; flying is now more commonplace. Women [are] once again ready to play a role; perhaps even much more active than in the previous war," she wrote. "War must affect thousands of women — indeed, hundreds of thousands — in various ways. Those who listened to a deeply interesting broadcast on the subject the other night heard of the difficulties of the teacher who is evacuated, of the woman writer and artist, and, saddest of all, of the refugee." Some things hadn't changed.

LONDON, England, December 1939. It was the first Christmas of the war, but no candles were flickering in the windows of London homes. Instead, blackout curtains shrouded windows and doors. In her weekly column, Mary described how Red Cross, St. John Ambulance, and ARP volunteers were spending hours at their first-aid posts, despite having nothing serious to do. Their inactivity made them the butt of jokes and criticism. The public was clearly becoming apathetic about the risks entailed by the war. Evacuated children and women were returning to London, and few people were carrying their gas masks.[41]

"When the King spoke on Christmas Day to his great family scattered around the world, he was thinking, as we all are, of what a new year may bring. 'If it brings peace,' said the King, 'how thankful we shall be. If it brings continued struggle we shall remain undaunted.... We shall bear whatever comes and remain undaunted and determined, united, and so far as the great majority is concerned, uncomplaining.'"

Mary had predictions of her own. "We look at the blank pages of the diaries and the engagement books with which we were dowered a few days ago and wonder, as one wonders every year, what the months will bring. Victory, one hopes. Courage and strength to carry on without the weakness of looking back and fretting for what is past. Sympathy and tenderness for those who suffer, and patience with those who strain that virtue. A largeness of mind which puts the work for the country's good first and ignores personal wrongs and slights. And we may be forgiven for hoping that those months may see from time to time a little pleasure, some happiness, and much hope."

LONDON, England, March 1940. In Mary's mind, there was little doubt about the nature of Britain's enemy. "While the Great War was going on and for all the years since it ended, we have been hearing that the older men threw the young into the hell of suffering and misery that had to be endured, and that the aftermath of that suffering was due to the selfishness and lack of imagination of a generation which did not itself fight. Now Lord Halifax puts on record that if the lamps are burning dim, if not actually going out, it is not due primarily to the selfishness and mistakes of an older generation but to a movement which is a Youth movement — Nazi youth. Our young men and our girls who are suffering too, both now and because of all which war must take from them, are fighting their own generation, which, because of evil guides and false ideals, has brought this calamity upon the world."[42] The flowers of Britain were once again to fall on the battlefield while, according to Mary, many of the survivors of the First World War were often being rejected for war service.

The record of Mary MacLeod Moore's life in journalism ends with the *Sunday Times* column "Home Front on Holiday," dated March 31, 1940; no further articles appear in *Saturday Night Magazine*. There was no "closing column," no explanation of why she was no longer writing for the *Sunday Times*. Perhaps her job was a victim of the war. The newspaper had the number of its pages cut by wartime paper restrictions from eighteen to twelve pages, and Mary's columns had shrunk from an average of fifteen hundred words in the 1920s to three hundred and fifty by the late '30s.

Mary may have also decided to leave London at the height of the war. Maps showing the impact of German bombing raids on the city reveal that the neighbourhood where she lived was badly affected, although Mary's apartment building emerged unscathed. Her will provides a tantalizing clue that she might have evacuated herself to Canada. She left money to fifteen relatives and friends in her homeland, "as a small token of affection and great appreciation for the kindness and sympathy extended to me during the war years and afterwards...."

Whatever the case, Mary's literary output abruptly ended, and she does not appear to have contributed to any publication after her relationship with the *Sunday Times* came to a close.

Since no papers exist for Mary for the remainder of her life, her biography essentially ends where her life as an active journalist ends. What remain are census records that reveal that in the late 1950s, Mary MacLeod Moore (Rees) entered the Belgravia Nursing Home in London, where she passed away quietly on February 26, 1960. She was eighty-nine.

Mary MacLeod Moore's funeral was a quiet affair, attended by her stepdaughter-in-law and a few friends. Her obituary recalled that the once well-known writer had "contributed to the *Sunday Times* under the pen name Pandora and worked as a journalist in Montreal, New York and London."[43] She was laid to rest under a tall stone Celtic cross in the Westminster Cemetery alongside her husband and mother. Unlike theirs, her name does not appear anywhere on the memorial.

At the close of the Great War, Mary wrote that "only the forgotten really die." The men who lost their lives were "part of the fabric of a new and better and nobler world; their example a portion of the great heritage of all Canadian children." Perhaps the same could be said of Mary, who — although seemingly forgotten — managed to leave behind an enduring record of the struggle of ordinary women and men to build a better world in the most trying of times.[44]

Chapter 12

Elizabeth Montizambert

Memory is like a basket full of flames.

— José Martí

GLOUCESTERSHIRE, England, August 1959. Elizabeth sat on the steel chair, back straight, hands folded in her lap. Her silver hair was carefully arranged, pearls at her throat, skirt and blouse neatly pressed. If it weren't for the report lying in front of the doctor, he would have assumed she was waiting for her prescriptions to be renewed, not for admission to an asylum for the mentally ill.

"I worked as a journalist in Paris," she said simply, her voice clear, watery grey eyes staring directly into his. "I know my memory is occasionally faulty, but I am quite capable of looking after myself. I have several assignments to finish. I would like to be driven back to my flat as soon as possible." She spoke with assurance, a woman used to getting her way.

This time, however, Elizabeth wouldn't be allowed to do what she wanted. After Harold Gibb died in 1941, she and Noel (Harold's widow) had continued their close friendship. When Elizabeth began to experience the usual infirmities of old age, the younger Noel had offered support and practical help. That burden became much heavier when Elizabeth began slowly slipping into dementia. The decline had started in 1955, when she was still enjoying a busy freelance career. It began with slips of memory and problems completing conversations. Gradually, she started to forget where she lived, and was unable to navigate streets she had known like the back of her hand. By 1957, Elizabeth had stopped writing altogether, and couldn't retain what she was reading. When friends gently asked if she was all right, she became angry and withdrawn.

Noel arranged for someone to stay with her at night in the expensive Knightsbridge flat, but this didn't prevent Elizabeth from slipping out during the day, wandering the streets of London. Finally, Noel, sixty-seven years old herself, couldn't cope any longer. She convinced her old friend that she was taking her for a drive in the country. Instead, there was a long ride to an expensive asylum in the Cotswolds. Noel had arranged for Elizabeth to be admitted to the Barnwood Institute, famous for its treatment of Great War poet Ivor Gurney. The hospital (according to its advertisements) was dedicated to "the care and treatment of ladies and gentlemen suffering from nervous and mental disorders.... Special accommodation is also provided at three villa residences, all of which stand in their own grounds and are entirely separate from the main Hospital. All the most modern methods of treatment including electric shock and prefrontal leucotomy are used."[1]

The doctor courteously asked Elizabeth a series of questions, jotting her responses (and his analyses) into a thick medical file. He noted that she was still distressed about the separation of her parents over fifty years earlier and that her fondest memories were connected with her work in Paris during the First World War. In those tumultuous years she had been full of vitality, courage, and independence. She would now turn to her intermittent and scattered recollections of that luminous time for comfort as she faced the inexorable decline of her body and mind.

PARIS, France, January 1919. Elizabeth was sipping tea at a small linen-covered table at Ciro's. It was early evening, but every one of the thirty-five tables was crowded with people. On the minuscule dance floor, Parisians were swinging their hips and thrusting their legs and arms into the air as they danced the "black bottom." The scents of Shalimar and Amour Amour mingled with sweat, while chiffon and tulle flew through the air like clouds; it was hard to tell who was dancing with whom. The seven-piece jazz band crowded into the corner shifted back and forth in time to a syncopated rhythm, the saxophonist swinging his instrument as fast as the dancers shimmying past him.

Before the war, Elizabeth would have found the gathering energizing, and been busily noting who was present, what they were wearing, and where the next fashion trends were going. Tonight, however, she felt only disgust as she scanned the dance floor. "[I]t seems as if the past four years had been utterly wiped out as soon as I entered the long narrow room which has now been enlarged to include another *salle* for its numerous customers," she wrote. "There were the same painted faces with eyes that ogled the same fat men with necks that bulged over the fur of their fur collars, the same vapid young men with olive complexions proclaiming them neutrals and nothing was wanted except a scarlet-coated Hungarian band and the cakes and sandwiches of other days to complete the pre-war illusion.... But if the profiteers *de la guerre* are so much in evidence, the war has certainly had a different effect on the great majority of the people who have suffered by its terrors, as well as the lesser number of those to whom it has surely brought a measure of happiness and prosperity of which they could never otherwise have dreamed."[2]

The men who had made their millions out of wartime industry could now flaunt their wealth openly. It sickened Elizabeth, for whom the human cost of war was still front-and-centre — 1,400,000 French soldiers killed, 1,100,000 disabled, three hundred thousand mutilated. Her beloved Paris was once again the city of light, but its new sparkle was illuminating the gaping wounds that the war had left behind.

PARIS, France, April 1919. A copy of *L'Oeuvre*, a left-leaning newspaper famous for its brilliant editorials, was spread across Elizabeth's desk. She was scanning it — and a dozen other Paris newspapers — for news and opinions relevant to the Paris Peace Conference. When she was finished, she would condense, translate, and type up the information for Prime Minister David Lloyd George, now in Paris for the conference,[3] delivering her translation each morning to the Hôtel Majestic where the British delegation was being housed.

"The Étoile quarter is almost entirely British since the huge Hôtel Majestic and its annex have been taken over to lodge all the members of the Conference," she wrote. The hotel's rooms were now filled with the army of typists, secretaries, and experts who had accompanied Lloyd George. One floor had been transformed into a hospital in case any members of the delegation should become ill. With the Spanish flu now sweeping through Europe, they couldn't take any chances with England's peacemakers.

The British delegation also had to be protected from crazed assassins and intrepid journalists. Even Elizabeth found herself having to run a gauntlet of security personnel each day as she delivered the morning's news. "The hotel is carefully guarded from the casual visitor. No one may enter without a pass and even if they are armed with such a document, they are only allowed to enter the ground floor; the passes are issued by security officers whose task must be no sinecure."[4]

The Peace Conference was a media event, with five hundred journalists in Paris covering the story. In the past, publicity surrounding affairs of state had been rigidly controlled.[5] The war had changed all that. The public had a tremendous stake in the proceedings and would no longer be content with tersely worded government announcements.

Having covered the war from start to finish, Elizabeth was deeply troubled about the growing misunderstandings between Britain and France being expressed at the Conference. "The French feel that they are not securing justice unless Germany is made to pay 140,000,000 francs for the damages to the country and 78,000,000 for pensions," she would later tell a Canadian press club. "It aroused their indignation to have people say that Germany was in no condition to pay, for the French believe that Germany would be able to pay later and they do not believe the price they pay then should be based on their present lack of funds."[6] Germany had not experienced anything like the destruction that France had endured, with its fields and villages torn apart by the war. It was little wonder that the French could not countenance any peace settlement that might ease Germany's burden of reparations in the decades following the Great War.

LONDON, England, 1919. Elizabeth was back in London. The *Montreal Gazette* had asked her to take on the role of London editor and she was glad to return to the city where she had spent so many happy years. She would write a monthly column entitled "Budget of London Topics," as well as assign and edit work by other journalists. In the busy interwar years Elizabeth would also write a syndicated column for the *Toronto Mail and Empire*, *Winnipeg Free Press*, *Gazette*, and *Vancouver Province*.

Elizabeth's work inevitably involved immersing herself in the city's busy social scene. There were lavish receptions at Lady Dunedin's mansion, dinners with Canada's high commissioner, and luncheon parties at the home of the prime minister. These glittering events brought maharajahs, ambassadors, royals, famous authors, and lords and ladies into Elizabeth's orbit and gave her plenty of fodder for her columns. She hadn't been able to focus on anything but the war for years; now she was immersing herself in current issues, art, music, and literature. She had also begun to explore her long-standing interest in London's rich social and cultural history by researching a book she would eventually call *Unnoticed London*.

Unnoticed London was "meant for the people who do not realise one-eighth of the stories packed into the streets of London, the city, which as Sir Walter Besant, that great London lover, once said, has an unbroken history of one thousand years and has never been sacked by an enemy," wrote Elizabeth. The book was intended for people who wanted to go beyond the usual tourist haunts and really see the London that she knew — the cobblestoned side streets, the ancient buildings, unknown museums, churches, and palaces. The book, pocket-sized with a deep-red cover, was filled with carefully researched information written in an appealing and conversational style. Tourists loved it;

within two months of publication, the first run was sold out. It would be reprinted five times.

Despite enjoying a busy and satisfying career in peacetime, Elizabeth, like most people, still couldn't escape from the memory of the war. It was in evidence everywhere; as she strolled to her office on St. Martin's Lane each day, she passed former soldiers standing on street corners, holding out trays of violets or lilies.[7] High rates of unemployment had forced many into transitory, menial jobs. Discouragement and anger, together with the lingering effects of acute wartime trauma, led to increased rates of alcoholism and violent behaviour.

Disabled veterans were having an even tougher time. "One of the most interesting of the groups of people who are co-operating to help the ex-Service men is the Friends of the Poor, who have a Disabled Soldiers Industry Branch at 42 Ebury Street," wrote Elizabeth. "There is absolutely nothing in this delightful little shop to show that the exquisite things it contains were made by men whose hands were once far more accustomed to handle a rifle than a needle."[8] Such "make work" schemes must have been galling for men accustomed to living life on a razor's edge during the war.

Many ex-servicemen suffered from psychological ill health, but few medical records survive that would illuminate their experience during this period. One Canadian statistic does indicate the depth of discouragement they were experiencing: in 1919 nearly 40 percent of reported suicides involved veterans.[9]

LONDON, England, January 1922. "Dear Miss Fischer, I have tried many times since your concert to get you on the telephone to arrange an interview, but always without success. I hear that you are leaving London shortly, and would be glad if you could see me tomorrow, Wednesday, the 1st February at a quarter to three...." Elizabeth was writing to Sarah Fischer, a twenty-five-year-old Canadian soprano who had recently made her London debut at the Old Vic as the Countess in Mozart's *Marriage of Figaro*. Always eager to promote Canadian artists, Elizabeth wanted to meet the rising young star.

Born in France and raised in Canada, Fischer was a statuesque woman with dark hair swept back from her face and a predilection for flowing gowns and capes. She came from humble beginnings; her father was a hatmaker, and she had first studied music at nights while working days as a telephone operator. In 1917, Fischer won a scholarship to study at the Royal College of Music, but because of the war was not able to claim the prize until 1919. In the interim, she studied and performed in Montreal and Quebec City. After the armistice she made her way to London, where she made friends with diva Emma Albani and began studying with prominent voice teachers. Fischer's talent was quickly noticed, and she was invited to join the British National Opera Company, where she sang the role of Micaëla in *Carmen* and debuted at Covent Garden in the role of Pamina in Mozart's *The Magic Flute*.

Despite these successes, Fischer faced some challenges. She was Jewish and reportedly lesbian,[10] two qualities that could have made her life difficult in the homophobic and anti-Semitic third decade of the twentieth century. She needed all the social contacts she could get to help propel her career forward, and Elizabeth was just the kind of person to make that happen. The two met early the next day at the breakfast table at Queen Alexandra's House, the women's residence at the Royal College of Music. As they chatted over coffee and soft rolls, they developed an instant rapport, and Elizabeth would become "a close and dear friend," according to Fischer,[11] introducing the talented young woman to people who could help her career.

It is not surprising the two women hit it off. Elizabeth may have had a privileged upbringing, but it had been a bohemian one in which she was exposed to all kinds of challenging ideas. Although we cannot say with any certainty that she herself was homosexual, many of her friends were. It was also abundantly clear that Sarah's Jewish identity would never stand in the way of their friendship. Quite the opposite; according to Fischer, Elizabeth introduced her not only to Lady Boscowen and Lady Northcote, but also to Lord Balfour. Balfour, an old acquaintance of Elizabeth's, was the author of the 1917 Balfour Declaration advocating the establishment of a national home for the Jews in Palestine. Elizabeth was keenly interested in that cause, attending parties with Lord and Lady Snowden and "noted men in the

Zionist movement,"[12] and commenting frequently on the situation in the Middle East.

LONDON, England, May 1924. Cicely Hamilton was back in London, writing and producing plays. Many of them — such as *The Child in Flanders: A Nativity Play* — were based on her wartime experiences. Hamilton, now sharing a house with her sister Evelyn, was struggling to make a living as a freelance writer. Publications often tried to avoid paying her after they had her copy in hand, and on at least one occasion she had to appeal to the Society of Authors to get the publisher of the *English Review* to pay her the pre-war rate of four guineas per thousand words for an article they had accepted. The Society intervened, and Cicely received her paycheque.

Cicely and Elizabeth frequently spent time together, with Elizabeth trying to help in whatever ways she could to enable her friend to make ends meet. Cicely repaid her by throwing her support behind Elizabeth's own projects. In 1924, Elizabeth's newest book, *London Discoveries in Shops and Restaurants*, was launched, and Cicely wrote a foreword heartily endorsing it.

"The accompanying volume literally bristles with information which the average Londoner might have acquired for himself — and which he very certainly hasn't," wrote Hamilton. "In future, when threatened with country cousins or overseas acquaintance, it is my firm intention to spend a previous hour or two in perusal of Miss Montizambert's pages; arising from their study primed with all that needs to be known anent [about] restaurants, hat shops, and the like." The book was exactly what Cicely suggested — a literary travel guide outlining some of the best places to buy everything from silk stockings to Ravenscourt pottery to French-language novels. London stalwarts like Gunter's Confectioners, which would disappear before the century was out, were described alongside businesses that would survive into the new millennium — famous names, including Harvey Nichols and Harrods.

The book revealed how Elizabeth liked to spend her time in post-war London. She still loved good food and wine, and *London Discoveries* listed her favourite haunts. Lunch often found her at the Green Tea Rooms on

Piccadilly or at the Ritz on St. James Street. For dinner, she might enjoy a "Spanish dish" at Joan's in Knightsbridge, the neighbourhood in which she lived. French shops such as the Galeries Lafayette and La Librairie Française were like a breath of Paris to Elizabeth, who missed the sophisticated society of the French capital.

Elizabeth's interest in art continued unabated, and an average afternoon might find her at the Alpine Club in Savile Row seeing an exhibition of Augustus John's paintings or going to a "private view" at the Leicester Galleries at the southeast corner of Leicester Square. According to Elizabeth, whenever "an exhibition of Max Beerbohm's drawings or Epstein's sculptures is presented, [it] brings together in the small rooms a gathering of people almost as interesting as the works of art."[13]

Fashion wasn't overlooked either; Elizabeth was still queen of the runways, whether in Paris or London. Predictably, she favoured Elspeth Phelps, the British couturier who designed for royalty during the first part of the twentieth century. "She has dressed all the famous actresses for the last twenty-one years; the first dress she designed was for Miss Ellen Terry, and she still designs personally for her own customers those eminently wearable frocks that are miracles of beauty and smartness."[14] Phelps's designs often appeared in *Vogue,* and she was one of the wealthiest and most successful dressmakers of the age. Elizabeth took a page out of Phelps's book, wearing smart, tailored dresses, thick fox furs, and elegant velvet hats decorated with plumes of feathers.

Nearly a century later, *London Discoveries* would continue to be used, not by shoppers or visitors to London, but as a detailed guidebook for grateful social scientists eager to plan their own journeys into the history of London's rich commercial and cultural scene of the 1920s.

LONDON, England, July 1928. Elizabeth's family had scattered to the winds. In 1916 her sister Beatrice had moved to an upscale apartment on West 57th Street in New York, where she exhibited watercolour portraits in a show by the Watercolor Club. By 1920 she had moved back to Montreal, where she joined the National Association of Women Painters and Sculptors and enjoyed a successful career painting miniatures for prominent members of the Quebec social scene.[15] Edith, the sister who had not pursued a profession, had moved to Berkshire to live with their mother, who began a slow decline into dementia and needed constant care. Elizabeth made frequent trips to visit them both, but in June 1924 that came to an end with the death of her mother at the age of seventy-four. Alice's death freed Edith to return to Canada. With the ties of family loosened, Elizabeth was now even freer to enjoy life in post-war London.

In her columns for the *Gazette*, Elizabeth described a day in the life of the capital that would be hard to imagine nearly one hundred years later. "I was crossing the road by Storey's Gate into St. James Park when I noticed in front of me a lady in a long blue dress with an unusually long skirt. Coming toward her was a small group of school children whose faces lighted up with pleasure when they caught sight of Mrs. Baldwin, the wife of the Prime Minister, who stopped to chat for some minutes."[16]

Elizabeth's article then went on to describe the nearby "open-air school" that Mrs. Baldwin was planning to visit. Such schools were being established across Britain for "delicate" children — those suffering from tuberculosis. Deaths due to the disease had risen steadily during the First World War, from 135 per 100,000 in 1913 to 169 in 1918. The idea behind the schools was a simple one: disease, it was believed, was the result of overcrowded, unsanitary conditions. Children affected by TB would be given the chance to spend much of their day outside as possible, getting fresh air. They would sleep in wards that were open to the elements and attend classrooms set up outdoors. The schools were residential, and some children would live there for much of their childhoods, while others stayed only for short periods.

This was, of course, only one of many actions taken to address the disease at this time. Infant and antenatal clinics were established to monitor infant and maternal health, and sanatoriums were built for those suffering from the disease. There would be a salaried midwife service introduced in 1936, and concerted effort to clear slums and build better housing. The result would be a fall in the TB mortality rate from 9.42 per 100,000 in 1922 to 6.12 in 1936.[17]

Elizabeth's article suggests that the schools were a progressive idea that needed to be celebrated. However, it is her simple description of a prime minister's wife, without bodyguards, unattended, not followed by a horde of journalists, that in some senses summed up the age — a time in Britain of innocent hope, rebuilding, peace, and health, a new world in the making. The economic collapse of the 1930s, the rise of dictators across Europe, and growing tensions among nations would soon sweep away that hope and replace it with a deepening realization that Britain and her allies would be forced to turn their human and material resources to fighting another global war.

LONDON, England, November 1931. The stars of London's rich theatre, literary, and feminist world were gathered around linen-covered tables at the Florence Restaurant. Hosted by Nigel Playfair, the actor-manager of the Lyric Theatre, the guests included novelist Ernest Raymond, actors Norman Kinnel, May Whitty, and Jean Cadell, and feminist and pacifist novelist Winifred Holtby. Elizabeth wouldn't have missed the celebration for the world. Speaker after speaker praised Hamilton's novels and plays: "Always an original thinker and a little ahead of her time, [Cicely Hamilton] has never had the recognition she deserved, but her work as a journalist and her delightful Christmas plays *The Beggar Prince* and *The Child in Flanders* are gradually winning their way all over the world because of their intrinsic worth."[18]

Cicely's friends also knew that she lived on a shoestring. Her freelance writing was sporadic, and her novels and plays brought her small returns. To make matters worse, her sister Evelyn had moved out in 1929, leaving the writer little kitchen equipment and only a few sticks of furniture. Elizabeth lent Cicely some furniture and canvased friends such as Winnifred Holtby to help fill other gaps. "That nefarious woman Elizabeth Montizambert, not content with spending a lot of time and furniture upon me, has now gone around blackmailing my friends on my behalf!" wrote Cicely to Winnifred. "Really, she ought not to, but the result is so magnificent that I can't be as angry with her as I ought to be. I never thought to have such knives and forks and spoons — I had Christmas dinner for four and they looked splendid!"[19]

Cicely would continue selflessly writing about issues she cared about — feminism, pacifism, the rise in fascism, and the difficulties faced by women seeking employment. But she was slowing down, and would face an even greater struggle to support herself. As a result of continued lobbying by Elizabeth and Cicely's other friends, in 1938 the writer would be granted a civil-list pension for her services to the Crown — in her case, the courageous work she did during the war years, and her continued concern for the poorest members of society.

LONDON, England, February 1934. "The expression of opinion throughout the British Commonwealth has today an enhanced value due to the fact that freedom of expression is under a ban in three great European countries, Russia, Italy, and Germany," wrote Elizabeth. The shadow of "Hitlerism" had begun to cross Europe, and her February column was dense with descriptions of political debates dedicated to issues such as disarmament, the German labour camp movement, and pacifism. Once more, her concern was with her beloved France, its government now deeply concerned about the growing militarism within Nazi Germany.

"The press has given prominence, naturally, to the problems of the French cabinet, the German reply to the French aide memoire on disarmament, the memorandum containing the British government's disarmament proposals, and the Nazi activity in Austria." In January, France had sent a letter to Germany demanding that it cease arming itself in contravention to the Treaty of Versailles. Germany had refused unless France would likewise disarm. British interventions between the two countries were, for the most part, weak and ineffective. Elizabeth, who covered the parliamentary debates on disarmament for the *Gazette*, was deeply concerned. Well aware of the persecution by Germany of its own citizens, she believed that war was highly likely. "Where great powers show themselves active, ruthless and not conscience-stricken in taking the blood of their own people," she wrote, "the moral force which should dissuade them from bloodshed in war seems but an ebb tide."[20]

Elizabeth was a member of the League of Nations Union, an organization formed in October 1918 to promote international justice and a permanent peace among nations based upon the ideals of the League of Nations, which had been created by the Allies as a result of the Paris Peace Treaties at the end of the First World War. But the League became discredited when it averted its eyes in October 1935 after Italy invaded Abyssinia, a fellow League member. Such inaction appalled Elizabeth, who believed that in light of growing militarism on the part of Germany and Italy, the government should strengthen its military and build up its stock of armaments. The fact that the government was hesitant to raise the money it needed by taxing people in hard economic times was short-sighted, according to Elizabeth. "In the present condition of affairs, the peace that the whole world longs for is only to be obtained if we are prepared to pay the price for it. It won't drop into our mouths."

LONDON, England, June 1936. *Michael's London* was finished. It described the adventures of a small boy and his governess as they visited some of London's most interesting historic sites. The book was essentially a guide to the capital designed for children by someone deeply concerned about the preservation and promotion of art, literature, and culture. "I feel very strongly that the present day child is liable to grow up with a very distorted idea of Beauty, surrounded as he is with Mickey Mouse and Dismal Desmonds and Golliwogs, so I want the illustrations in this book to have a vigorous loveliness with none of the abnormal monstrosities for which they have no innate liking," wrote Elizabeth to her publisher, Hamish Hamilton. Disney would prove her wrong — children would indeed have an "innate liking" for Mickey Mouse.

In *Michael's London*, a boy named Michael travelled around London with his governess, Maretta. Together they listened to the story of

Cleopatra's Needle, went on a scavenger hunt in St. James Park, and played under the statue of King Charles in Trafalgar Square. The book received excellent reviews and would become a popular school award. Together with *Unnoticed London* it would lead to an unexpected honour for Elizabeth: in the late 1930s she would be one of the few women to be made an honorary member of the Royal Institute of British Architects.

After *Michael's London* was published, Elizabeth was commissioned to write another children's book, this time for London Transport. *London Adventure* was part of their "London-in-your-pocket" series and was designed for young people touring the city with their parents. It was a scaled-down version of *Michael's London*, with the same protagonist. The inexpensive guidebook was part of an overall strategy by London Transport to help reignite the local economy with tourist dollars. Unfortunately, the pocket guide would be published in 1939, when urban tourism would be the last thing on people's minds.

―

VIMY, France, July 1936. Elizabeth looked down the rolling park flowing down from Vimy Ridge. The landscape was in sharp contrast to the giant memorial, with its slices of gleaming limestone soaring into the sky and twenty giant figures representing faith, justice, peace, honour, charity, truth, knowledge, and hope looming over the crowds below. Over one hundred thousand people had come to the unveiling of the memorial, including more than eight thousand Canadian veterans of the 1917 battle. Widows and mothers, British and French ex-servicemen, and hundreds of children were settled wherever they could best witness the ceremony marking the battle that had taken nearly thirty-six hundred Canadian lives.

Elizabeth may have been thinking of one life in particular. Her cousin Violet Walker (the daughter of her Uncle Frederick) had lost her oldest son, Norman, at Vimy on April 13, 1917. A graduate of Upper Canada College, he had enlisted in 1915. He was just twenty years old when he was killed. Elizabeth might well have felt she was representing her cousin as she stood in the shadow of the great memorial.

The two-hundred-and-fifty-acre park that surrounded the monument was covered with tufts of grass that barely disguised the pock-marked landscape where the Canadians had fought so many years before. It had taken nearly three years to remove the majority of the war detritus from the area. Deep beneath the ground, unexploded munitions, old wartime tunnels, and bits of human beings remained buried, while some trench systems were already being preserved for the battlefield tourists and historians of the future.

Elizabeth listened intently as Canada's minister of justice, Ernest Lapointe, declared that the "grandest tribute we could offer to Canadian soldiers is to affirm that their sacrifices have contributed to the introduction into our civilization of its highest modern conception — that of universal Peace founded on recognition of the basic right of people to life and justice."

King Edward VIII spoke briefly. Then he pulled a cord to release the Union Jack, revealing the statue of "Mother Canada," her head bent as she overlooked the Douai Plain, the strategic objective so many Canadians had died to achieve. Then the plaintive sound of the "Last Post" filled the air, while veterans removed their ceremonial berets and wiped tears from their faces.

LONDON, England, August 1937. Despite the terrible downturn in the country's economy during the Depression, Elizabeth was still able to live at a fashionable address in Westminster and hold expensive luncheons for friends. It took a lot of effort to maintain that lifestyle; Elizabeth worked full-time and carried a heavy load of freelance writing. Her correspondence with book publishers and magazine editors reveals a successful writer who demanded (and received) higher fees for her work than many of her colleagues.[21] The archives of publishers Hamish Hamilton and J.M. Dent and Sons bulged with correspondence from her ensuring that her royalties reflected her status as a prominent journalist and that adequate attention was paid to the proper production and promotion of her books.

Elizabeth was exacting in her expectations, and angry when she didn't get the response she expected from editors and reviewers. Writing to

Hamish Hamilton, she says, "I have had 24 [reviews] so far and send you the list.... All were complimentary except a catty one in the *Catholic Herald*, whose writer had, I suppose, discovered from my praise of Edward VI that I do not belong to the church...."[22]

Despite her heavy workload, Elizabeth still managed to keep in close touch with her wartime acquaintances. She enjoyed luncheons with friends such as Evelyn Baird Murray OBE, who had overseen King George and Queen Mary's Club for the Overseas Forces; Louise Weiss, author of memoirs about the First World War; and Lieutenant-Colonel Oswald Balfour, the nephew of the former prime minister and a champion of the movement for a Jewish homeland.[23]

Elizabeth also regularly returned to France, where she often stayed with her close friends Prince Reginald and Princess Marie de Croÿ. The de Croÿ estate was located near Mons on the Franco-Belgian border. At the outset of the war, the pair had transformed their château into a Red Cross hospital, and during the occupation had hidden British soldiers on the run from the German army. It was dangerous work, and cost their friend, the nurse Edith Cavell, her life. After Cavell's execution, the Germans imprisoned the princess and sentenced her to ten years of hard labour, keeping her in solitary confinement for nearly two years, during which time her health broke down.

In the decades after the war, de Croÿ's heroism was forgotten. Thankfully, she penned a memoir entitled *Wartime Memories*, which was published in 1932. In 1937 she wrote to Elizabeth asking for help publishing a similar book by an unnamed countess. Elizabeth once again did what she could for her old wartime friends. "I have just had a letter from Princess Marie de Croy asking me to send her the address of a publisher who would care to publish a volume of most amusing and sprightly war memoirs she has just finished translating for a French friend, a countess whose château was in the war zone and saw a great deal of the English H.Q.," she wrote to Hamish Hamilton. "I saw it in manuscript last summer and was interested, but I do not know how much Princess Marie felt bound to omit, as a lot of it was too personal for publication."[24] In her correspondence, Elizabeth did not name the writer of the memoir, nor did she describe the parts of the memoir that may have been omitted as "too personal." Like Elizabeth's own wartime writings, there would always be gaps, especially involving information about some of the more traumatizing moments of the war. Elizabeth, like so many female journalists of her generation, would all too frequently attempt to frame their work as "amusing" and "sprightly" recollections, and it would be up to historians to root out the serious underpinnings of their wartime writing.

LONDON, England, September 1939. Britain was once again at war. In response to Germany's invasion of Poland, Prime Minister Neville Chamberlain had presented an ultimatum to Hitler. On September 3, at 11:00 a.m., Chamberlain announced to the nation that the ultimatum had expired and the country was at war with Germany. Twenty minutes later, the first air-raid sirens were sounded in London. They were a false alarm, but they reminded any Londoner who had lived through the Great War of the very real possibility of destruction raining down from the skies.

Elizabeth was penning a new yet familiar column for the *Gazette*, this time titled "London in Wartime." It would describe her adventures navigating London during air raids and report on the political and social upheavals caused by the war, as well as the day-to-day life of Londoners struggling to eke out an existence on limited rations and without husbands, brothers, and sons.

One silver lining in an otherwise dark time was the return to London of Elizabeth's friend Sarah Fischer. In 1937, Fischer had travelled to Austria to live and work. The *Ottawa Citizen* reported that in February 1938 the soprano was in Salzburg, singing at the Franciscan Church. It was a bittersweet moment, just before Austria was to be subsumed by Nazi Germany. Fischer threaded haunting English, French, and German songs throughout her program. The international flavour of her music would not be lost on her audience; she was performing before a group of Austrian aristocrats, many in their military uniforms.

Her last concert in Austria was a program of Canadian folk songs performed in Vienna. In March, Germany annexed Austria and quickly applied anti-Jewish legislation to the capital, excluding Jews from economic, cultural, and social life. Elizabeth was worried about her friend, and sent a letter urging Sarah to consider moving home. "It seems to me that there is so much that you could do in Canada to set the young on the right path of the 'bel canto' as well as showing the way by example."[25] But it wasn't the *bel canto* so much as the fear that her dear friend would end up in a concentration camp that was uppermost in Elizabeth's mind. In columns as early as 1933, she had been ringing alarm bells about the German persecution of the Jews and supporting relief efforts for those who managed to escape to Britain.[26]

Sarah was fortunate enough to be able to leave and move to London, her Canadian passport in hand. It was tough to find work in the capital, despite Fischer's sterling international record. Covent Garden had been closed for the duration, and just two weeks after the war began, Elizabeth was again urging her friend to consider returning to Canada. "Why don't you do what I have so often wanted you to do … go back and enrich the life of our country with your gift. Surely you could make a good income there as well as be among your own people and though you may be loth [*sic*] to break ties you may have formed over here, yet you would have the deep satisfaction of feeling you are bringing to Canada something she needs. Do think it over and don't stay in this country where you may suffer much. You weren't even on this side in the last war so you have no conception of what a bombed city is like. I was in France and I'd like to spare anyone who can possibly keep out of it."

It was advice that Fischer would eventually heed, but galvanized by her experience in Vienna, she was determined to stay in London for now and contribute to the war effort. She would soon be given that opportunity, gaining a very real "conception of what a bombed city is like" in the process.

LONDON, England, June 1940. England was enjoying the relative peace of the "phony war," but on the Continent, French and British troops were bravely trying to fend off Germany's invasion of France. Elizabeth's predictions about what Britain's lack of military preparedness might cost her were coming true. In early June, the Allies were overpowered, and three hundred thousand British troops were hurriedly evacuated at Dunkirk and another one hundred and fifty thousand from ports along the coast. By June 14, Nazi soldiers were parading in Elizabeth's beloved Paris, and on June 24, France surrendered to Germany and a puppet government was installed in the capital.

Some Britons saw France as traitorous, but not Elizabeth. "I can't write about France," she anguished. "When an English transport driver said to me a few days ago 'aren't you sorry you worked for the French in the last war?' I couldn't answer her. I felt as if she had struck me, and through me all the brave, generous, self-sacrificing French people whose friendship has honoured me."[27]

LONDON, England, October 1940. "Hitler once said 'one cannot overestimate the stupidity of the bourgeoisie.' In Germany, yes, or he would not be where he is. But this week I saw more clearly than ever what a colossal mistake he has always made about this country when I went about London to see some of the many places that have suffered damage after four weeks of intensive bombing," wrote Elizabeth. It was the height of what became known as the Blitz, the bombing campaign that rained destruction and terror on London. It began on the afternoon of September 7, 1940, when German bombers made their first appearance in the skies over London. Previously, their targets had been radar stations and RAF airfields. In an attempt to demoralize the population and force Britain to call for peace, they would now bomb civilian targets. Three hundred and forty-eight bombers and 617 fighter planes would drop bombs on the city for two hours, beginning at 4:00 p.m. After a two-hour-long reprieve, they would start again, blasting targets until 4:30 the next morning.

For the next fifty-seven days, London was bombed day and night. "I saw historic churches [bombed] like St. Giles, St. Dunstan-in-the-East, St. Magnus the Martyr, hospitals like St. Thomas's and the Great Ormonde Street one for children, museums such as the Tate and the

Public Record Office, famous shops and little shops, one of them with the inscription 'Owing to Hitler, our premises is littler.'"[28] These historic buildings, which Elizabeth had described in *Unnoticed London*, now faced certain destruction.

As the bombs dropped and air-raid sirens screamed, Elizabeth often found herself rushing into nearby tube stations where "neat rows of dingy expectant cushions and blankets folded against the wall" were always ready for their nightly tenants, who lived a "troglodyte existence." One afternoon while walking in Westminster, she was also forced to shelter in the underground site of London's only surviving Roman baths, a place she had never visited before. "It took Hitler to show me this curious place and the two-thousand-year-old wooden pipes."[29] The next day she went farther afield, visiting a bombed cathedral-like factory. She watched as men and women worked in the dim and dusty light, sorting and salvaging anything they could from the broken building. "London has now been bombed every night for over a month and the marks of damage inflicted are everywhere," she wrote, "but there are 692 square miles of London filled with stubborn people, and since every bombed church, hospital, shop, or private dwelling only fills them with fiercer determination to win the war, Hitler may as well try and devise some fresh means of shaking their morale."[30]

One morale booster for stressed Londoners was the performances of music and drama that were subsidized by the government. Locals could now "see and hear some of the best talent in town for twelve pence." Myra Hess was holding noon-hour concerts at the National Gallery, the Three Arts Club was providing ballet for a shilling, and Shakespeare was being performed in the Waterloo Road neighbourhood. Elizabeth's old friend Sarah Fischer had also organized a "12:00 Concert Series" at Wigmore Hall, featuring herself and other London-based Canadian artists. After the first few months of the Blitz were over, she would take Elizabeth's advice and return home to support the work of her compatriots, ultimately establishing the Sarah Fischer Concert Series, in which Canadian musicians and new Canadian talent would be presented at four concerts per year. The series would continue until Fischer's death three decades later.

LONDON, England, May 1943. It was a softly warm May afternoon, but instead of flowerbeds, Elizabeth couldn't help but notice the vivid posters covering the wooden hoardings surrounding so many bombed-out homes. There were images of bowls full of potatoes, women cheerily creating new dresses from old, and thick black lettering declaring "Go Easy with Bread, Eat Potatoes Instead," "Don't ride for fun unless your fun is Work," "Wage War with War Savings," "Re-model and Mend Your Old Clothes." But there was also a more serious and heartfelt message for those who had suffered the loss of their homes in the recent blitz: "If you are bombed out of your house and have nowhere to go, ask the Air Warden to direct you to the LCC [London County Council] Rest Centre. Here you will be helped to find another home."

As she stood on the sidewalk, the breeze ruffling the edges of one of the loose posters, Elizabeth suddenly felt old. The bombing, the destruction of the city she loved so well, Londoners taking it on the chin from bombing raids — although at least it wasn't the concentrated, incessant rain of bombs, which had finally ended in May 1941. But already there were rumours of a new, even more devastating German weapon.

Elizabeth tried to shove those thoughts from her mind; she was on her way to interview some young land girls from the "dominions," now volunteering to "do their bit" in the war. It reminded her of that earlier war, interviewing Canadian girls serving as ambulance drivers on the Western front. "Born in London, [Joan West] told me she had lived all her short life in British Columbia. Coming to England on a hiking holiday, covering 800 miles in Southern England, she was caught up by the war, and in spite of not then knowing what a tractor looked like, has been doing successful farm work for 2 ½ years on a farm of 5,000 acres."[31] She would write a chatty article describing the girls with their rosy cheeks and strong backs, ready to help the war effort. But her heart wasn't in it anymore. She was sixty-eight years old, hair grey and wispy, eyes weakening. She was just tired of war.

LONDON, England, July 1944. Hitler's secret weapon was no longer such a secret. The V1, or "doodlebug," was a jet-propelled missile packed with high explosives designed for terror bombing. It made a strange buzzing sound as it made its murderous journey to earth. More than six thousand people would be killed by this new, lethal weapon (another nine thousand would die as a result of its replacement, the more lethal V2). "Great pity that Goebbels can't see for himself the precise effect of this ultimate boomerang, but no doubt he hears and reads enough to enrage him," wrote Elizabeth. Interviewing people standing near the wreckage created by one of the bombs, she reported that "the chief reaction is a deep-seated resentment at the futility of the whole thing, that precious lives should be lost and homes destroyed, merely because the twisted mind saw in such tragedies material for lying propaganda to prop their shaking morale." Britons weren't going to be cowed by this latest threat. "There is no confusion, no panic, no visible sign of the sleepless nights or the work to be faced in the day. This is the bulldog breed that no German will ever, ever understand."[32]

Elizabeth's columns were getting shorter as the war lurched to its end. Her last column ran in December 1944, and after its publication she retreated to the country to rest and recuperate. Retirement from the *Gazette* didn't mean, however, that she stopped writing entirely. There were still the occasional articles for magazines such as *The Canadian*, *Lancet*, and the *Illustrated London News*. But there was no longer the constant demand of heavy deadlines and the editing of other people's articles into shorter and shorter lengths as the amount of newsprint available was cut back by government order.

The war years and the immediate post-war period were a time of great loss for Elizabeth. Her cousin Harold died in 1941, and her sister Beatrice passed away one year after the war ended. Her friend Cicely died of heart failure in 1952; the furniture Elizabeth had lent her friend so many years earlier was then returned to its rightful owner. She also witnessed the decline of another acquaintance whom she much admired: Cornelia Sorabji, India's first female lawyer, had burst onto the London scene decades before, speaking out about the challenges facing women in her home country. In 1947, at the age of eighty, while suffering from osteoarthritis, she was institutionalized and diagnosed with incipient dementia.

Elizabeth visited Sorabji as often as she could, and believed that the once-active crusader was getting inadequate care, being "transferred to a public ward which she shares with rather more-or-less deranged women."[33] Sorabji's biographer would later report that Elizabeth's fears were well founded, and suggested that jealous family members had simply wanted to put the now-frail Sorabji in a home where her condition would not be made public.[34] There was little Elizabeth could do to help her friend, but Sorabji's treatment would make a lasting impression on the now-elderly Elizabeth.

In 1957, Elizabeth stopped writing entirely. That decision may have come more from necessity than choice. Her memory had begun to decline sharply. She eventually forgot her correct age and where she lived. In August 1959, the sophisticated intellectual who had hobnobbed with royalty and rubbed shoulders with famous artists would find herself sitting in a metal chair, being interviewed for admission to the Barnwood Institute.

"She has always had a very full life, plenty of friends — lots to do and she is very anxious that she should not be left to rot in bed," the doctor scrawled in thick black ink. He concluded that a possible cause of Elizabeth's dementia was her heavy burden of literary work and the late hours that she had kept. There are other, more likely explanations. Elizabeth may have been suffering from the symptoms of post-traumatic stress disorder (PTSD) due to her years as a journalist in France. PTSD by itself can be a contributing factor in the development of dementia. Another explanation is simple genetics. Her mother had lapsed into senility in her final years, and now Elizabeth was doing the same. It was a fate she had long feared, now come to pass. After seeing how her friend Cornelia had been treated when her faculties had begun to decline, it was little wonder she resisted admission to an institution where she could no longer avoid facing the reality of her illness. Despite her fears, she would live a quiet and seemingly pleasant life at the Barnwood Institute for the next five years. In August 1964, Elizabeth fell and fractured her femur. She died a few days later.

Despite having been a fashion and culture reporter in London and Paris as well as a war correspondent during two global conflicts, in her final years, as her life ebbed away, Elizabeth could no longer remember the historic events she had once covered with such style and intelligence. Fortunately for us, we can recreate her memory simply by turning the dial of a microfilm reader or tapping information into a search engine. As the years fly by, hundreds of articles emerge, as fresh today as they were nearly a century ago. As we scan the pages, we can see life again through the eyes of an aristocratic young woman in a silk tunic and lavender hobble skirt munching a butter-covered baguette, watching and writing history as it was made.

Afterword

Writers whose work is wildly popular during their lifetimes are often forgotten after death. Who, after all, kicks back and reads the works of Fanny Burney, a hugely popular satirical novelist of the nineteenth century, or Madame de Stael, an eighteenth-century writer and intellectual who gathered admirers in her Paris salon? They were once famous and respected, their lives the subject of gossip and speculation. Yet after their deaths, their language was seen as difficult or dated, and the issues about which they were passionate stopped resonating with a new generation. Mary MacLeod Moore, Beatrice Nasmyth, and Elizabeth Montizambert were no exception to this rule. They rubbed shoulders with some of the most influential writers and opinion-shapers of their day and produced literally thousands of articles for an eager public. Yet their prodigious output did not guarantee their survival in the public imagination. Like a good meal, their work was consumed by hungry readers, then quickly forgotten. And as their writing faded into obscurity, so too did any interest in the women who produced it.

So why should we bother revisiting their lives and work? For three reasons. They reveal much to us about a period in our history that had a profound effect on our development as a nation; they provide fresh insights into women's lives and contributions during those tumultuous times; and they can provide inspiration to a new generation of journalists. Moore, Montizambert, and Nasymth witnessed (and occasionally made) history, exploring and recording the experiences of women affected by the First World War. As professional journalists, they also broke through the gender barrier, covering hard news in an era when few women were allowed outside the confines of the "women's page."

Today, at a time when many Great War historians unrelentingly draw from the diaries, first-person accounts, and analyses of men, the writings of Moore, Montizambert, and Nasmyth are a necessary corrective to an unbalanced and biased view of history. As Louise North, author of *The Gendered Newsroom*, writes: "If it is mostly men who decide and shape news then we are seeing the world through the values and views of men."

Moore, Montizambert, and Nasmyth faced significant challenges while doing their work. They were barred from areas thought too "dangerous" for women, but found themselves in the line of fire anyway while doing their jobs in supposedly "safe" areas. Both Montizambert and Nasmyth narrowly escaped when bombs landed near their homes and work sites, and Nasmyth found herself caught in a fire in an underground subway station. They also faced sexual harassment and had to fight hard to be paid fairly. None of the women experienced income security from their work as journalists.

It is difficult to be absolutely sure, but it appears that all three women relied on freelance income to make their livings. Beatrice Nasmyth was on the staff of the *Daily Province* before the war, but went to London as a freelancer. Although the *Province* did pay her fare to England, she was paid strictly on a fee-per-article basis. In her family's personal archive is a neat stack of calling cards, on the backs of which Bea recorded the titles of every article she wrote, how much she was paid for it, and when it appeared. Mary wrote a regular column for *Saturday Night*, but her name did not appear on any staff list for the magazine. She was a contributor, albeit a frequent and regular one. Her brother William provided her with free lodgings in London, and when he could no longer do that she lived modestly in shared rooms with her mother, supporting them both with a prodigious output of freelance work. Elizabeth was the only journalist of the three who managed to achieve a staff position, as London editor of the *Gazette*, her name listed on the company's masthead. Yet she only received this position after the Great War, and even then, supplemented her income with her own inherited wealth and through well-paid freelance work and her own regular syndicated columns.

Yet despite having to work long hours for low pay in challenging circumstances, all three women still managed to find the time to champion the groundbreaking work of other women — playwright Cicely Hamilton, writer Radclyffe Hall, and nurse-politician Roberta MacAdams all received significant, life-changing support from these journalists.

Perhaps most important, the work and experience of Moore, Montizambert, and Nasmyth provide us with a comparative lens through which we can re-examine the lives and work of modern female war correspondents. Sadly, when we ask whether female journalists today are treated more respectfully and given the same opportunities as their male colleagues, the answer is still a resounding "no." Despite the efforts of generations of women writers, *The Global Report on the Status of Women in the News Media in 2010* reported that men hold close to two-thirds of the jobs in journalism in the world. The gap is wider at the top, with men holding 73 percent of top management positions.

In Canada, many newsrooms seem to have equal numbers of men and women, but there is more to the story than that. Once inside the newsroom, male reporters still tend to get assigned to report on so-called "hard news," while women are expected to introduce stories, read the weather, and report on traffic. And women aren't being promoted up the ladder in equivalent numbers, either, despite the plethora of female talent. We need only look at the top levels of management in established news organizations such as the Canadian Press to see evidence that the glass ceiling is still very much intact. In 2014, at Canada's largest twenty-five newspapers, only four had female publishers, and only four had female editors-in-chief.[1]

Women also continue to face obstacles at the beginning of their working lives as journalists. Canadian newsrooms are simply not "family-friendly," a major concern for young women entering the field. The pressures of "getting the story" no matter what time it is or where you are mean that women with young children (especially if they are primary caregivers) have to make a hard choice between family and work. The same was true for Mary, Elizabeth, and Beatrice. When she married and had children, Beatrice stopped working for the *Province*, while childless Mary and Elizabeth continued to work full-time, going from strength to strength.

Yet despite obstacles as current today as they were one hundred years ago, Moore, Montizambert, and Nasmyth managed to cover the Great War. They did this while under the gaze and direction of male publishers, military brass, and censors, something that affected their work but did not entirely control it. They were subversives, writing about women's experience of war as honestly and directly as they could, providing a much-needed corrective to the traditional notion of global conflict as something that (impossibly) occurred in isolation from women, children, and other non-combatants. Today, we can join them in that struggle, pushing back the veil of narrow scholarship about the Great War by unearthing and reclaiming the insights and lives of Moore, Montizambert, and Nasmyth — three intrepid war correspondents, writers, and adventurers in a dangerous age.

Acknowledgements

This book has taken me on a journey across Canada, to Britain, and to France. Many wonderful people contributed to the research and writing of this book. Heather Boyd (formerly western bureau chief, Canadian Press), Marjorie Lang (author of *Women Who Made the News*), and blogger and researcher Annette Fulford (ww1warbrides.blogspot.ca), who were extremely generous with their time and feedback. As the book entered the publication process, I received invaluable encouragement from historians Sandra Campbell, David Marshall, Barbara Freeman, Sarah Carter, Nancy Janovicek, journalist Vivian Smith, librarian Kalin Jensen, and Canadian biographer Charlotte Gray. I cannot thank them enough for their assistance.

Librarians and archivists are the hidden heroes of most biographies and *Firing Lines* is no exception. I was given extensive assistance by librarians and archivists at Library and Archives Canada, Galt Archives, Stratford-Perth Archives, Elgin County Archives, City of Vancouver Archives, Bishop Strachan School Archives, Whitehern Museum and Archives, Ontario Archives, and the Bristol University Library Archives. Writers and researchers who provided helpful information and details include Mary Anderson (author of *The Life Writings of Mary Baker McQuesten: Victorian Matriarch*), Stratford researcher Kate Jacob, and British military historian Julian Putkowski.

Beatrice Nasmyth's children — Harry Furniss and Monica Newton — generously shared photographs, memories, and piles of newspaper and magazine clippings written by their mother. Jonathan Morgan, library technician at the University of Waterloo, spent many hours looking through microfilm of the *London Sunday Times* and sending me copies of columns by Mary MacLeod Moore. My mother, Rosemary Lewis, and late stepfather, Herb Heidinger, took me on trips to Stratford to visit Beatrice Nasmyth's childhood home and to the Stratford-Perth Archives. Dorothy Reid, a descendant of the Montizambert family, shared often humorous memories of Elizabeth and her sisters. Sally Cline, author of *Radclyffe Hall: A Woman Called John*, kindly provided me with many insights into the character of Radclyffe Hall and her friendship with Mary MacLeod Moore.

I cannot thank Dundurn Press enough for their unflagging support of my book and Canadian women's history in general. The editorial process has been a great pleasure for me; my manuscript benefited greatly from the meticulous and perceptive work of editor Allison Hirst. Former war correspondent Anna Maria Tremonti generously contributed the foreword to *Firing Lines*. Just like Nasmyth, Montizambert, and MacLeod Moore, she has broken ground for the next generation of female journalists.

I am especially thankful for the support of my partner, Heather. Together we spent many hours driving to obscure towns and villages, cemeteries, and archives, searching for fragments of information about Mary, Elizabeth, and Beatrice. As always, Heather's interest, companionship, and encouragement made the research and writing a pleasure.

At the end of the day, I am most grateful to Beatrice Nasmyth, Mary MacLeod Moore, and Elizabeth Montizambert, three women who I have never met but whose work has deeply affected me. *Firing Lines* took seven years to research and write, including hundreds of hours spent reading microfilmed articles written nearly one hundred years ago. Those columns and features spoke to me across time, as did the lives of the women who wrote them. It is my hope that *Firing Lines* will provide a wide-open window into the complex, compelling characters of these three remarkable, courageous Canadian journalists and bring them to life again for a new generation of readers.

Notes

Prologue: Reclamation
1. This is a rough calculation based on a comparison of the Canadian censuses of 1911 and 1921.
2. An exception is historian Marjory Lang's excellent history of female Canadian journalists entitled *Women Who Made the News* (Kingston: McGill-Queen's University Press, 1999). However, there is only a very brief section on female war correspondents.
3. Martin Farrar, *News from the Front: War Correspondents on the Western Front, 1914–18* (Phoenix Mill: Sutton Publishing, 1998), 5.
4. Ibid., xiii.
5. Jeffrey Keshen, *Propaganda and Censorship During Canada's Great War* (Edmonton: University of Alberta Press, 1996), xiii.
6. Ibid., xiv.

Chapter I: The Suffragette
1. Historian Annette Fulford tracked down the reference to the *Calgarian* in www.theshipslist.com.
2. Harry Furniss, "Furniss: Some Notes on the Family," 1977, unpublished essay, 4.
3. James Hope Nasmyth, "The Nasmyth Family," unpublished genealogy

research, compiled sometime in the late 1960s.
4. Canadian Family Census Forms, 1852–1891, Stratford-Perth Archives, Stratford, Ontario, Canada.
5. Information provided from directories by Kate Jacob, Researcher, Stratford-Perth Archives.
6. Carolyn Bart-Riedstra and Lutzen Riedstra, *Stratford: Its History and Its Festival* (Toronto: James Lorimer and Company, 1999), 18–20.
7. Carolyn Bart-Riedstra, *Images of Canada: Stratford* (Charleston: Arcadia Publishing, 2002), 8.
8. For articles citing the success of both men, see *Stratford Daily Beacon*, "City's Leading Druggist: Mr. C.E. Nasmyth," August 1, 1914; *Stratford Daily Beacon*, "Former Druggist in City Succumbs," August 4, 1936; Sally Newton, "Biography of Beatrice Sifton Nasmyth Furniss," unpublished essay, n.d.).
9. *The Canadian Encyclopedia* (Toronto: McClelland & Stewart, 1999), 2289.
10. Furniss, "Furniss: Some Notes on the Family," 3.
11. Ted Byfield, Editor, *Alberta in the Twentieth Century: Volume II, The Birth of the Province 1900–1910*, Edmonton: United Western Communications, 1992), 52.
12. "Mary Ella Dignam — Artist and Educator," posted on www.coolwomen.ca, November 2, 2006.
13. Sally Newton, "Biography of Beatrice Sifton Nasmyth Furniss," unpublished essay, 1, Newton Collection.
14. Letter from Beatrice Nasmyth to her father, September 5, 1896, Newton Collection. This letter contains numerous poems describing Bea's time at Glenwilde.
15. Sally Newton, "Biography of Beatrice Sifton Nasmyth Furniss," unpublished essay, n.d.
16. This reconstruction was based on information provided in Sally Newton's "Biography of Beatrice Sifton Nasmyth Furniss." The event was so important to Beatrice that when she was well into her eighties, she shared it with her granddaughter. The names of her teacher and principal were not recorded; pseudonyms have been used in their place.
17. From the Elgin County Archives website, www.elgin.ca/alma_college.htm, accessed October 31, 2006. The Archives holds extensive records from the college.

18. Ibid.
19. Sally Newton, "Biography of Beatrice Sifton Nasmyth Furniss," unpublished essay, nd.
20. Ibid., 10.
21. "A Woodstock Girl: Miss Beatrice Nasmyth Lady Champion at Lake Mary Regatta," undated clipping, Newton Collection.
22. Ibid., 11.
23. Marjory Lang, *Women Who Made the News* (Kingston: McGill-Queen's University Press, 1999), 221.
24. Ibid., 13–14.
25. (Undated) 1913 newspaper photo of Beatrice Nasmyth, "Newly Elected President of the Vancouver Branch of the CWPC."
26. Charlotte Gray, *Flint & Feather: The Life and Times of E. Pauline Johnson, Tekahionwake* (Toronto: Harper Flamingo Canada, 2002), 380.
27. Rick Craig, *Racial Discrimination: Asian Immigrants in B.C.* (Vancouver: Legal Services Society of British Columbia, 1982), 41–42.

Chapter 2: Military Daughter

1. "Personages and Personalities: Our London Correspondent," *Saturday Night Magazine*, August 29, 1925.
2. In fact, there wouldn't even be a female editor of the *Star* until Doris Giller (after whom the Giller Prize is named) was appointed editor of the entertainment section in 1979.
3. "Personages and Personalities: Our London Correspondent," *Saturday Night Magazine*, August 29, 1925.
4. "Mrs. M. Rees Dies," *Sunday Times*, February 28, 1960.
5. *Quebec Directory for 1851* (London: Genealogical Research Library, reprint, n.d.), 22.
6. Reginald V. Harris, "Col. William James Bury MacLeod Moore: Soldier and Freemason," in C.E.B. LeGresley, ed., *Papers of the Canadian Masonic Research Association*, no. 7 (1951): 96–113.
7. *Dictionary of Canadian Biography*, www.biographi.ca, 1/4/2007, entry for George Anthony Barber, by Frederick H. Armstrong.
8. Baptismal records, St. Luke's Anglican Church, La Prairie, Quebec.

9. This is a reconstruction based on details provided by Mary in her short memoir "Personages and Personalities: Our London Correspondent," *Saturday Night Magazine*, August 29, 1925.
10. Ibid.
11. Ibid.
12. Ibid.
13. Ibid.
14. Ibid.
15. Reginald V. Harris, "Col. William James Bury MacLeod Moore: Soldier and Freemason," in C.E.B. LeGresley, ed., *Papers of the Canadian Masonic Research Association*, no. 7 (1951): 113.
16. "Personages and Personalities: Our London Correspondent," *Saturday Night Magazine*, August 29, 1925.
17. Henry Morgan, editor, *Canadian Men and Women of the Time* (Toronto: William Briggs, 1912), 819. The various newspapers for which Mary worked are listed in the entry under her name. The only weekly appears to have been the *Metropolitan*.
18. "Personages and Personalities: Our London Correspondent," *Saturday Night Magazine*, August 29, 1925.
19. Marjory Lang, *Women Who Made the News: Female Journalists in Canada, 1880–1945* (Montreal: McGill-Queen's University Press, 1999), 8.
20. Ibid., 10.
21. "Personages and Personalities: Our London Correspondent," *Saturday Night Magazine*, August 29, 1925.
22. Ibid.
23. Letter from Mary MacLeod Moore to Calvin McQuesten, January 6, 1907, Whitehern Museum and Archives.
24. Mary Anderson, "Rev. Calvin McQuesten," www.whitehern.ca/c_calvin.php, accessed September 28, 2005.
25. McGill University Theatre Playbill with notation by Calvin McQuesten, Whitehern Museum and Archives.
26. "Personages and Personalities: Our London Correspondent," *Saturday Night Magazine*, August 29, 1925.
27. Letter to Rev. Calvin McQuesten from Mary MacLeod Moore, January 6, 1907, Whitehern Museum and Archives.

28. Grace Brockington, "A World Fellowship: The Founding of the International Lyceum Club for Women Artists and Writers," www.academia.edu/876236/A_World_Fellowship_The_founding_of_the_International_Lyceum_Club_for_Women_Artists_and_Writers, accessed October 4, 2016.
29. Leonard Rees, *In Memoriam*, January 19, 1932.
30. Ibid.

Chapter 3: The Aristocrat

1. This is a reconstruction of an early encounter between Alice Gibb and Charles Montizambert. It is likely that they met through one of the many carefully chaperoned parties held by the Gibb family and other elite families in Quebec City.
2. Dictionary of Canadian Biography online, February 13, 2007, entry for James Gibb by Pierre Poulin, http://www.biographi.ca/en/bio/gibb_james_8E.html.
3. George W. Crawford, *Remember All the Way: The History of Chalmers-Wesley United Church, Quebec City* (Montreal: Price Patterson, 2006), 151.
4. "From hence I went in an open Carriole (which is a sort of Phaeton body on a sledge or Runners shod with Iron instead of Wheels) to Woodfield to call on Dr. Mabon's sister. It is 3 miles from Quebec, a beautiful Situation among Woods on the Steep & high banks of the St Lawrence, & within a mile from Wolfes Cove the spot where Gen'l Wolfe Landed," www.archives.gov.on.ca/en/explore/online/simcoe/simcoe-quebec-city.aspx, accessed October 4, 2016.
5. Quoted by George W. Crawford in *Remember All the Way: The History of Chalmers-Wesley United Church, Quebec City* (Montreal: Price Patterson, 2006), 152.
6. *Montreal Daily News*, "Munificent Bequests," undated clipping from unknown newspaper, courtesy Shirley Nadeau.
7. Obituary, *Quebec Chronicle*, August 1, 1905. Quoted in Montizambert family tree, provided to author by Janet Beale, November 1, 2005. See also photocopy from *Who's Who*, 644.
8. Register of Chalmers Presbyterian Church, May 21, 1867; see also marriage announcement, *Quebec Chronicle*, May 23, 1867.

9. Email correspondence to the author dated Thursday, March 1, 2007, from Jocelyne Milot, Director, Museum of the Royal 22nd Regiment, Citadelle, Quebec.
10. 1871 Recensement, courtesy Quebec City Archives.
11. Louisa Blair, *The Anglos: The Hidden Face of Quebec City*, Vol. II (Quebec: Editions Sylvain Harvey, 2005), 6.
12. Jack Granatstein, *Canada's Army: Waging War and Keeping the Peace* (Toronto: University of Toronto Press, 2002), 27.
13. For references to the kinds of food served by military wives during the nineteenth century, see Dianne Graves, *In the Midst of Alarms: The Untold Story of Women and the War of 1812* (Quebec: Robin Brass Studio, 2007).
14. According to the 1881 England Census.
15. Elizabeth Montizambert, "London in Wartime," *Montreal Gazette*, December 27, 1939.
16. Louisa Blair, *The Anglos: The Hidden Face of Quebec City*, Vol. II (Quebec: Editions Sylvain Harvey, 2005), 46.
17. "The Bishop Strachan School for Young Ladies," course outline, 1890, courtesy Bishop Strachan School Archives.
18. Katharine Wallbridge Clarke, "The Story of the Bishop Strachan School," undated article, Bishop Strachan School Archives.
19. "The Bishop Strachan School for Young Ladies," course outline, 1890, courtesy Bishop Strachan School Archives.
20. This reference came from researcher Annette Fulford.
21. From an interview with Dorothy Reid, 41 Gypsy Roseway, Willowdale, Ontario, M2N 5Y8. According to Reid, a descendant of one of Elizabeth Montizambert's cousins, "Alice Montizambert caught her husband with the maid and left him. She had money of her own — something like $50,000, which was a lot of money in those days — and she got mad at her husband and took the girls all over Europe. As soon as a man got interested in one of them, she'd move again."
22. Robin S. Harris, *A History of Higher Education in Canada, 1663–1960* (Toronto: University of Toronto Press, 1976), 116.
23. From interviews with Dorothy Reid, 41 Gypsy Roseway, Willowdale, Ontario, M2N 5Y8, a relative of Elizabeth Montizambert.
24. Information from www.wolman-prints.com.

25. Jay Winter and Jean-Louis Robert, eds., *Capital Cities at War: Paris, London, Berlin, 1914–1919* (Cambridge: Cambridge University Press, 1999), 32.
26. Letter from Elizabeth Montizambert to Miss Fischer, January 31, 1922, Library and Archives Canada, MG 30, Series D207, Vol. 18.
27. John Collins, *Post-Impressionist Masterworks from the National Gallery of Canada* (Ottawa: National Gallery of Canada, 2004), 24.
28. Elizabeth Montizambert, "Causerie de Paris," *Montreal Gazette*, April 6, 1912.
29. Jay Winter and Jean-Louis Robert, eds., *Capital Cities at War: Paris, London, Berlin, 1914–1919* (Cambridge: Cambridge University Press, 1999), 51.
30. Ibid., 264–65.
31. Elizabeth Montizambert, "Causerie de Paris," *Montreal Gazette*, March 28, 1912.
32. Ibid., September 18, 1914.

Chapter 4: Called to the Colours

1. Mary MacLeod Moore, "London Letter," *Saturday Night Magazine*, August 22, 1914.
2. Ibid., December 12, 1914.
3. Ibid., August 22, 1914.
4. The days in which banks are closed in Britain are usually observed as public holidays known (then as now) as "bank holidays." These were originally meant to provide working-class people with rare opportunities for relaxation and time with family.
5. Mary MacLeod Moore, "London Letter," *Saturday Night Magazine*, August 29, 1914.
6. Ibid.
7. Richard van Emden, Steve Humphries, *Veterans: The Last Survivors of the Great War* (London: Leo Cooper, 1998), 20.
8. Letter from Mary MacLeod Moore to Calvin McQuesten, 1916, courtesy Whitehern Museum and Archives.
9. Elizabeth Montizambert, "Causerie de Paris," *Montreal Gazette*, August 25, 1914.
10. That move occurred on September 2, 1914, according to Martin Gilbert in *The Imperial War Museum Book of the Western Front* (London: Pan Books, 2001), 18.

11. Jay Winter and Jean-Louis Roberts, eds., *Capital Cities at War: Paris, London, Berlin: 1914–1919* (Cambridge: Cambridge University Press, 1997), 152–53.
12. Ibid., 30–31.
13. Elizabeth Montizambert, "Causerie de Paris," *Montreal Gazette*, September 1, 1914.
14. Ibid., September 18, 1914.
15. This is an approximate figure. Jay Winter and Jean-Louis Robert, eds., *Capital Cities at War: Paris, London, Berlin 1914–1919* (Cambridge: Cambridge University Press, 1997), 139.
16. Elizabeth Montizambert, "Causerie de Paris," *Montreal Gazette*, September 28, 1914.
17. Ian Sumner, *French Poilu, 1914–1918* (Oxford: Osprey Publishing, 2009), 39.
18. Elizabeth Montizambert, "Causerie de Paris," *Montreal Gazette*, September 8, 1914.
19. Mary MacLeod Moore, "London Letter," *Saturday Night Magazine*, September 5, 1914.
20. Ibid.
21. Martin Farrar, *News from the Front: War Correspondents on the Western Front, 1914–18* (Phoenix Mill: Sutton Publishing, 1998), 5.
22. Ibid., xiii.
23. Mary MacLeod Moore, "London Letter," *Saturday Night Magazine*, September 12, 1914.
24. Ibid.
25. Ibid., December 5, 1914.
26. Elizabeth Montizambert, "Causerie de Paris," *Montreal Gazette*, September 18, 1914.
27. Holger Herwig, *The Marne, 1914* (New York: Random House, 2009), 155.
28. *Record of the 4th Royal Irish Dragoon Guards in the Great War, 1914–1918* (Canterbury, 1925), 3.
29. Martin Gilbert, *The Routledge Atlas of the First World War*, Second Edition (London: Routledge, 2003), 16.
30. Elizabeth Montizambert, "Causerie de Paris," *Montreal Gazette*, September 28, 1914.
31. Holger Herwig, *The Marne, 1914* (New York: Random House, 2009), 126–27.

32. Beatrice Nasmyth, Letter to James Nasmyth, September 25, 1915, Monica Newton Collection.
33. Beatrice Nasmyth, "Visiting England in Wartime," *Daily Province*, March 31, 1915. This article described Beatrice's experiences in September 1914.
34. Beatrice Nasmyth, "Canadian Soldier Lads See World's Metropolis," *Daily Province*, November 27, 1914.
35. Ibid.
36. Mary MacLeod Moore, "London Letter," *Saturday Night Magazine*, December 19, 1914.
37. Elizabeth Montizambert, "Causerie de Paris," *Montreal Gazette*, January 14, 1915.
38. Ibid.

Chapter 5: Total War

1. Elizabeth Montizambert, "Causerie de Paris," *Montreal Gazette*, February 15, 1915.
2. Ibid.
3. Mary MacLeod Moore, "London Letter," *Saturday Night Magazine*, January 16, 1915.
4. Mary MacLeod Moore, "The Cost of Living in London," *Saturday Night Magazine*, December 5, 1914.
5. Mary MacLeod Moore, March 10, 1916 letter to Calvin McQuesten, Whitehern Museum and Archives. See also her article "The Cost of Living in London," which appeared in *Saturday Night* in November 28, 1914. She uses almost identical language to describe her "rooms with attendance" in this piece.
6. Beatrice Nasmyth, "Little Scenes in England in Wartime," *Daily Province*, April 24, 1915. This piece reflects events that occurred around February 1915.
7. Ibid.
8. Elizabeth Montizambert, "Causerie de Paris," *Montreal Gazette*, April 14, 1915.
9. Ibid.
10. Ibid., December 1, 1915.
11. Mary MacLeod Moore, London Letter, *Saturday Night Magazine*, May 29, 1915.

12. Ibid., June 5, 1915, 28.
13. Elizabeth Montizambert, "Causerie de Paris," *Montreal Gazette*, April 14, 1914.
14. *Illustrated London News*, July 25, 1915.
15. Mary MacLeod Moore, "London Letter," *Saturday Night Magazine*, August 14, 1915, 28.
16. Arthur Marwick, *Women at War: 1914–1918* (London: Fontana Paperbacks, 1977), 73.
17. According to GWL Nicholson's history of the Great War, this office was the predecessor of the famous Canadian War Records Office established by Max Aitken/Lord Beaverbrook.
18. Letter from Beatrice Nasmyth to James Nasmyth, September 25, 1915, Newton Collection.
19. Jay Winter and Jean-Louis Robert, eds., *Capital Cities at War* (Cambridge University Press, 1997), 265 and 270.
20. Beatrice Nasmyth, "Where Every Canadian Regiment Is Represented," *The Province*, November 1915.
21. Ibid.
22. Letter from Beatrice Nasmyth to James Nasmyth, September 25, 1915, Newton Collection.
23. Neil Hanson, *First Blitz: The Secret German Plan to Raze London to the Ground in 1918* (London: Corgi Books, 2009), 43–44.
24. Letter from Beatrice Nasmyth to James Nasmyth, September 25, 1915, Monica Newton Collection.
25. Beatrice Nasmyth, "When the Zeppelins Hurled Bombs on London," *Daily Province*, October 6, 1915.
26. Date and description of air raid based on essay in www.firstworldwar.com/airwar/bombers_Zeppelins.htm by Ari Unikoski.
27. Letter from Beatrice Nasmyth to James Nasmyth, October 13, 1915, Monica Newton Collection.
28. Letter from Beatrice Nasmyth to James Nasmyth, September 25, 1915, Monica Newton Collection.
29. Pádraig Ó Siadhail, "Katherine Hughes, Irish Political Activist," in Bob Hesketh and Frances Swyripa, eds., *Edmonton: The Life of a City* (Edmonton: NeWest Publishers, 1995), 83.
30. Byfield, 422.

31. Letter from Beatrice Nasmyth to Deborah Nasmyth, February 3, 1916, Monica Newton Collection.
32. Elizabeth Montizambert, "Causerie de Paris," *Montreal Gazette*, Friday, December 10, 1915.
33. Ibid.
34. Ibid.
35. Ibid.
36. Beatrice Nasmyth, "Rambles in Dark but Interesting London," *Vancouver Daily Province*, December 3, 1915.
37. Beatrice Nasmyth, "Writes of Ladies' Day at London Press Club," *Daily Province*, February 12, 1916.

Chapter 6: Who Dies If England Lives?

1. Beatrice Nasmyth, "Penny Buns and Coffee Becoming a National Institution in the Old Country," *Daily Province*, February 19, 1916. According to the *Virago Book of Women and the Great War*, edited by Joyce Marlow (London: Virago Press, 1999), by the end of the war, 7,973,825 soldiers had been fed at station buffets.
2. Beatrice Nasmyth, "Scotch Nurse Who Trekked Through Serbia," *Daily Province*, February 1916.
3. Ibid.
4. *British Journal of Nursing*, January 1, 1916: 5–7.
5. Ibid.
6. Caroline Moorehead, *Dunant's Dream* (New York: Carrol & Graf, 1998).
7. Ibid.
8. Ibid.
9. Mary MacLeod Moore, "London Letter," *Saturday Night Magazine*, March 18, 1916.
10. Mary MacLeod Moore, "London Letter," *Saturday Night Magazine*, August 26, 1918.
11. Letter from Beatrice Nasmyth to Deborah Nasmyth, February 3, 1916, Monica Newton Collection.
12. Letter from Beatrice Nasmyth to Deborah Nasmyth, February 23, 1916, Monica Newton Collection.
13. Beatrice Nasmyth, "Only One in Millions," *Province*, March 31, 1916.

14. Letter from Mary MacLeod Moore to Calvin McQuesten, March 10, 1916, Whitehern Museum and Archives, Hamilton, Ontario.
15. Ibid.
16. Mary MacLeod Moore, "London Letter," *Saturday Night Magazine*, February 5, 1916.
17. Elizabeth Montizambert, "Causerie de Paris," *Montreal Gazette*, May 11, 1916.
18. Ibid.
19. Mary MacLeod Moore, "London Letter," *Saturday Night Magazine*, August 5, 1916.
20. Joyce Marlow, ed., *Virago Book of the Great War* (London: Virago Press, 1999), 157.
21. Military records of Frederick George Sutton, held by the National Archives of Canada.
22. Elizabeth Montizambert, "Causerie de Paris," *Montreal Gazette*, Wednesday, July 26, 1916.
23. Eileen Crofton, *The Women of Royaumont: A Scottish Women's Hospital on the Western Front* (East Linton, Scotland: Tuckwell Press, 1996), 69.
24. *The Women of Royaumont: A Scottish Women's Hospital on the Western Front*, 72.
25. Ibid., 77.
26. Lis Whitelaw, *The Life and Rebellious Times of Cicely Hamilton, Actress, Writer, Suffragist* (Columbus: Ohio State University Press, 1990), 146.
27. Elizabeth Montizambert, "Budget of London Topics," *Montreal Gazette*, December 21, 1935.
28. Beatrice Nasmyth, "Greater Than Any Yet Told Is to Be Future Story of Last of Last Great West — Peace River District," *Province*, October 14, 1916.
29. This eyewitness account is quoted but not attributed by Terry Copp in "Canada's National Army, Canada's National Interest 1918–2008," *Journal of Military and Strategic Studies*, 10.3 (2008): 10. This was the 2008 Ross Ellis Memorial Lecture in Military and Strategic Studies.
30. Desmond Morton and J.L. Granatstein, *Marching to Armageddon* (Toronto: Lester and Orpen Dennys, 1989), 120.

31. Elizabeth Montizambert, "Causerie de Paris," *Montreal Gazette*, January 23, 1917.
32. Ibid.

Chapter 7: Women's Work

1. Elizabeth Montizambert, "Causerie de Paris," *Montreal Gazette*, March 12, 1917.
2. Margaret Darrow, *French Women and the First World War* (New York: Oxford, 2000), 195.
3. Elizabeth Montizambert, "Causerie de Paris," *Montreal Gazette*, June 9, 1917.
4. Eileen Crofton, *The Women of Royaumont: Scottish Women's Hospital on the Western Front* (East Lothian: Tuckwell Press, 1977), 120.
5. www.history.co.uk/explore-history/history-of-london/london-goes-up-in-flames-again.html, accessed March 4, 2013.
6. Mary MacLeod Moore, "London Letter," *Saturday Night Magazine*, February 17, 1917.
7. Ibid.
8. Elizabeth Montizambert, "Causerie de Paris," *Montreal Gazette*, Tuesday, April 10, 1917.
9. Ibid.
10. Ibid., Saturday, July 7, 1917.
11. This was Beatrice's perspective, not the officer's. Beatrice Nasmyth, "Many Prohibited Areas Today in London," *The Daily Province*, April 20, 1917.
12. Nasmyth, "Many Prohibited Areas Today in London," April 20, 1917.
13. Mary MacLeod Moore, "London Letter," *Saturday Night Magazine*, February 10, 1917.
14. *The Observer*, April 8, 1917.
15. Elizabeth Montizambert, "Causerie de Paris," *Montreal Gazette*, Thursday, June 14, 1917.
16. Ibid.
17. Margaret Darrow, *French Women and the First World War* (New York: Oxford, 2000), 195.
18. Margaret R. Higonnet, *Lines of Fire: Women Writers of World War I* (New York: Plume Books, 1999), xlv.

19. Elizabeth Montizambert, "Causerie de Paris," *Montreal Gazette,* June 30, 1917.
20. Ibid.
21. Desmond Morton and J.L. Granatstein, *Marching to Armageddon: Canadians and the Great War* (Toronto: Lester and Orpen Dennys, 1989), 147.
22. Elizabeth Montizambert, "Causerie de Paris," *Montreal Gazette,* June 14, 1917.
23. Cicely Hamilton, quoted in Liz Whitelaw, *The Life and Rebellious Times of Cicely Hamilton* (Columbus: Ohio University Press, 1990), 157.
24. Letter from Beatrice Nasmyth to her father J.H. Nasmyth, August 16, 1917, Monica Newton Collection.
25. Ibid.
26. Letter of Harold McGill to Emma, September 24, 1917, Glenbow Archives (M742 File 7).
27. Letter from Beatrice Nasmyth to her parents, February 15, 1918, Monica Newton Collection.
28. Beatrice Nasmyth, "Tells of Life in London Suburb," *Daily Province,* April 1, 1918.
29. The unnamed British newspaper was quoted in "Alberta's Women MPP's" in the December 19, 1917, issue of *The Globe* (Toronto).
30. Desmond Morton and J.L. Granatstein, *Marching to Armageddon: Canadians and the Great War* (Toronto: Lester and Orpen Dennys, 1989), 165.
31. *London Gazette,* No. 30573, March 13, 1918.
32. Mary MacLeod Moore, "London Letter," *Saturday Night Magazine,* December 15, 1917, 31.
33. Ibid.
34. Elizabeth Montizambert, "Causerie de Paris," *Montreal Gazette,* November 24, 1917.
35. Ibid.
36. Ibid.

Chapter 8: Lines of Communication

1. Mary MacLeod Moore, "Somewhere in France, the Veil Lifted," *Saturday Night Magazine,* January 26, 1918.
2. Morton and Granatstein, 169.

3. Howard Palmer with Tamara Palmer, *Alberta: A New History* (Edmonton: Hurtig Publishers, 1990), 186.
4. Mary MacLeod Moore, "Somewhere in France, the Veil Lifted," *Saturday Night Magazine*, January 26, 1918. In the introduction to this article, Mary makes clear that the tour was designed for the "purpose of describing the work of women behind the lines."
5. Margaret Higonnet, *Lines of Fire: Women Writers of World War I* (New York: Plume Books, 1999), xlvii.
6. Beatrice Nasmyth, "Lifts the Curtain on Life of Canadian Troops on Soil of France," *Daily Province*, February 16, 1918.
7. Debbie Marshall, *Give Your Other Vote to the Sister: A Woman's Journey Into the Great War* (Calgary: University of Calgary Press, 2007).
8. Beatrice Nasmyth, "Red Cross Has an Army All Its Own," *Daily Province*, February 18, 1918.
9. Mary MacLeod Moore, *The Maple Leaf's Red Cross* (London: Skeffington and Sons, 1919), 164.
10. Ibid., 222.
11. Beatrice Nasmyth, "Once Cow-Shed; Now Modern Operating Room with All Equipment," *Daily Province*, March 6, 1918.
12. Ibid.
13. Debbie Marshall, *Give Your Other Vote to the Sister: A Woman's Journey Into the Great War* (Calgary: University of Calgary Press, 2007), 184.
14. Mary MacLeod Moore, "Somewhere in France, the Veil Lifted," *Saturday Night Magazine*, January 26, 1918.
15. Mary MacLeod Moore, "War Zone Sketches," *Saturday Night Magazine*, June 1, 1918.
16. "Forgotten Heroes: A Million Horses Were Sent to Fight in the Great War — Only 62,000 Came Back," *Daily Mail Newspaper*, July 15, 2014.
17. Mary MacLeod Moore, *The Maple Leaf's Red Cross* (London: Skeffington and Sons, 1919), 167.
18. Beatrice Nasmyth, "Canadian Girls Drive Ambulances and Think It Fun," *Daily Province*, March 2, 1918.
19. Ibid.
20. Mary MacLeod Moore, *The Maple Leaf's Red Cross*, 187.
21. Beatrice Nasmyth, "Canadian Girls Drive Ambulances and Think It Fun," *Daily Province*, March 2, 1918.

22. Elizabeth Montizambert, "Causerie de Paris," *Montreal Gazette*, February 6, 1918.
23. Douglas Gill and Julian Putkowski, *The British Base Camp at Étaples: 1914 to 1918* (Étaples: Musée Quentovic, 1997). Most of the facts used in this chapter concerning the Étaples military camp come from this superb study.
24. Mary MacLeod Moore, "Canadian Women in the War Zone," *Saturday Night Magazine*, March 16, 1918.
25. Beatrice Nasmyth, "Once Cow-Shed; Now Modern Operating Room with All Equipment," *Daily Province*, March 6, 1918.
26. Mary MacLeod Moore, "Somewhere in France, the Veil Lifted," *Saturday Night Magazine*, January 26, 1918.
27. Ibid.

Chapter 9: When Your Boy Comes Back to You

1. Beatrice Nasmyth, *Daily Province*, March 17, 1917.
2. Letter from Beatrice Nasmyth to James and Deborah Nasmyth, February 15, 1918, Monica Newton Collection.
3. Mary MacLeod Moore, "London Letter," *Saturday Night Magazine*, April 27, 1918.
4. Quoted in Malcolm Brown, *The Imperial War Museum Book of the Western Front* (London: Pan Books, 2001), 294.
5. Desmond Morton and J.L. Granatstein, *Marching to Armageddon: Canadians and the Great War 1914 to 1919* (Toronto: Lester and Orpen Dennys, 1989), 178.
6. Mary MacLeod Moore, "London Letter," *Saturday Night Magazine*, April 27, 1918.
7. Wikipedia, "Paris Gun," http://en.wikipedia.org/wiki/Paris_Gun.
8. Elizabeth Montizambert, "Causerie de Paris," *Montreal Gazette*, April 27, 1918.
9. Ibid., May 1, 1918.
10. Ibid.
11. Ibid., April 27, 1918.
12. Letter from Beatrice Furniss to Blanche Hume, April 27, 1918, Monica Newton Collection.
13. Letter from Beatrice Nasmyth to James and Deborah Nasmyth, February 15, 1918.

14. Letter from Harry Furniss to Guy Furniss, dated February 24, 1918, Monica Newton Collection.
15. Description of wedding from undated clipping, *Woodstock Sentinel Review*, Monica Newton Collection.
16. Elizabeth Montizambert, "Causerie de Paris," *Montreal Gazette*, May 20, 1918.
17. Mary MacLeod Moore, "London Letter," *Saturday Night Magazine*, May 4, 1918, 22.
18. Letter from Harry Furniss to Dorothy Furniss, undated (c. October 1918), Monica Newton Collection.
19. www.warmuseum.ca/firstworldwar/history/battles-and-fighting/land-battles/arras-and-canal-du-nord-1918.
20. Elizabeth Montizambert, "Causerie de Paris," *Montreal Gazette*, December 18, 1918.
21. Mary MacLeod Moore, "London Letter," *Saturday Night Magazine*, January 11, 1919.
22. Ibid.

Chapter 10: Beatrice Nasmyth

1. Victor Sauntry, "Canadian Newspapers and the Paris Peace Conference of 1919: A Study of English-Language Media Opinion" (Master's Thesis, University of Waterloo, 2008), 27.
2. Undated clipping, "Woodstock Woman at Versailles," Monica Newton Collection.
3. Harold Nicolson, *Peacemaking 1919* (Grosset and Dunlap, 1933).
4. Harry Furniss, *Memoirs* (self-published, 1994).
5. Alan Bowker, *A Time Such as There Never Was Before: Canada After the Great War* (Toronto: Dundurn Press, 2014), 194–221.
6. Michael Huberman, Denise Young, "Hope Against Hope: Strike Activity in Canada, 1920–1939," *Explorations in Economic History 39*, 315.
7. The information about the strike at the *Gazette* and Guy's role as a non-union engraver came from conversations between Guy Furniss and his son Harry, recorded in Harry's privately published memoir, dated 1994.
8. Beatrice Furniss, "Without References," manuscript. It is not known whether or not this story was published. It was written sometime in the 1920s.

9. Beatrice Furniss, "Lawyer's Letter," *Modern Woman Magazine*, n.d. (but likely 1934), 26.
10. Telegram from Guy Furniss to Beatrice Furniss, March 27, 1928, Monica Newton Collection.
11. Canadian National Railroad (CNR) menu, c. 1928.
12. Letter from James Nasmyth to Guy Furniss, April 3, 1918, Monica Newton Collection.
13. Email correspondence from Monica Newton to Debbie Marshall, February 17, 2001.
14. Harry Furniss, *The Flying Game, Volume I* (Victoria: Trafford Publishing, 1995).
15. Information about COTC at McGill accessed January 28, 2015, from www.archives.mcgill.ca/public/exhibits/mcgillremembers/cotc.htm.
16. Unattributed newspaper clipping entitled "Exhileration [sic] ... Depression," labelled in ink "1945." Monica Newton Collection.
17. Harry Furniss, *The Flying Game, Volume I* (Victoria: Trafford Publishing, 1995).
18. Media Club of Canada, "Canadian Women of Note" (microfiche), 1981, 649.

Chapter II: Mary MacLeod Moore

1. "Captain W. MacLeod Moore Sudden Death in Brussels," *Sunday Times*, April 13, 1919.
2. Canadian War Graves Registers (Circumstances of Casualty), 1914–1948 for William MacLeod Moore.
3. "Captain W. Macleod Moore: Sudden Death in Brussels," *Sunday Times*, April 13, 1919.
4. Mary MacLeod Moore, "In the Track of the War God," *Sunday Times*, April 27, 1919.
5. Ibid.
6. Ibid.
7. Mary MacLeod Moore, "The War Zone Re-Visited," *Sunday Times*, August 1, 1920.
8. Mary MacLeod Moore, "In the Track of the War God," *Sunday Times*, April 27, 1919.
9. Mary MacLeod Moore, "London Letter," *Saturday Night Magazine*, April 19, 1919.

10. Ibid., March 15, 1919.
11. Ibid., April 19, 1919.
12. These were the best figures Mary had at hand. Today the Commonwealth War Graves Commission lists 888,246 United Kingdom war dead.
13. Mary MacLeod Moore, "London Letter," *Saturday Night Magazine*, July 26, 1919.
14. Mary MacLeod Moore, *The Maple Leaf's Red Cross* (London: Skeffington & Son Limited, 1919), 165.
15. Mary MacLeod Moore, *Cassells Weekly* article quoted in *Saturday Night Magazine*, August 29, 1925, 24.
16. Harold Hobson, Phillip Knightley, and Leonard Russell, *The Pearl of Days: An Intimate Memoir of the Sunday Times: 1822-1972* (London: Hamish Hamilton, 1972), 122.
17. Mary MacLeod Moore, "Easter Preparations," *Sunday Times*, March 26, 1933.
18. *Evening Post*, "Power of Journalism: Ignorance Abroad, Need for Dissemination of Truth," March 31, 1922.
19. Mary MacLeod Moore, "Silent Legion," *Sunday Times*, April 1, 1923.
20. Mary MacLeod Moore, "Do You Remember?" *Sunday Times*, July 15, 1923.
21. "Editor's Wedding," *Sunday Times*, Sunday, June 10, 1923.
22. After Leonard Rees's death, Mary would remain close to his son Lawrence and Lawrence's wife, Sandra Rees.
23. Sally Cline, *Radclyffe Hall: A Woman Called John*, 197.
24. Ibid., 241.
25. Hall wasn't the only person the couple knew who had fought very publicly against censorship. In July 1929, Mary and Leonard were invited to an intimate dinner with Sir John Keane, an Irish baronet and politician who had opposed the banning of *The Tailor and Ansty*, a book considered at the time to be sexually provocative.
26. Mary MacLeod Moore, "Armistice Day," *Sunday Times*, October 20, 1929.
27. The information about Flora Lion's studio comes courtesy of Colin Cohen's site, www.resurgam.info/missingportraits/Painters/floralionatwork.html.
28. "Leonard Rees: Editor of the *Sunday Times* for 31 Years, January 1932," Obituary Pamphlet.
29. "Signor Mussolini's Play," *The Times*, May 7, 1932.

30. Claudia Baldoli, *Exporting Fascism: Italian Fascists and Britain's Italians in the 1930s* (Oxford: Berg Publishing, 2003), 103.
31. Mary MacLeod Moore, *Sunday Times*, October 22, 1933.
32. Mary MacLeod Moore, "Northern Sunshine," *Sunday Times*, September 9, 1934.
33. Mary MacLeod Moore, "Choosing the Presents," *Sunday Times*, December 17, 1933.
34. Mary MacLeod Moore, "Valentine's Day and Lent: Flatlets for Poor Ladies," *Sunday Times*, February 11, 1934.
35. Mary MacLeod Moore, "And a Happy New Year," *Sunday Times*, January 1, 1939.
36. Mary MacLeod Moore, "Matters of Defence," *Sunday Times*, January 15, 1939.
37. Rob Baker, "Two Perfect Women: The Meeting of Prunella Stack and Gertrud Scholtz-Klink in 1939," www.nickelinthemachine.com/2011/12/two-perfect-women-the-meeting-of-prunella-stack-and-and-gertrud-scholtz-klink-at-claridges-in-1939.
38. Mary MacLeod Moore, "Do We Want a Woman Chief?" *Sunday Times*, March 12, 1939.
39. Mary MacLeod Moore, "Our Patron Saint," *Sunday Times*, April 23, 1939.
40. Mrs. Leonard Rees, "Britain the Great Protector," *Echoes Magazine*, Autumn 1939, 13.
41. Mary MacLeod Moore, "This War of Nerves," *Sunday Times*, December 17, 1939.
42. Mary MacLeod Moore, "Home Front on Holiday," *Sunday Times*, March 31, 1940.
43. Anonymous, "Mrs. M. Rees Dies," *Sunday Times*, February 28, 1960.
44. Mary MacLeod Moore, "London Letter," *Saturday Night Magazine*, January 11, 1919.

Chapter 12: Elizabeth Montizambert

1. Advertisement, *Journal of Mental Science*, January 1953: iv.
2. Elizabeth Montizambert, "Causerie de Paris," *Montreal Gazette*, February 15, 1919.
3. Anonymous, "Charming Canadian Acclaimed by Press Club," *Toronto Telegram*, May 20, 1922.

4. Elizabeth Montizambert, "Causerie de Paris," *Montreal Gazette*, February 15, 1919: 14.
5. Zara Steiner, "The Treaty of Versailles Revisited," in Michael Dockrill and John Fisher, eds., *The Paris Peace Conference, 1919* (Basingstoke: Palgrave MacMillan, 2001), 13–33.
6. "Charming Canadian Acclaimed by Press Club," *Toronto Telegram*, May 20, 1922.
7. Elizabeth Montizambert, *London Discoveries in Shops and Restaurants* (London: Women Publishers Limited, 1924), 88.
8. Ibid., 63.
9. Active History website, http://activehistory.ca/2014/03/soldier-suicide-after-the-great-war-a-first-look.
10. In her memoir, Canadian opera singer Maureen Forrester sarcastically suggested that Fischer was "interested in more than my voice."
11. Handwritten note by Sarah Fischer on letter from Elizabeth Montizambert to Fischer, dated January 31, 1922. Available in Sarah Fischer fonds at Library and Archives Canada MG 30 Series D207, Vol. 18, file 1922.
12. Elizabeth Montizambert, "Budget of London Topics," *Montreal Gazette*, August 3, 1929.
13. Elizabeth Montizambert, *London Discoveries in Shops and Restaurants* (London: Women Publishers Limited, 1924), 69.
14. Ibid., 81.
15. Anonymous, "Montizambert Miniatures on View at Studio Sale," *Montreal Star*, December 1, 1920.
16. Elizabeth Montizambert, "Budget of London Topics," *Montreal Gazette*, August 18, 1928.
17. Martin Gorsky, "Public Health in Interwar England and Wales: Did It Fail?," www.ncbi.nlm.nih.gov/pmc/articles/PMC2647660.
18. Elizabeth Montizambert, "Budget of London Topics," *Montreal Gazette*, December 12, 1931.
19. Lis Whitelaw, *The Life and Rebellious Times of Cicely Hamilton: Actress, Writer, Suffragist* (Michigan: Women's Press Limited, 2008), 209.
20. Elizabeth Montizambert, "Budget of London Topics," *Montreal Gazette*, March 3, 1934.
21. See correspondence between Elizabeth Montizambert and Hamish

Hamilton in the Hamish Hamilton fonds of the Bristol University Library Archives.
22. Letter from Elizabeth Montizambert to Buchanan Clarke, editor of Hamish Hamilton, Bristol University Library Archives, DM1352/Ii.
23. Court Circular, *London Times*, January 31, 1930.
24. Letter from Elizabeth Montizambert to Hamish Hamilton, August 1, 1937, Bristol University Archives, DM 1352/I.
25. Letter from Elizabeth Montizambert to Sarah Fischer, October 15, 1937. Available in Sarah Fischer fonds at Library and Archives Canada MG 30 Series D207, Vol. 18, file 1937.
26. Elizabeth Montizambert, "Budget of London Topics," *Montreal Gazette*, June 17, 1933.
27. Elizabeth Montizambert, "London in Wartime," *Montreal Gazette*, November 14, 1940.
28. Ibid., November 2, 1940.
29. Ibid.
30. Ibid.
31. Ibid., June 8, 1943.
32. Ibid., July 5, 1944.
33. Letter from Elizabeth Montizambert to Dorothy Sayers, September 19, 1947, the Marion E. Wade Center, Wheaton College, Wheaton Illinois, Ref. 379/14.
34. Suparna Gooptu, *Cornelia Sorabji: India's Pioneering Woman Lawyer*, Oxford University Press: 2006, 207. Available online at www.oxfordscholarship.com/view/10.1093/acprof:oso/9780195678345.001.0001/acprof-9780195678345-chapter-9.

Afterword

1. Vivian Smith, *Outsiders Still: Why Women Journalists Love and Leave Their Newspaper Careers* (Toronto: University of Toronto Press, 2015), 10.

Bibliography

Newspapers, Journals, Magazines

British Journal of Nursing
Chatelaine
Daily Province
Evening Post
Explorations in Economic History
Globe
Illustrated London News
Journal of Military and Strategic Studies
London Sunday Times
London Times
Montreal Daily News
Montreal Gazette
Papers of the Canadian Masonic Research Association
Quebec Chronicle
Saturday Night Magazine
Stratford Daily Beacon
Toronto Telegram
Woodstock Sentinel Review

Books

Anderson, Mary, ed. *The Life Writings of Mary Baker McQuesten: Victorian Matriarch*. Waterloo: Wilfrid Laurier University Press, 2004.

Baldoli, Claudia. *Exporting Fascism: Italian Fascists and Britain's Italians in the 1930s*. Oxford: Berg Publishing, 2003.

Bart-Riedstra, Carolyn. *Images of Canada: Stratford*. Charleston: Arcadia Publishing, 2002.

Bart-Riedstra, Carolyn, and Lutzen H. Riedstra. *Stratford: Its History and Its Festival*. Toronto: James Lorimer and Company, 1999.

Blair, Louisa. *The Anglos: The Hidden Face of Quebec City, Vol. II*. Quebec: Editions Sylvain Harvey, 2005.

Bowker, Alan. *A Time Such as There Never Was Before: Canada After the Great War*. Toronto: Dundurn Press, 2014.

Brown, Malcolm. *The Imperial War Museum Book of the Western Front*. London: Pan Books, 2001.

Byfield, Ted. *Alberta in the Twentieth Century: Vol. II, Birth of the Province, 1900–1910*. Edmonton: United Western Communications Ltd., 1992.

Canadian Encyclopedia. www.thecanadianencyclopedia.ca.

Cline, Sally. *Radclyffe Hall: A Woman Called John*. London: Overlook Books, 1999.

Craig, Rick. *Racial Discrimination: Asian Immigrants in B.C.*, Vancouver: Legal Services Society of British Columbia, 1982.

Crawford, George. *Remember All the Way: The History of Chalmers-Wesley United Church, Quebec City*. Montreal: Price Patterson, 2006.

Crofton, Eileen. *The Women of Royaumont: A Scottish Women's Hospital on the Western Front*. East Linton: Tuckwell Press, 1996.

Darrow, Margaret. *French Women and the First World War*. Oxford: Berg Publishing, 2000.

Dictionary of Canadian Biography. www.biographi.ca/en/index.php.

Farrar, Martin. *News from the Front: War Correspondents on the Western Front, 1914–18*. Phoenix Mill: Sutton Publishing, 1988.

Furniss, Harry. *The Flying Game, Vol. I*. Victoria: Trafford Publishing, 1995.

———. *Memoirs*. Vancouver: self-published. Gilbert, Martin. *The Imperial War Museum Book of the Western Front*. London: Pan Books, 2001.

———. *The Routledge Atlas of the First World War, Second Edition*. London: Routledge, 2003.

Gooptu, Supama. *Cornelia Sorabji: India's Pioneering Woman Lawyer*. Oxford: Oxford University Press, 2006.

Granatstein, Jack. *Canada's Army: Waging War and Keeping the Peace*. Toronto: University of Toronto Press, 2002.

Graves, Dianne. *In the Midst of Alarms: The Untold Story of Women and the War of 1812*. Quebec: Robin Brass Studio, 2007.

Gray, Charlotte. *Flint and Feather: The Life and Times of E. Pauline Johnson, Tekahionwake*. Toronto: Harper Flamingo Canada, 2002.

Hanson, Neil. *First Blitz: The Secret German Plan to Raze London to the Ground in 1918*. London: Corgi Books, 2009.

Harris, Robin. *A History of Higher Education in Canada, 1663-1960*. Toronto: University of Toronto Press, 1976.

Herwig, Holger. *The Marne, 1914*. New York: Random House, 2009.

Heskith, Bob, and Frances Swyripa. *Edmonton: The Life of a City*. Edmonton: NeWest Publishers, 1995.

Higgonet, Margaret, ed. *Lines of Fire: Women Writers of World War I*. New York: Plume Books, 1999.

Hobson, Harold, Phillip Knightley, and Leonard Russell. *The Pearl of Days: An Intimate Memoir of The Sunday Times: 1822-1972*. London: Hamish Hamilton, 1972.

Keshen, Jeffrey. *Propaganda and Censorship During Canada's Great War*. Edmonton: University of Alberta Press, 1996.

Lang, Marjory. *Women Who Made the News*. Kingston: McGill-Queen's University Press, 1999.

Marlow, Joyce. *The Virago Book of the Great War*. London: Virago, 1999.

Marshall, Debbie. *Give Your Other Vote to the Sister: A Woman's Journey into the Great War*. Calgary: University of Calgary Press, 2007.

Marwick, Arthur. *Women at War: 1914-1918*. London: Fontana Paperbacks, 1977.

Montizambert, Elizabeth. *London Adventure: A Guide to Old Treasure in New Ways*. London: London Passenger Transport Board, 1939.

———. *London Discoveries in Shops and Restaurants*. London: Woman Publishers, 1924.

———. *Michael's London: A Book for Children in Any City*. London: Hamish Hamilton, 1936.

———. *Unnoticed London*. London: J.M. Dent and Sons, 1922.

Moore, Mary MacLeod. *The Maple Leaf's Red Cross*. London: Skeffington and Sons, 1919.

Moorehead, Caroline. *Dunant's Dream*. New York: Carrol and Graf, 1998.

Morgan, Henry, ed. *Canadian Men and Women of the Time*. Toronto: William Briggs, 1912.

Morton, Desmond, and J.L. Granatstein. *Marching to Armageddon: Canadians and the Great War*. Toronto: Lester and Orpen Dennys, 1989.

Nicholson, Harold. *Peacemaking 1919*. London: Grosset and Dunlap, 1933.

Palmer, Howard, and Tamara Palmer. *Alberta: A New History*. Edmonton: Hurtig Publishers, 1980.

Putkowski, Julian, and Douglas Gill. *The British Base Camp at Étaples: 1914–1918*. Étaples: Musée Quentovic, 1997.

Quebec Directory for 1851. London: Genealogical Research Library, reprint, n.d.

Record of the 4th Royal Irish Dragoon Guards in the Great War, 1914–1918. Canterbury: 1925.

Sumner, Ian. *French Poilu: 1914–1918*. Oxford: Osprey Publishing, 2009.

Van Emden, Richard, and Steve Humphries. *Veterans: The Last Survivors of the Great War*. London: Leo Cooper, 1998.

Whitelaw, Lis. *The Life and Rebellious Times of Cicely Hamilton, Actress, Writer, Suffragist*. Columbus: Ohio State University Press, 1991.

Winter, Jay, and Jean-Louis Robert, eds. *Capital Cities at War: Paris, London, Berlin: 1914–1919*. Cambridge: Cambridge University Press, 1999.

Image Credits

Page 16	Photo courtesy of Monica Newton.
Page 24	Photo by the author.
Page 27	Photo courtesy of Monica Newton.
Page 29	Photo courtesy of Monica Newton.
Page 36	Photo courtesy of Monica Newton.
Page 72	Photo courtesy of Bishop Strachan School Archives.
Page 124	Photo courtesy of Monica Newton.
Page 138	Photo courtesy of Bernie Quigley.
Page 146	Photo courtesy of Monica Newton.
Page 147	Photo courtesy of Monica Newton.
Page 156	Author's collection.
Page 163	Photo courtesy of Monica Newton.
Page 165	Photo courtesy of Monica Newton.
Page 204	Photo courtesy of Monica Newton.

Index

Adams, Charles, 121–22, 143–44
Air Raid Precautions (ARP) wardens, 240, 243
airmen, 137–40
Alberta, 144–47, 161–62
Alberta Agent General's office, 117–18
Allied army, 93–94, 136–37, 186, 195–96
Alma College, 32–33
ambulances, 93, 177–79, 188
American army, 186
anti-war demonstrations, 75–77
Armistice Day, 196–98, 233
art and artists, 25, 28, 50–51, 67, 69–70, 97, 103–04, 107–08, 192–93, 255
Asian immigrants, 36–37
Assistance Publique, 87

Association de l'Enrôlement Volontaire des Françaises, 154–55
atrocities, 90, 241
Australian military, 167, 175, 195–96

Barber, Emily Susan, 41–42
Battle of the Somme, 136–37, 141, 148
Beaverbrook, Lord, 171
Belgium, 86, 90–91, 93, 101–02, 105–06, 134, 221–22
bias against women, 17, 52, 272–74
Blair, Louisa, 60–61
bombing raids, 102–03, 109–10, 113–16, 120, 161, 166, 180, 187–88, 194, 214–15, 245, 265–68
See also shelling
Boutroux, Aline, 154–55

British Expeditionary Forces, 84–85, 87–88, 93–94, 137–38
British vs. Canadians, 91–92
Brockington, Grace, 50–51
Brunner Mond explosion, 152–54

Cambrai, 195–96
Canadian military, 60–61, 63–65, 82, 92–93, 105–06, 116–17, 143–44, 148–50, 158, 167–68
Canadian Pay and Records office, 111–12, 117–18
Canadian Women's Press Club (CWPC), 35, 49
Canadians vs. British, 91–92
casualties, 88, 104, 106, 113–16, 131, 137, 147–48, 152, 158, 167–68, 171–72, 180, 189, 194–96, 224, 249
casualty clearing stations, 130, 140–42, 177
See also hospitals
censorship, 16, 84–85, 90, 116, 157
Christmas truce, 96
Christmases, 95–96, 181–82, 236, 243–45
clubs, 23, 35, 49–51, 53, 60–61, 86, 118, 212, 255
Collum, Vera, 141
Concerts at the Front, 160–61
conscription, 79, 134, 171
Croÿ, Marie de, 262–63
Currie, Arthur, 167, 181, 203

Daily Province, 111
Declaration of Unity, 134–35

Defence of the Realm Act (DORA), 16, 85
dementia, 248, 256, 269–70
dictatorship, 241
Dignam, Ann, 26
Dignam, Deborah Eliza. *See* Nasmyth, Deborah
Dignam, Hugh, 26
Dignam, Mary Ella, 28
Dignam, William, 26
dilution, 81–82, 108–09, 154–55, 172–73, 178–79
Dinard, 97–98
Durham, Mabel, 34–35
Duval, Pierre, 98

economics of war, 80–81, 99–100, 108–09, 116–17, 127–28, 133, 154–55, 158–59
education for girls, 32–33, 65–67
Elder, John, 174–75
employment of women, 45–46, 68, 71, 80–81, 108–09, 127–28, 154–55, 172, 272
Étaples, 18, 177, 179–80
evacuations, 126–27

family dynamics, 111
Farrar, Martin, 16
fashion, 14, 48–49, 70, 80–81, 103, 158, 192, 229, 255
feminism, 28, 34–35, 83
Ferdinand, Francis (Archduke), 76
First Battle of Mons, 87–88
First Battle of Ypres, 94
First Nations peoples, 63–64

Fischer, Sarah, 252–54, 263–64, 266
flame-throwers, 135–36
France, 264–65
    pre-war, 55–58
    See also Paris
Franco-Prussian War, 55, 79, 87
freelancing, 52, 208, 210, 254, 257, 261, 272–73
French, Sir John, 88–89
French Army, 87–89, 93–94, 110
Furniss, Guy Mackenzie, 13–14, 37, 164, *165*, 190–92, *204*, 207–10, 212, 217–18
Furniss, Harry, 24, 191, 195–96
Furniss, Harry (son), 208, 210–16
Furniss, Monica, 208, 210–11, 214, 216–17

gangrene, 141, 174–75, 180
gas attacks, 105–06, 167, 177, 229, 240, 243
German army, 76, 86–89, 93–94, 144, 186
German tactics, 103
Germany, 237–38, 240–42, 258
Gibb, Alice, 56, 59, 61, 65–66
Gibb, Harold, 80, 88, 135, 247
Gibb, James Lawson, 57–59
Glenwilde, *29*, 30, 211

Haig, Douglas, 167
Hall, Radclyffe, 230–32
Hamilton, Cicely, 69, 142, 149–50, 160–61, 254, 257–58, 268
Hardie, Keir, 75–76
Hitler, Adolf, 237

Horne, George, 168
horses, 175–76
hospitals, 97–98, 101, 109–10, 119–20, 135–38, 140–43, 148–49, 173–74, 177, 179–80
Hughes, Katherine, 49, 117–18

"In Flanders Fields," 106
Inglis, Elsie Maud, 140–41
internationalism, 228
Italy, 235–36
Ivens, Frances, 142

Johnson, Pauline, 35, 210
journalists, 13–14, 17, 48–49, 51, 84–85, 171, 205, 272
journalists' tour, 13–14, 170–82, 226

Keshen, Jeffrey, 16
Kitchener, Lord, 15–16, 84
Komagata Maru, 37

L'art de la Mode, 48–49
La Prairie, 40–41
land girls, 267
Lang, Marjory, 35, 46
League of Nations, 205, 228, 237, 259
letter writing, 28, 34, 101, 111–12, 131–32, 168–69, 195
lines of communication, 170, 174–75, 186, 226
Lion, Flora, 233–34
living conditions, 85–87, 99–100, 104, 113, 151–52, 157, 159, 183–85, 223–24, 238, 252, 256–57
Llandovery Castle, 194–95

Index 307

London, 49, 51, 62, 68, 82, 89, 91, 98–99, 107, 118, 120–21, 152–54, 196–97, 265–67
London Discoveries in Shops and Restaurants, 254–55
"London Letters," 52, 187
London Sunday Times, 14
Lusitania, 106–07
Lyceum Club, 50–51, 53

MacAdams, Roberta, *14*, 162, *163*, 164, 166–67, 170, 216
MacPherson, Grace, 178, 180
Maple Leaf's Red Cross, The, 225–26
marriages, 190–92, 214, 229–30
Martin Farrar, 16, 85
McCrae, John ("In Flanders Fields"), 106, 174
McPhedran, Florence, 170
McQuesten, Calvin, 47–48, 131
Métis, 63–64
Michael's London, 62, 259–60
midinettes, 158–59
military awards, 149, 168
modus Vivendi, 95–96
Montizambert, Alice. *See* Gibb, Alice
Montizambert, Beatrice, 60, 65, 255–56
Montizambert, Charles, 59–61, 63, 65–66, 68
Montizambert, Elizabeth, 13, *14*, 54–58, 61–62, 65–67, 69, 72, 78–79, 89–91, 95–98, 102–04, 142–43, 169–70, 187–90, 197–98, 247–48, 256, 259–63, 268–70

Montreal Gazette, 14, 55, 69–70
Montreal Herald, 46–47
Montreal Metropolitan, 45, 47
Montreal Star, 38–40, 48
Moore, Mary MacLeod, 13, *14*, 18, 38–40, 42–49, 51–53, 76, 78, 82–86, 95, 98–100, 106–07, 127–29, 131–34, 136–37, 152–54, 168, 170, 185–87, 193–94, 196–200, 235, 239, 245–46
Moore, William MacLeod, 41–42, 44, 134, 147–48, 173–74, 220–21
Motor Ambulance Convoys, 18
munitions factories, 108–09, 128–29, 152–55
Mussolini, Benito, 235–36

Nasmyth, Alexander, 25
Nasmyth, Beatrice, 13, *14*, 17, 23–25, *27*, 28–35, *36*, 37, 91–93, 100–102, 111–18, 120–23, *124*, 129–31, 137, 140, 144–45, *146*, 161–66, 170, 183–85, 190–92, 203, *204*, 208–19
Nasmyth, Charles, 25–26
Nasmyth, Deborah, 25–26, *27*, 32
Nasmyth, George, 25
Nasmyth, James, 25–26, 29, 35, *124*, 210
Nasmyth, James (great-uncle), 25
Nasmyth houses, *24*, 26, *28*
New York School of Applied Design for Women, 45
Noyes, Alfred, 77, 235
nursing, 84, 126, 177

Operation Michael, 186–87
Owen, Wilfred, 15, 179

Pankhurst, Emmeline, 83, 108
Paris, 55–58, 70–72, 78–81, 86–87, 89–90, 95, 97, 102–04, 107–09, 134–35, 151–52, 154–55, 187–90, 192–93, 197–98, 248–49
Paris Peace Conference, 249–50
Paris Press Syndicate, 109, 119
Passchendaele, 167–68
patriotism, 128–29
and the declaration of war, 78
Pelletier, Madeleine, 81–82
poetry, 35, 210
prisoners, 126–27, 132
pseudonyms, 46–47, 52, 70, 239

Quebec, 40–41, 58, 61, 171
Queen Alexandra's Imperial Military Nursing Service (QAIMNS), 84

rationing, 151–52, *156*, 183–84, 197, 267
Red Cross, 132, 148, 172–73, 225–26
Rees, Leonard, 52–53, 133, 229–32, 234–35
refugees, 101–02, 189–90
Remembrance Day. *See* Armistice Day
Riddell, Florence, 129–31
Riel, Louis, 63–64
riots, 36–37, 61, 179–80, 225
Royaumont, 140–43, 148–50, 160

Sassoon, Siegfried, 15, 133
Saturday Night Magazine, 14, 44, 52, 99
Saturday Sunset, 34
Scholtz-Klink, Gertrud, 240–41
Scottish Women's Hospital (SWH), 140–43
"Second Battle of Ypres," 105–06
Second World War, 213–16, 242–45, 263–68
shelling, 88–89, 94, 115, 121–22, 139, 144, 156, 188–90
See also bombing raids
Sifton, Arthur, 27–28, 118, 161, 203, *204*
Sifton, Clifford, 27–28
Sifton, Elizabeth, 26–27
Sifton, John, 26–27
Silvertown, 152–54
Smedley, Constance, 50
Smith-Ryland, Adria "Noel," 135, 247–48
soldiers, 82, 93, 95, 98–99, 111–12, 121–22, 124–25, 130–31, 155–57, 181
Soldiers' and Sailors' Families Association, 85–86, 118–19, 132
soup kitchens, 87, 104, 107, 169, 189–90
St. George's House, 113
Stratford, 25–26, 30
suffragism, 35, 48, 83, 161–62, 166–67, 171–72, 198–200
Sutton, Fred, 137, *138*, 139–40

Index 309

Torrance, William, 57
train trips, 23–24, 30, 39–40, 49, 109–10, 118–20, 125–27, 144–46, *147*, 175
training camps, 92–93, 101, 117, 243
trench warfare, 93, 96, 117, 121–22, 137, 147–48

Unnoticed London, 251–52, 260

Vancouver Province, 14, 23–24, 205
Vancouver World, 34
Vassilieff, Marie, 107
Verdun, 119–20
Versailles Peace Treaty, 203–07, 224
veterinary hospitals, 175–76
Vimy Ridge, 157–58, 260–61
voluntary aid detachments (VADs), 84
volunteer work, 85–86, 109–10, 119–20, 123–25, 132

wages, 95, 99–100, 109, 111, 129, 155, 158–59
war
    Boer War, 77–78
    declaration of, 24, 77–78
    end of, 196–98, 206
    North-West Rebellion, 64–65
    opposition to, 159–60, 171
    preparations for, 239–40
    thoughts about, 77–78, 106, 125, 132, 144, 185–86, 232, 244–45

war work, 82–83, 85–86, 117–18, 123–25, 142, 154–55, 172–73, 243
See also dilution
Ward, Mary Augusta, 13–14
Western Front, 95–96, 152, 172, 182
women
    and war industries, 108–09, 128–29, 227
    as journalists, 13–14, 17, 48–49, 51, 171, 205, 272
    roles of, 17, 45–46, 61–62, 68, 71, 81–83, 100, 158, 172, 227–28
    See also nursing
Women's Army Auxiliary Corps (WAAC), 172, 180–81
Women's Emergency Corps, 83–84
women's medical units, 126–27
women's writing
    subjects of, 15, 17, 84, 96, 99–100, 208–09, 226–27
    writing styles, 46, 51, 226–27, 263–64
Woodstock, 32
Woodstock Collegiate, 32
Woodstock Sentinel Review, 33
worker strikes, 158–60, 207, 224
wounded troops, 90, 109–10, 135–36, 140–43, 174, 178

Ypres, 93–94, 105–06, 228–29

zeppelins, 102–03, 109–10, 113–16, 130

dundurn.com
@dundurnpress
dundurnpress
dundurnpress
dundurnpress
info@dundurn.com

FIND US ON NETGALLEY & GOODREADS TOO!

DUNDURN